VOLUME 4

THE URGENT
NEED
FOR CHRISTIAN
RENEWAL

*The Collected Works
of H. Evan Runner*

PAIDEIA
PRESS

VOLUME 4

THE URGENT
NEED
FOR CHRISTIAN
RENEWAL

The Collected Works
of H. Evan Runner

H. EVAN RUNNER

SECOND EDITION

EDITED BY
KERRY JOHN HOLLINGSWORTH
STEVEN R. MARTINS

PAIDEIA
PRESS

www.paideiapress.ca

The Urgent Need for Christian Renewal
The Collected Writings of H. Evan Runner | Volume 4

This four-volume second edition is a publication of Paideia Press (P.O. Box 1000, Jordan Station, Ontario, Canada L0R 1S0) and the Reformational Digital Library (www.reformationaldl.org).

Editorial Team: Kerry J. Hollingsworth, Steven R. Martins, Jenny Hultink
Book Design: Steven R. Martins, Project Manager, Paideia Press

ISBN 978-0-88815-283-1

Printed in the United States of America

This four-volume re-publication of *The Collected Works of H. Evan Runner* is the fulfillment of a promise made to Prof. Runner by the editor of the first edition, Kerry John Hollingsworth, and the publisher, John Hultink, to bring all of Dr. Runner's writings into print.

Table of Contents

APPENDIX 237

Editor's Preface to the
First Edition

THE VOLUMES THAT COMPRISE *The Collected Writings of H. Evan Runner* contain over a thousand pages of text. The collected writings contain Professor Runner's early review articles, along with lectures, papers, and public speeches that range from 1940 through to the 1990s. The public lectures he gave at Unionville, a village just north of Toronto, Canada, from 1959 through 1961, are also included. These lectures have already been published in one form or another, and in some cases, reprinted many times. The range of material treated in these volumes covers almost the entire encyclopedia of the sciences, while the way Runner treats this material has proved to be significantly instructive and inspiring for several generations of students. Runner's analysis is always radical; it always gets to the "heart" of the matter. Central to the radicality of this core analysis was Runner's commitment to "the Word of God as the directing Principle of our whole life." Indeed, it was the centrality of this latter principle in his analysis that always made his speaking and writing style so charismatic, so gripping, and so much to the point.

Hence the reader will discover in these volumes that Runner's writings are just as relevant today for the core issues that Christian men and women face in their everyday lives as they were when they were written, in some cases sixty and seventy years ago.

At the Unionville Conference in 1961, in the presence of his revered mentor Professor D.H.Th. Vollenhoven, Runner articulated the central grounding principle that animated both his work and the work of his teachers, Herman Dooyeweerd and Dirk Vollenhoven. That grounding principle was the unshakable subjection to the *dunamis*, the power of the Word of God to direct the hearts of those who would but commit their "ways" to its demands.

Even as a systematic philosopher, Runner made it abundantly clear that what he was about, whether in the classroom, the lecture hall, or a public forum, was the concrete working out of the central thrust of the Word of God for ALL of our life's activities. It was NOT about philosophy in the first place, even the Philosophy of the Cosmonomic Idea, as important as it was for him. And it was certainly not about theology, which also has its rightful place as a scientific discipline. It was about RELIGION, religion understood as "the human response to the Word of God."

"In the beginning," man emerges as God's final act of creation who is set into the midst of the creation order in a wholly dependent relationship, a religious relationship that Runner always emphasized encompasses his entire being. His entire life is religion and, in order to give form to the creation, he must listen to God's Word for his entire life's activities. The directing power of God's Word provided him with an entrée into the structural order of creation. Hence the *Direction* provided by God's Word for the life of mankind within the *Structure* of creation is absolutely symbiotic; *Structure* and *Direction* are completely dependent on each other. Without the direction of the Word of God, man's activities in God's good creation can only be a pale parasitic distortion of what God's life-giving Law Word lays out for humanity.

Therefore, Runner argued that when man no longer believes God but believes Satan's lie instead, his misdirected belief distorts his form-giving activities within the structure of creation. It is important to understand at this point that man's fall into sin did not disturb the structure of God's good creation; it only distorted the *religious response* of mankind to the Word of God for his activities within the bounds of creation. The religious response of all mankind in all their life activities is still entirely characterized by belief. Believing is the inescapable condition of all mankind. Therefore, after the fall, Christians do not live in one world and non-Christians in another. Everyone lives in exactly the same world and must respond to the structures of God's creation for his or her life in one way or the other. That is, the difference between Christians and non-Christians is always a question of belief, except that there is now a *directional antithesis* in the common response to the structure of creation. Man's common response to the structure of creation is now expressed in terms either of *rightly directed belief*, or *misdirected belief*. Christians and non-Christians "are not doing different things – they are doing the same things differently (motivated by a different root commitment)."

Within the structure of creation, then, human experience does not admit of unbelief, since there is no such thing. Every person holds to a belief of some kind or another whether it be pagan, secular, or Christian, and each person acts on those beliefs. Indeed, the empirical results of humanity's formative activities throughout the ages bear tragic witness to the reality of Runner's claim regarding the directional antithesis that emerges in all of life's activities.

It was precisely this directional antithesis in the life of humanity that Runner sought to work out in a systematically coherent way in his teaching, lectures, and public speeches. But it was not the power of Philosophy that he was so passionate about, at least not in the first place. At the very heart of all that Howard Evan Runner was advocating was the plea to allow the radical power of the Word of God to direct all of our life's activities, including our philosophical analysis.

Kerry John Hollingsworth
Editor of the First Edition, 2016
Paideia Press; Reformational Digital Library
www.reformationaldl.org

Editor's Preface to the Second Edition

THE FIRST EDITION OF *Walking in the Way of the Word: The Collected Writings of H. Evan Runner* was published in two volumes, the first in 2016, and the second in 2009. Both volumes, published seven years between each other, were not as ideally paired as intended in terms of their formatting. This first edition, however, was considered the first step towards presenting Runner's work and legacy to the world. This second edition, a four-volume-set, slightly re-organizes Runner's writings into a uniform formatting, making it more reader-friendly and accessible, while more polished than the first edition. Additionally, with the advances of the book publishing industry, this four-volume-set will have a broader and wider distribution reach than its first edition. In consultation with the first edition's editor, the four volume set has been divided as follows:

Volume I: Early Book Reviews and Writings from 1940 to 1957

Volume II: Writings from 1961-1964, the Unionville Lectures, The Scriptural Religion and Political Task, and Select Lectures

Volume III: Writings from 1967-1977 and Can Canada Tolerate the CLAC? to Dooyeweerd's Passing

Volume IV: Writings from 1979-1994, Interview with Dr. H. Evan Runner, and a Brief Chronology of his Life

It was both a monumental and mammoth task to collect all of H. Evan Runner's works together and to publish them, and the editor of the first edition, Kerry J. Hollingsworth, who did the heavy-lifting for its composition, and the founder of Paideia Press, John Hultink, who joyfully commissioned the work, accomplished a great feat in that they brought to the world an invaluable treasure that can be said to contain the biblical *antidote* to the religio-cultural problem that the church faces today, a problem that is not only religious but also philosophical in nature. Hollingsworth fleshes that out in his introduction to the first edition, the religio-cultural and philosophical problem, and the solution rooted in a Scriptural world-and-life view provided by Runner, whose roots run deeper in D.H.Th. Vollenhoven and Herman Dooyeweerd's thinking than in anyone else's. Hollingsworth's introduction to the man Howard Evan Runner is included in the first volume of this four-volume set, a most comprehensive, concise, and yet brief biography of the man behind the writing.

New to this second edition is an article that serves as an excellent personal introduction to Runner written by John Hultink, which suitably follows Hollingsworth's in the first volume, for while Hollingsworth provides a "bird's-eye" view of Runner and his life, with snapshots of his heart, pains, and struggles, Hultink complements this introduction with a personal testament of what it was like to have Runner as a professor. One could say that Runner's heart is brought into fuller view with Hultink's writing, thanks to the context provided by Hollingsworth's introduction. Both are excellent and remarkable compositions, neither one or the other takes away from each other, instead, they strengthen each other and provide the reader with all he or she needs to better understand, not only the writings of the man Howard Evan Runner, but the faith and heart of the man himself. May there be more men who take after Runner's reformational spirit, for as is true of Vollenhoven and Dooyeweerd, Runner can too be considered a trailblazer in his own right.

It is the earnest hope and heart of all those involved in this publication project that this four-volume set prove to not only be beneficial for the reader, but potentially life-changing as it steers the reader towards Christ, His Word, and a proper understanding of the world and our place in it. If we hope to *live* Christianly, we must learn to *think* Christianly.

Steven R. Martins
Editor of the Second Edition, 2021
Project Manager, Paideia Press
www.paideiapress.ca

Interview of
Dr. H. Evan Runner

(Reproduced from: Hearing and Doing: Philosophical Essays
Dedicated to H. Evan Runner, *Wedge, 1979)*

...So you see, if it were not for the fact that I had learned all that Greek in high school, college, and graduate school, I would not have been able to work with Vollenhoven and test the significance of what he was doing. The point I want to make is, we must not go on as Christians the way the Evangelicals generally are still doing in the United States, just suddenly trying to get into culture by going to a university and saying, "Now we'll go to a philosophy class and find out what philosophy is all about," for then you'll get some tradition which has been with us all these years, or in the history of philosophy you get some big textbook that has been written according to the American norm, or older books which were translations of German books from the end of the 19th century. *That is not our task.* Our task is as Christians ourselves to study those Greek texts as closely as we can as we try to understand what was going on, what they were doing *in the light of the full revelation that we have in the Scriptures.* That, to me, is a very important thing that Vollenhoven taught us, and we have only just begun to work that way – we have only just begun. And as I look back over my early years and call to mind all those apparently insignificant events, I see – well, you have to speak from out of your faith – I see that the Lord was preparing me in those simple things.

But you wanted to know about my early background. Well, I grew up in a Presbyterian church in Philadelphia. My father was

17

Scotch-Irish and Welsh. His grandfather was a Presbyterian minister who had come to this country from Ulster with his congregation at the time of the potato famine in the 1840s. They established a little community in Pennsylvania – Runnersville, not too far from Oxford and very close to the Pennsylvania-Maryland border, a region of some importance shortly thereafter in connection with the Civil War – and became farmers. But my grandfather – shows how short a time ago that is – he ran away from home and became a bugler in the Civil War on the Northern side. I remember him as a retired farmer; he lived to be 92 years old. My father was born in 1878, and he lived to be 84. He was a "hard-shell" Baptist until he married my mother.

My mother was English and Pennsylvania Dutch. Her father's name was Watterson; her mother's name was White. They lived in that rural area too, but they belonged to one of the more prominent churches in Oxford, the Presbyterian church. Grandfather Watterson was a schoolteacher, and as he got older he sold insurance, and then was retired. I can remember that I used to sit on his lap and pull at his long white beard. My mother worked in a dry-goods store for a number of years before she was married in 1912. I was born in 1916. My father had been married twice before, but his second wife and his only son died in the same winter, of pneumonia, and his first wife had also died. So I was the only child and a good deal of emotion was attached to me, and that probably was not good. Anyway, before I was two years old we moved to Philadelphia because, as they told me later, they wanted me to have the opportunity to study and to advance.

The church I grew up in was Westminster Presbyterian Church at 58th and Chester Avenue. Our pastor – the only one I had until I went away to college – was Warren R. Ward. He was a graduate of Princeton Seminary, but he had been a Methodist all his life. He used to organize a summer Bible school every July. It was excellent. I have never run across anything as well regulated and accoutered. The church also had a very good prayer service on Wednesday evenings. As many as 150 to 200 people would turn out. The prayer period was half the hour; and the other half was spent studying the Scriptures. The minister went through Bible books verse by verse and word by word. I remember going through Ephesians, Romans and Revelation. And we of the younger generation were encouraged in that church to memorize the Shorter Catechism. But the strangest thing, the sermonizing was Arminian! And the pastor encouraged us to attend the Keswick Conferences in New Jersey, which taught a form of perfectionism. We also had the Scofield Reference Bible recommended to us, and we heard a lot of preaching about the rapture and the millennium. And we would have men from Moody Bible Institute. But at the same time Mr. Ward would tell us about his teachers at Princeton: J. Gresham Machen, Robert Dick Wilson, and Oswald Allis. But I'll come back to that.

What I used to read as a boy? Oh, novels having to do with the French and Indian wars, everything about the frontier, Daniel Boone – all that sort of thing. And I began to read Dickens. I just devoured Dickens. In the summer months you could always find me at the public library, you know, the local branch. And that is where I first started taking out philosophy books – that is right! It just comes back to me. It was in a cool, shady part of the general reading room. I would stand in front of the shelf that had books on logic and epistemology and so on, and I would take one home and leaf through it and saw that I could not understand it and take it back later. Ha, ha! But I wanted so badly to understand what was in those books!

I went to Anna Howard Shaw Junior High School, at 54th and Warrington Avenue. It is a very bad neighborhood now, I am told, with street gangs and stabbings sometimes taking place at night in the streets and alleys. But I have fine memories of that place! Especially the Latin teacher, Miss Catherine I. Smart. She took a great interest in her students and fired us with a desire to be able to read and work with Latin. She was an unmarried Roman Catholic lady of middle age, straight black hair, and false teeth that would regularly fall to her desktop when she burst out laughing as we, one after the other, recited *hic, haec, hoc.*

After that I went to West Philadelphia High School. It was more than a half hour's walk, but we walked in groups, picking up friends on the way. I remember I had a number of Orthodox Jewish friends, who would invite me in for just a moment while they put on their prayer caps and quickly said their prayers, saying, "Watch how I do this," and then we would go out and walk on to school together. I remember in my last year of high school one of them invited me in and I wondered what was coming. Then he pulled out something and said: "Look, I just bought a prayer rug; I have converted from Judaism to Islam." So he would take his prayer rug to school from that day on.

Sometime during my high school years there was a "Million Dollars Testament Campaign" all across America, and I became an agent for that. I got a number of students together, and we would stand in the fire escapes (because we weren't allowed in the school building, but the fire escapes were enclosed in the building actually) and distribute New Testaments, until that was forbidden. And then, with the help of one of the teachers in the English department, we held a little Bible study group right after school hours, in one of the classrooms. We just felt the need of Christian fellowship, because there was no such thing. You know, our life in school and during the week was just so different from Sunday and Wednesday night at the church! We were growing up in a working-class neighborhood with many Irish Catholics and just three or four blocks from a very heavy Jewish community with a big synagogue, so you associated with these kids all the time. The only time you weren't with them was when you were in your own church, in the prayer meetings on Wednesday night and at young people's society and all day Sunday. So you felt the pull of two worlds very strongly.

My mother never let me go to school in the morning without having me get down on my knees with her in prayer. Every morning. Just a short prayer for the day, you know, and for my work. And we might remember my father (he would be off to work already) and our Korea missionaries and people that we knew as well as Christian work that we knew about. She had me do that every school day. Actually, when I left home for college, quite a tug was needed to pull away from that form of piety. Meanwhile, our minister was undergoing a change and started giving altar calls in the evening services. At first only three or four times a year, but gradually it became fairly regular: at the last hymn there would always be an altar call, and you could come forward and kneel in the front benches. The idea was to have your sins forgiven and to repent, that is, to expect not to engage in those sins again. But of course you did. So of course, although it was meant to be a once-for-all thing, you would find yourself going up more than once. It has a terribly wearing and tearing effect on the emotional life of a puber. And then those sermons inviting you to give your life to the Lord, which you felt you hadn't done completely unless you volunteered to be a minister or a foreign missionary–what they called "full-time...

> Young people today lack order or structure in their thinking about the Bible. That is a strange thing; for the Bible is a revelation to us of the order of God in His creation. And it is the insight into this order (proper Bible-knowledge) that gives perspective to our life-in-the-world (Kingdom service). The second flows out from the first. Thus it is not surprising that our young people also have no clear-cut convictions about what Kingdom service is (Rom. 12:1-2). [1963][1]

...Christian service." What I appreciate in it is that a person has to come to a point of decision, and that it is important that he make it known before the whole congregation. But whether in this way, at that moment, perhaps under the impression of some words you have just heard – I question whether that is good for a young person. At any rate, that is not what I would mean by "hearing and doing"!

But to get back to our pastor's interest in Princeton. Towards the end of the 1920s it was threatened with reorganization by the General Assembly, which would take away its distinctive Reformed character and make it more representative of all the movements in the church. This led in 1929 to the founding of Westminster Seminary, and our pastor was fully behind that. He would have some of these men come out and preach for us, and there would be a special offering for the

---

1. (The indented quotations have been selected from Dr. Runner's writings and are intended to clarify and expand on the comments he makes in the interview.)

new seminary. I remember hearing Robert Dick Wilson, J. Gresham Machen and Oswald Allis in this way. And I was taken by my parents to the very first opening exercises of Westminster Seminary and to its first graduation exercises. I clearly remember Robert Dick Wilson giving his final exhortation to Westminster's first graduating class.

I went to Wheaton College in the fall of 1932. That first semester my father lost his job. He was a typesetter with a firm that printed law cases and also railroad timetables and things like that. It was a very good company to work for – until the depression and the linotype machine came... So here he was – unemployed at 54! He sold Fuller brushes, did anything to make a little money. It was bad. He had savings in one of the savings and loan associations, and I remember taking a long walk with him one evening – we walked to save money, that is how tight it was – to their office, and when he came out he said to me, "Well, I do not expect to see any of that money back." I wanted to quit school, but they insisted that I continue. How they managed to support me during those years I do not know. I myself managed to get some scholarship aid.

Right from the beginning, I chose philosophy as my major. There were always these two strains in me: my love for philosophy and a classical education – I mean the sense of the continuity of our experience of Western civilization – *and* the desire to be a missionary, to Korea first, later to China, to come to grips with that whole civilization, to make the Christian religion relate to it somehow. And that lasted right up until I was at the Free University of Amsterdam (the Netherlands), in 1946-47, where Harry Boer and I had rooms next to each other. He had been in Nigeria already, and we would sit till three or four in the morning discussing whether I should go to China. But it looked bad in China then. The northern march of the Communists was taking place: it was the demise of the Kuomintang. On the other hand, I was feeling increasingly that the Christian base at home was eroding. And that is when I finally decided I would work here, in the West.

Often as a child and adolescent, and indeed even later, I wondered why there were no longer any Christian martyrs. Could it be that the Spirit of Christ had conquered the world, and there was no opposition? But then I began to see that there were no struggles, no contesting of spirits, for the simple reason that the Christians had withdrawn into their own little house, the organized church, and through a spirit of gradual accommodation had abandoned the world to a spirit alien to Christ's to give form to nine-tenths of our society. [This could not but greatly affect their own spirituality!] [1967]

In my first two years at Wheaton they had only one man in philosophy. As a sophomore, I had to write a paper about values in his Medieval Philosophy course. The question was whether good was good and God was good because He participated in goodness, or whether goodness was good because God willed it so. And I felt – I think that this came from reading the Scriptures – that goodness was what it was because of the way God had made the world, that it must issue ultimately from God's Creator-will. But the professor took what I would call the more platonic view, you know, that there is some kind of subsisting goodness in which God participates and is therefore good. And I got quite upset about it. So when I went home in the spring vacation, I went right down to Westminster Seminary, which was still in session, and I – I was generally quite shy when I was young, but I was determined to make this paper good – I went up to some students and asked them, "Where can I find Dr. Van Til?" And they led me to him, and I told him I was a student at Wheaton and was thinking of coming to Westminster but that I had this problem on my hands just now, and would he have any syllabuses or anything that would provide me with material for this term paper? He piled me up with stuff which I took home and tried to devour in the few days I had.

Of course, I also took Greek in college. I had had three years of it in high school, and we had read Xenophon and three books of Homer. But at Wheaton they had only one professor, a retired Methodist minister. He was about eighty-some years old, and he would just drone out a translation. But they put me in junior Greek, and we read Herodotus the first year, and what did we read the second year? Euripides' *Alcestis*. Just one play in the whole semester. It was not good. So, mainly for that reason, in my third year I went to the University of Pennsylvania, where I took a lot of Greek with a man named Bates (a well-known editor of Sophocles). I studied hard that year and neglected a lot of other things. But that year I got much better instruction in philosophy too. I had a year course in modern philosophy from Henry Bradford Smith, one of America's best logicians. He was the one who at the end of the first lecture dared us to leave the faith of our homes behind us and follow the course with an open mind. He said:

> This class is made up of all kinds of people – orthodox Protestants, liberal Protestants, Orthodox Jews, liberal Jews, Reform Jews, Roman Catholics, Greek Orthodox Christians, and unbelievers like myself. How can we possibly discuss together unless we have some common basis? And since it cannot be any of those things, what else is there except that we can build up a fund of rational ideas together? And that is what modern philosophy is all about.

Well, I was impressed with that. That is the day I walked home through the park and stood in front of a tree and took out my pocketknife and scratched my initials in the tree and thought: "Do I dare or do not I dare?" I finally decided I didn't dare let go of my faith. I learned from that later how important it is to grab a student in the first month – even the first week – when those fundamental decisions are being made that determine the whole direction of his life.

> At the end of the period, as we were already leaving the room, the professor dared us to free ourselves of our past and make a new beginning on a rational basis that would be acceptable to all reasonable persons. What would you have done? I was a serious student; I wanted more than anything else at that moment to enter into the beckoning mysteries of the history of modern philosophy. Well, I did not follow the advice of my professor, but I almost did, humanly speaking. Yet I must say this here: I did not know what was going on, and for years I was unable to say why it was not right to take the professor's "reasonable" dare. I know many Christians who took similar advice, usually with the most disastrous consequences.

Permit me one more brief illustration. Many years later when I was doing graduate work in a research society at Harvard University it happened at a dinner that a professor suddenly looked up laughing into my face and asked if I could still believe that Jesus had gone "up" to heaven. He meant, of course, that with the modern scientific picture of the world that had arisen out of the work of Copernicus, Bruno, Kepler, Galileo, and others "up" could be anywhere and thus nowhere in particular. By this time I was more mature and knew something about what was going on. But the disdainful attitude still hurt; it was as if you were being cut off from any body of scholars that might be expected to do useful work... A statement about the sunset does not refer to the earth and the sun in their mutual relations as a result or their physical motion in space: it is language which gives expression to our experience of life from out of our central (religious) human position as lords of the creation (Ps. 8). All the arguments about no longer being able to believe that man is the center of the created world, and the earth the scene of the great drama of the covenanted fellowship between God and men, stem from making the physical aspect of life the whole of life. The scientistic thinker (not, be it noted, the scientific thinker!) has identified all proper knowledge with scientific knowledge, in particular with the mathematical methods of physics or with other areas of science that attempt to apply its methods. When we look at the earth and the sun and their mutual relations *in this particular manner*, then there is no place for a sunset. The scientistic thinker characteristically concludes that the concept "sunset" belongs to a primitive pre-scientific generation and straightway excludes it from the body of true and valid knowledge.

The same sort of thing was involved in the Harvard professor's laughing remark to me about the ascension of Christ. From the point of view of our present scientific conception of the motions of physical bodies in space it is not possible to conceive of any absolute "up"; such a concept the scientistic thinker would describe as "medieval" and "obscurantist." We need to take a slightly closer look at what is involved here. What the medieval men had done was to accommodate scriptural revelation to an old Greek science. Medieval Christians read the Greek scientific meaning back into the revelation, so that the "up" of Jesus' ascension became confused with the "up" of the Ptolemaic world-picture. But science, a human activity, has a history. And when subsequently the Ptolemaic picture was cast aside by men like Bruno and Copernicus, the effect upon the Church and upon the attitude of men towards the Word of God was disastrous. Not because science had disproved the scriptures, but because the medieval church had accommodated the supra-temporal Word of God to a time-conditioned scientific piece of work, understanding the former in the light of the latter, thus reversing the natural order. The science in the synthesis was indeed primitive.

I suppose this was in the mind of that Harvard professor that day. But, as I have already told you, there was no opportunity on that occasion to explain to him how I thought about the matter. Actually, however, his observation had no more bearing on my thought than that other half-rhetorical question once put to me by one of Harvard's most distinguished professors: "How can you believe in God in these days when space has become so vast: where do you put Him?" For all the scriptures say about the ascension is that Jesus led the disciples to a place over against Bethany and that while they looked on He was taken up, and a cloud received him out of their sight. It ought to be clear that the "up" here simply refers to the very ordinary, everyday experience of those disciples who remained standing on the earth, the place appointed by God to be man's home.

The fatal original error of scientists was to take such a word as "up" and insist that the only "true" meaning it could have was the scientific meaning that refers abstractly to relations of physical motion. In logical terms, such words were thought of as being "univocal," i.e., as having one and only one meaning.

This scientism is still essentially the faith of the men comprising the teaching staffs of our modern universities. From my observation of Christian students over a period now of slightly more than twenty-five years *I am convinced that almost without exception the student is lost to integral Christianity not somewhere down the years of his university experiences, but at the very outset. The innocent freshman does not realize that the very existence of the university involves the philosophical problem as to its place, as to the place of science* (die Wissenschaft) *in the whole of life.* [1960]

For my senior year I went back to Wheaton. I had heard that they had a new instructor for Greek, a young Ph.D. graduate of Dr. Oldfather's (University of Illinois, trained, as J. Gresham Machen had been, in Gildersleeve's classical seminar at the Johns Hopkins University in Baltimore, Maryland). Harriet Jamieson was her name, and she was indeed excellent. I had two courses with her. We read the *Agamemnon* of Aeschylus, and we read two books of Thucydides' *History*. I became an assistant in the department and graded papers.

I had always had seminary, particularly Westminster, in mind (as well as the idea of becoming a missionary, at first to Korea, later to China), but more and more as I got into Greek I thought about getting a doctorate in classical languages and becoming a Greek teacher. And as a matter of fact, in my senior year Miss Jamieson recommended me for a scholarship that would have enabled me to go to the University of Illinois to study with Dr. Oldfather. You could get a doctorate in three years. It was a strong temptation. I asked her, "How many days do I have to think it over?" And she said, "Well, I ought to have your answer in three days." So I went into my room and just thought and thought and thought, and prayed, and I decided: No, I am not going to do it. If I do that, I'll do it after seminary. So I gave it up. I hated to give it up, because money was scarce in those days and I had never had much of it. In the summer following my graduation I taught a course in Plato's dialogues in the Greek department at Wheaton, and then in the fall of 1936 I began my studies at Westminster Seminary.

It was at Westminster that I learned about the revival of the Reformed religion in the nineteenth century. And I remember in my second year there that Dr. Van Til said to me: "If you want to become a Reformed thinker, you had better think about learning the Dutch language, because most of the writing in which this developing thought has been embodied will not be translated in your lifetime, if ever, and there is no way to get at it except to learn Dutch and read it well." So right then and there, I made up my mind to learn Dutch.

To Professor Van Til I am indebted in many ways. He first opened my eyes to the possibility of a Christian method in philosophy and from him I first heard about the serious effort being made at the Free University of Amsterdam to formulate a philosophy in the light of scriptural revelation. From him too I first learned to read the Dutch language, an accomplishment which has become a source of ever-increasing blessing and joy to me, chiefly in enabling me to follow the remarkable reformational work which the Spirit of God has wrought in the Netherlands since the days of Da Costa, Bilderdijk and Groen van Prinsterer. This historic movement has come to be for me what Athens was to the fourth-century Greek, the nursery of genuine *paideia*. [1951]

And then Professor Klaas Schilder of the Theological Faculty of Kampen, the Netherlands, came to Philadelphia. He had come to America at the invitation of some Christian Reformed men in New Jersey and Michigan to talk, among other things, about common grace. But at any rate, in April of 1939, Schilder stopped off at Westminster Seminary and gave three lectures. He dealt with Karl Barth's Gifford Lectures on the Scottish Confession of 1560, and he had some very critical remarks to make about how the work had been translated and interpreted. I listened very intently to those lectures, and I liked them very much. He was a brusk type of person, but I took to him, and at Dr. Van Til's suggestion I went to him to talk about my plans for the future. Since my high school days I had wanted to study at a German university. "Well," he said, "there is a high probability that there will be war very shortly, but why do not you come to Kampen for a year first? Then you can get a much better idea of what we have to offer in the Netherlands, and after a year you can decide whether you still want to go on to Germany. I can always give you references to people in Erlangen." And he tried to sum up what my expenses would be in Kampen, going into all kinds of detail about room and board, laundry, and so on... Anyway, I was persuaded to go to Kampen.

I was keen on going to Europe. At this stage of my development, however, it was not to learn more about the Reformed view of life and all that; it was almost exclusively in the interest of studying theology. I was not thinking much beyond that. I was just an idealistic young fellow who had grown up in the American Evangelical world, and we had this distinct phenomenon of Westminster Seminary, and the struggle was to keep our Presbyterian heritage. You see, the one Presbyterian Church in the United States split during the Civil War. Afterwards the North industrialized and prospered, and the northern seminaries began to send many of their brighter students to Germany, where the Ph.D. programs had developed. They began to get their professors back newly trained under Von Harnack and people like that, and so the *religionsgeschichtliche Schule* came into the seminaries. The big battle was whether Princeton would slowly but surely be caught up in the maelstrom and undergo the same influences, or whether it would stand apart from that development as a kind of rock of traditional Scottish-American Presbyterian orthodoxy – which really meant, philosophically, as I came to see later, Scottish Realism and back to the Cambridge Platonists and the idea of reason as having its own, if not scientistic at least practicalistic *a priori* and all that. I didn't realize those things then. I was simply caught up in that struggle of preserving our Presbyterian heritage over against the Modernism in the church that we had still recently been part of, and I wanted to be able to work with the best theoretical-theological tools available. That was the framework. That is why I went to the Netherlands. It was part and parcel of that notion that theological science gets at the finesses of the Christian religion. It was part of that confusion, that hearing the Word of God is doing and writing theology, that it is *there* that you are closest to the Word of God and are working out its finest meaning. It was the Greek faith in *theoria*.

> In the Christian world a particularly striking example of the insidious working of the scientistic frame of mind is the confusion of the immediate awareness of the integral Truth of the Word of God in our hearts with a scientific (theological) body of propositional statements about this Truth. So much attention has been devoted to the latter that the necessary earlier possession of the former has largely been overlooked... But the Reformation taught us that men are free from the theologians in understanding and interpreting the Word of God. Life

precedes science, and in life God makes us aware of (reveals to us) the Truth... The *terra firma* of God's truth ought not to be called theology, or we might get an unfortunate canonization, no, worse, declaration of infallibility of Berkhof or some other theologian (depending of course, on the speaker's preferences). Let us not be the cause of any theologian's becoming canon for us, or a stuffed shirt. [1960]

I sailed for Europe on August 24, 1939, the day the newspaper headlines read: *ROOSEVELT ADVISES AMERICANS TO LEAVE EUROPE.* The war broke out the day we arrived. Most of the Americans never got off the boat. They said: "We are going right back to the States," but I, a brash 23-year-old, who for so long had wanted to experience Europe and European education, finally said to myself, "I am staying here, no matter what." I settled in Kampen (where before the war the circumstances of the nineteenth century still surrounded you on every hand and some things reminded you strongly of the Middle Ages) on September 16 to live at the Hospitium of the Theological School.

Schilder appeared to have a very busy life. He published a lot, was editor of a weekly, served on a synodical committee, and during all this he would just rush into class almost out of breath and start lecturing. He never had a note in front of him, but he would talk, for example, about some point in dogmatics, about when it first became a matter of articulated doctrine of the church at some medieval council or in the debates between Abelard and Bernard of Clairvaux, or something like that, and he would quote the Latin text of the decision of the Council of Soissons out of the big collection of Hefele-Leclercq from memory. He was treating the *Locus de Deo*, and he was handling the difference between *cognitio Dei insita* and *cognitio Dei acquisita* as it developed in Reformed theology in the seventeenth century, and in connection with that how Descartes and the Cartesian school dealt with the whole problem of the innate knowledge of God.

Well, that was very much to the point for me, a young systematic theologian who knew something about the history of philosophy and could collate the two things. That is what attracted me to him. And although he didn't elaborate on it so explicitly, I slowly began to see in his lectures that behind that development or combined with it was this whole history of modern rationalistic philosophy and the Cartesian notion of the *a priori* which was bound up with the notion of *ratio*. And this is what made me begin to see that you can get partitioned off into theology and its history, while other people get siphoned off into philosophy and its history, and that that just isn't the way to get insight into what happened, because there is some common element behind them both that causes them to run parallel. There is a parallel in the phenomena of the several sciences. It is one *Geistesentwicklung* which took place. After six months of Kampen, I returned to America when the consulate advised us to leave Europe. It was the end of February, 1940.

My immediate problem was how to continue my education. Get a doctorate... but in what? I was in theology and had seen these lines running parallel in modern philosophy and modern theology. So that made me want to get to know more about church history. But I had to get help somewhere, so I sent out letters to about six graduate schools. The best answer I got was from Harvard Divinity School. It offered me six hundred dollars, which was good in those days, and on that basis I decided to go there. And I thought the best thing to do was to take Philosophical Theology or Church History, and I decided on Church History because I saw that I needed a lot more historical information than I had if I was going to be precise about what I did philosophically. Also, I had seen in their catalogue that George LaPiana (formerly of the Gregorian University in Rome) was there, and I thought this man might just be a good man to work with. I went to see him as soon as I got to Cambridge and told him I wanted to become a good historian and learn all the techniques, the ancillary disciplines, and whatever else was necessary. So basically I worked with LaPiana that year.

At the end of that year I was recommended by two men of the Divinity School faculty to the Society of Fellows of Harvard University on the basis of two papers I had written – one on some aspects of Augustine's *De Trinitate* and the other on Kierkegaard's *Abschliessende unwissenschaftliche Nachschrift* (at that time not yet available in

English). Well, I was appointed to the Society of Fellows. In those days I was studying Syriac. I had studied it at Westminster and was taking it at Harvard from Professor William Thomson, and I had started to read a certain man named Ephraim Syrus, and I got the idea, in connection with my studies in philosophy, that it might be a good thing to read some of the Syrian writers about dogma and some Greek writers like the Apologists and the Antignostic Fathers and see whether the structures of Greek philosophy were much less visible in the Syriac writers than in the Greek writers. That was the idea I had and that was the project I presented for the three years I would be a Junior Fellow...

I had an office to myself in the Widener Library near the section I would be using the most. So a lot of patristic stuff was right outside my office. And we had keys to the stacks – oh, it was an ideal set-up! As a Junior Fellow I could audit any courses I felt would be helpful. One I attended was by Edward Kennard Rand, who wrote *The Building of Eternal Rome* and *The Founders of the Middle Ages* (which has an excellent chapter on Boethius). Rand gave a course on the classical heritage of the Middle Ages, and one day he talked to me and I told him about myself and about my Syriac project. He said. "You know, a man you want to know is right upstairs – Werner Jaeger, formerly of the University of Berlin. I am going to see that you get introduced to him." So about a week later there was a note from Rand under the door of my office introducing me to Professor Jaeger.

Jaeger told me about his vow to Wilamowitz to finish the critical edition of Gregory of Nyssa, and that he had a number of people working for him and was looking for people to collate manuscripts to make a critical edition. And I said, "Oh, I would be interested in knowing a little more about that. Do you think it would be possible...?" I immediately jumped at the thing because I thought if you could work with him day by day you would learn many things. Perhaps I jumped too fast giving up this other project – I just said it on the spur of the moment, actually, but I have always felt the greater desirability of being educated by an outstanding *person*.

And he said, "Well, why do not you come and read for me some day?" So one day I went to his office and he gave me a page of Gregory of Nyssa to translate. Somehow I managed that, and he got up and smiled – he was always so gracious – and said, "Well, if you would like to be part of my institute, I think we could find work for you." Two days later I was up there getting photostats.

Our job was to collate manuscripts and then to determine the critical text. I was assigned a sermon of Gregory's that dealt with the resurrection. Meanwhile, Jaeger himself was continually going through catalogues of libraries in Europe, trying to find new manuscripts that might include work by Gregory and just thinking his way through manuscript history and manuscript dissemination. I learned a lot of things from Jaeger in terms of historical method, but I have had little chance to use them. I have always wanted to make an edition of something. I think it is important to get some project like this started with your students and to get an institute started. Christians ought to be doing this kind of work – in their own schools.

After three years at Harvard, I taught English and Latin at a Christian high school in Paterson, New Jersey, and began working for a Th.M. degree at Westminster. I would come down to Philadelphia for a week or a long weekend and spend a lot of time there. I completed it in 1945-46 while I stayed with my parents again, and I did substitute teaching in the public school system. I concentrated on two areas: the ancient church, especially the fourth and fifth centuries, Gregory of Nyssa, the Cappadocian Fathers and the men right around there in that part of the world; and secondly, the beginnings of Protestant scholasticism – Geneva, France, the men around Beza, Gomarus, Voetius, Cocceius. Also, what the differences were between the Genevan so-called decretal theology and the later covenant theology. I made big charts with hundreds of names and their writings.

Gradually, however, I was becoming a little bit skeptical about the meaning of my research projects. I was just accumulating facts, facts, facts, but my ability to unify them and to see sense in them wasn't keeping pace. And as for the relation of philosophy to the history of theology – I just felt I didn't have the key to that. And then there was the limitedness in my personal life: living in the city, attendance at public schools, voting Republican, growing up with the Shorter Catechism, the Keswick Conferences, the Scofield Bible – the dualism that characterizes so many American fundamentalists was my life too, and I began to feel I couldn't live that way any longer. My life was just a lot of bits and pieces; it wasn't pulled together. So I thought, my first task is to see my own life in a greater unity – get it all together – but I didn't know where I could get help unless it would be from that philosophical movement at the Free University. So as the war was coming to an end, I secretly in my heart longed to go back to the Netherlands.

So you see, my reason for going to the Netherlands again after the war was once more to a large extent theoretical – to gain clarity about the coherence of the history of philosophy and theology. And it was not until I began to study the *Wijsbegeerte der Wetsidee* more seriously that I began to sense the depth-dimension of man in the heart and the answer that a man gives and has to give to revelation. That took me years, but gradually I began to see the religious background of all human work, pre-theoretical as well as theoretical, and that our *certainties* – the problem Husserl wrestles with, and the problem Heidegger wrestles with, and they have not resolved it really – where does the apodicticity, the certainty, the universal validity, where does it come from? Husserl got it from Brentano and from British empiricism, but if it is to arise out of our experience of sense-data and our observation of factual situations, there is no possible explanation for an absolutely universal validity. There is no way to explain that, and you fall flat on your face. The idea that there is a *revelation*, that God's creation is of a law-order, and that that law-order somehow revelationally impinges upon us, and that our nature as religious beings in the covenant...

> It is difficult, Professor Vollenhoven, highly esteemed promoter, to express in words what these five years of association have meant to me. I marvel that just at the time when I threatened to succumb to the widespread pestilence of historical relativism, my footsteps were directed to you. For under your tutelage the divine antidote was with remarkable skill accommodated to the peculiar symptoms of my disease. [1951]

...of God is to walk with Him and to know this revelation in some immediate religious confrontation with God – that began to give me a new hope, the hope that I could deal with complex factual situations and that I could rest at any given moment because my knowledge of law or of universal validity (I am using later terminology; I wasn't all that conscious of those things then) wasn't derived from, or dependent upon, the building up of all those facts, so that I would collapse in the accumulation of them, but there was a deeper dimension constantly at work while I was studying history – in short, it was the religious background of the *Wijsbegeerte der Wetsidee* that put solid rock under my feet.

I got to Amsterdam in the fall of 1946. Holland was just pulling out of the war situation. Fuel was rationed, and so was food. I stayed in the Hospitium of the Free University on the Keizersgracht, and there I got to know Leo Oranje, and then in that winter of 1946-47 some very important things happened.

It was a very severe winter, and by February they ran out of fuel. We sat in our rooms with our overcoats on, hats on, earmuffs on, gloves – you would take the glove off, turn the page, put the glove back on – we had boots on, and so we sat and studied! And Oranje came to my room on a Friday afternoon – it was bitter cold and I was very uncomfortable – and he said, "You cannot study in this cold all weekend. I am going to my girl's house; they'll have a little heat there. Would you like to come along?" So I said okay and I went along. And that weekend I met Elisabeth Wichers, who was to become my wife! She was the older sister of Leo's girlfriend. That was in Badhoevedorp.

Later Oranje took me to Breukelen to his own family. His father was very active in all kinds of Christian causes; he was principal of a Christian day school, and he was in the Antirevolutionary Party, and he was in a Christian social organization called Patrimonium – I do not know what all. And once Leo Oranje casually remarked to me, "You take everything too theoretically." Well, he was a law student himself, but he turned to me and said, "You take everything too theoretically. Why do not you see something of our Reformed *life* in the Netherlands?" I said, "All right, but how do I go about it?" And he said, "Why not start with a visit to the Kuyperhuis? They'll be able to tell you something about it there." So I got on the phone and it was answered by Dr. Rutgers, the one who had been governor-general of the West Indies. When they found out that there might be more students interested, they arranged a day for us. So a group of us – myself, Harry Boer, a fellow from South Africa, and a few others – we all went down to The Hague and spent a whole day with the staff of the Kuyper Foundation. And we met Dr. Gerbrandy, who had been premier in London during the war, and we met and talked with a daughter of Abraham Kuyper who was already very old. But, typically Dutch, they had three people read papers to us: Mekkes, and Bruins Slot, and Van Riessen all read papers, each an hour long.

As I went home and thought it all over, I began to realize that there was a broad spectrum of reformed life, and that I had never experienced anything like this before. And I began to ask myself: Where did all this come from? There was the theology that I was used to, there was the philosophy that I was busy studying, but now I learned there was also a practical life. How were they related? I do not remember how I first got steered to Groen van Prinsterer – probably through talks with Leo at some meal or so at the girls' home – but I bought myself a copy of Groen's *Ongeloof en Revolutie*, i.e., *Unbelief and Revolution*, and read it. And I read about Isaac da Costa and Bilderdijk and Groen and about the differences between them. And then the problem that I originally had between philosophy and theology as two forms of scientific life got broadened out to also include pre-scientific life – what lies behind all this? And I began to sense the importance of the religious dimension of the heart and the covenant of God and what that means – that we live with God in His covenant, and that all the various aspects of our life are embraced in that, and how that openness or closedness of the heart to His revelation, which impinges upon us and to which we must respond, gives direction to all the various expressions of our life, whether they are scientific or pre-scientific. That began to take on some shape, but only gradually, and I do not think I got that all worked out until I had begun to teach at Calvin, really.

Early in 1948 it looked very much as if the Italians and the

French would all vote Communist at the general elections that were coming up, and there was general talk that the Russian armies would just come in and march right up to the Channel. One day at the end of February, my wife and I were sitting in De Roode Leeuw across the street from De Bijenkorf drinking coffee after doing some shopping when we noticed that the man at the next table was holding a newspaper which read in big headlines: *MASARYK COMMITS SUICIDE.* I didn't believe it. I thought he had been forced to do that, so I said: "It is time for us to get out of here." We left Europe somewhere early in March.

For a year we lived in Philadelphia, and then rented a cottage in Pella, Iowa, at the suggestion of Glenn Andreas, who lived there. Glenn and I have been close friends ever since we met at Wheaton, and he has been a source of encouragement to me in many ways all these years. I had all my Aristotle books with me and worked on my thesis. In March, 1950, we were back in the Netherlands to get the dissertation finished and approved and to receive my degree. I worked very closely with Vollenhoven. He was himself working on the development of Aristotle at this time and was preparing something for publication because I had to be able to refer to it in my thesis.

> The work of Vollenhoven makes claim to have penetrated far beyond the present insight into the nature and relations among the philosophical results of individuals and "schools" in antiquity... Can the promise which the method of Vollenhoven holds for getting Aristotelian research out of the impasse into which it has fallen indeed be realized? May we now look forward to the possibility of getting an interpretation of the Aristotelian corpus more in accordance with historical fact? It was such questions as these that induced me to undertake the present study... In sharp contrast to the opinions [of Nuyens and Jaeger] is the view of Vollenhoven, according to which almost every phase of Aristotle's development is represented in various parts of the *Physics.* Here is room, apparently, for more thorough textual analysis than has hitherto been forthcoming. [1951]

I tried to meet S.G. de Graaf this time, and I was very disappointed to hear that it was no longer possible because of his condition. You see, by this time I had begun to realize the importance of men like Sikkel and de Graaf and of that new covenantal preaching which had arisen and which was really the religious setting of the development of the *Wijsbegeerte der Wetsidee*. Also, I again participated in a series of gatherings at the Kuyperhuis for foreign students. I was doing a lot of thinking that year, and it involved my background. Knowing that Calvinism in America had generally meant Puritanism, I began to think: "How do I distinguish what I have come to see – how I have come to read the Scriptures and understand them – from the Puritanism which the word *Calvinism* had always meant to me?" And I made notes of important points that I would want to get across to students once I was back in the States and teaching. There were something like fifteen to twenty points, and when I rediscovered those…

> We must distantiate ourselves from the Pilgrims and Calvinists of New England, as well as from previous attempts to erect a "Christian political party" on this continent. (Cf. Schlesinger, *Age of Jackson*, p. 56.) We are not conservatives. Conservatives are one wing of the humanistic bloc, which, as times get increasingly severe, loses to the liberals or radicals. Train young college students to think of these things, and awaken through them the Christian people. [1950]

…notes years later and looked down the list, I saw that practically every one of those points had already been met in some way or other by the work that had been done in the meantime in the Groen Club. But we'll get to that in a moment.

I began teaching at Calvin College in the fall of 1951. For my course in Greek philosophy I chose one of the standard textbooks. But I thought to myself, "I am a beginning teacher. If I use the book to group our class discussions around, I will come more and more into that American way of talking and putting the problem, and that will be the end of *me*." So immediately I started making a syllabus. I used to sit up till two in the morning writing it out, and the next day I would dictate the few pages that I had ready.

We confess that God created us men and that He deals with us by way of covenant (Westminster Confession of Faith, ch. VII). Since the Fall however, men are in two different ways related to God by way of covenant: some, by virtue of the gracious restorative work of God the Spirit in their hearts... are once again in principle obedient to God, submissive to Him and His sovereignly declared will...: others are in a state of active revolt against God and His rule... These latter, though they cannot escape Him in this world of His creation, confronted as they are on every side with His works and working, make every effort of which their created nature is capable to demonstrate that the world is self-sufficient, i.e., capable of sustaining (ontology) and explaining (epistemology) itself. This dual relation in which men stand to God has always had, and of necessity must have, much to do with their *philosophizing*. It has always affected their – thus also our – study of the *history of philosophy*. In the sequel this will become increasingly clear and meaningful. For the present we shall merely say that it is because of the radical (from the Latin "radix," root) influence of our confession upon our philosophical work that this syllabus is a necessity. We do not, nor may we, feel at home in the philosophical studies of non-Christians. [1952]

Then in my second year at Calvin, in the Christmas holidays, one evening after dinner three men came to my door. They were Mr. Steven Harkema, Mr. Peter Boonstra, and Mr. Jacob VanderWilp. And they wanted me to speak for a group. It seemed that there was in Grand Rapids a group of immigrants who had formed a choir which met regularly, and these men wanted to deepen the meaning of the thing by getting conversations going in this group about the dangers of humanism in American public life. They thought that out of the membership of the choir there could be set up a Calvinistic Culture Association, and they asked me if I would speak for them at a public meeting to inaugurate such an Association. I agreed to do it. *And that is how it all got started!* In my speech I said basically that to start this separate Christian organization for cultural action was to throw the rudder over and launch out in a new direction. And I attacked the prevailing notion of common grace as though it could form a basis for cooperation in existing organizations inspired by humanism. Well, some of my colleagues who were present didn't like that at all! But some of the students who were present came to me later that spring and asked me if we could not get together more regularly to discuss these issues.

> The meeting was held on the evening of February 5, 1953, in the Eastern Avenue Christian Reformed Church, and the title of my address that evening was "Het Roer om!" (which, I have been informed, should be translated into English as "Rudder Hard Over!"). A number of Calvin professors were present, and several of them, unfortunately, were made exceedingly angry. There had also been a very good number of students present... Almost at once discussion, heated and persistent, began. To be sure, everything did not happen at once. But there must have been a great deal of talk among the Canadian students and Dutch immigrant students of the United States. Finally, I think early in March, Jan Kunst and Bernie Zylstra, who were together in my afternoon logic class, came to me one afternoon after class... and asked me if I would be willing to give one evening out of every fourteen days to some students who felt the need of discussion of such matters as Christianity and culture, and particularly the necessity of Christian cultural organization. I accepted immediately, before they had a chance to think twice... [1963]

That summer I drew up a program of study. It has never been completely worked out yet. It involved the question of who the Puritans were, the meaning of the Enlightenment, its influence in America, the basic ideas of the Declaration of Independence and the Constitution, the nature of Scholasticism, particularly as manifested in Reformed theology, the concept of natural law, the religious ground-motives that have successively given order to the experience of Western man, the origins of capitalism, the rise of the labour movement, and so on and so forth. And I had it divided according to topics: there were something like eight, but we started with about five, since there were around twelve or fifteen students who joined the club, and so two or three fellows started working on each of these topics. And then we would have meetings together. We would read the Scriptures and pray together and talk about our academic life and the meaning of it all, and then we would have a report on what work was being done in each of these groups. That is what we originally did.

And gradually out of these study groups came fuller and fuller reports. But then the students wanted to do something more on their own. And just at that time Mr. Harkema – he and I had talked a great deal at the beginning – and Mr. Boonstra had a painting business together. These men hadn't had much formal education themselves, but they kept saying, "We have got to form a group of students!" So when I was approached by these students, I must have told Harkema almost immediately, and shortly after that he brought me a whole set of folders which had been published by the Anti-Revolutionary Party for their leadership courses. (Each folder contained 15 to 20 lessons on a certain topic.) I took a quick look at the set and saw that most of them were not helpful (they were full of details about the Dutch political system and party history), but the first one was what came to be referred to as the Groen Club syllabus: *The Bible and the Life of the Christian*. I showed that one to these students at board meetings during that first year, and we came to the conclusion that we needed something like that in English, and then we decided to translate it. So that is how that got started. Now let's see…

> The following lessons have been translated and adapted by students of Calvin College and Seminary under my general supervision in the Groen van Prinsterer Society. After we had twice used them ourselves we felt so enthusiastic about them that we decided to make them more generally available. *They have helped us greatly*, and we feel confident they will help many others… *Do* books of human words ever help here unless the Divine Word – singular, thus a *structure!* – gets through, which alone is the POWER that can grip a human heart, draw it together into one and give it direction? In how many of our books, sermons, catechism classes, etc. does that happen? Or do we too often get lost in unrelated facts, individual persons in the Bible about whom we can moralize, etc.? No wonder so many of our words are POWERLESS! They do not convey the WORD!

The thing to do in the circumstances is not to fume and fuss but to *provide the insight* for which our young people are unwittingly hungering and thirsting, and for lack of which they will surely utterly lose their bearings. That is exactly what we think these lessons will do. [1963]

...oh yes, I was also persuaded that we needed to get into Groen van Prinsterer's *Ongeloof en Revolutie* (Unbelief and Revolution) so I assigned it chapter by chapter, and we had just begun it when I also decided that we ought to try our hand at translating it, to get more deeply into the work and into the meaning of it. That all happened in those early years, and although I myself only half knew where it would take us, we soon felt sure in our hearts that we were working in the right direction.

And then in 1956, in Toronto, the Association for Reformed Scientific Studies was founded – by ministers like the Reverend Henry Venema and the Reverend François Guillaume, and by Mr. Peter Speelman and Mr. Vande Riet, who were booksellers, and by a number of other men. Their second public meeting was held that fall, and Steven Harkema and I attended on behalf of the Calvinistic Culture Association. I remember, we drove over one Friday evening in Harkema's car. It was pouring rain as we crossed the Canadian border. Several fellows of the Groen Club came along – cannot remember who... Henk Hart, John Vander Stelt, Jan Kunst, Jan Groen, John Van Dyk (big John), Bernie Zylstra, Albert Huls (now deceased) – about five of those fellows. Well, it became quite apparent at this meeting, to me at least, that their ultimate aim, goal, was to establish a Reformed university in North America, but that they didn't really, apart from possessing a general vision, know how to go about it. I mean, they had only a very vague notion of what that meant and what it involved: a Reformed university, higher education that could really be called Reformed. And there was opposition from some of the American home missionaries in Ontario, who felt that their experience and guidance needed to be consulted more and who may have felt that this thing would mean competition for Calvin College. The Canadian men wanted to provide guidance for their Christian schoolteachers. They were thinking of making a night school of it. So plans were discussed to give evening courses in a Toronto church basement. I got up at one point and said some things about, you know, the true significance of the Reformation, and its decline, and its revival in the nineteenth century, and the need to make this a *national* movement, bringing in the western Canadian provinces.

> Every effort, anywhere in the world, at building Reformed Christian (institutions of) higher education is doomed to certain failure if, before it assembles large faculties from this or that trusted church denomination and builds appropriate buildings, it does not possess *insight into the inner point of connection* between God's revelation of Himself in Jesus Christ and the materials of the several areas of theoretical investigation and cultural forming. [1965]

There won't be time to go into how the Unionville Conferences came to be organized, starting with 1959 – three days of lectures for our college and university students. These gave the A.A.C.S. (then still called the A.R.S.S.) a tremendous momentum...

> This Study Conference... is designed... also to call attention to the really desperate need that exists here in Canada for *a center of scholarly research and university instruction of our own*, where we can, above all, just be ourselves, where, I mean to say, we can quite naturally and happily go from Scripture to our field of research and back again, glorying in our God and Father, Who is above all and blessed forever. [1959]

> Mr. Chairman, for the third successive year I have the honour of being one of your lecturers here at the Unionville Conference. I alone, of your speakers, have had the wonderful privilege of seeing this Conference grow to what, in the brief span of these three years, it has already become... The experiences I have had at these conferences I count among the most precious of my life. God has been pleased in our midst to perform a mighty work. In these conferences we are experiencing a recovery of the Word of God in its integral meaning as directing Principle of our *whole* life, or our "walk" in life, that is, of our life-dynamics. Specifically, as students we have been brought to view the whole of the scientific enterprise as a "moment" of our religion... And what is this

blessed thing that we have been experiencing here at this place if not a re-discovery of the Biblical "hearing and doing"...? [1961]

There is a tempo in human affairs. We cannot keep attracting students with mere *promises* of development and brief suggestions with respect to it. The *development* will have to come. There must be produced in our midst *a body of scripturally directed scientific knowledge*. This is what our students are waiting for. [1962]

After many years of hard work it was finally possible in 1967 to open the Institute for Christian Studies in Toronto. I was invited to give the opening address and for four years (1970-74) I had the privilege of...

We come today introducing into the life of this nation and of this continent a new institution. More weighty is the fact that for the English-speaking world it is even a new, an unheard of, kind of institution. The emergence of this new thing means that a new concentration of forces is taking shape. It signifies a re-organization of our human and material resources to accomplish a task not yet undertaken. There is a re-alignment with the avowed purpose of carrying out the Christian Mission in higher education in a manner and to a degree never hitherto attempted on our continent. This is a radical Christian proposal for radical times. [1967]

We do not put our confidence in rituals and liturgies, in our denominational histories or our theological systems. That is not to deny the relative importance of any or all of these when they are themselves scripture-directed. But our confidence is in the life-producing, life-sustaining, life-developing Word of our God... in the Word of God alone. The God who came near in Jesus Christ is our strength; His Word is our life. Mindful of our calling to be agents of reconciliation, our hearts cry out in the words of an Old Testament prophet: O earth, earth, earth, hear the Word of God and *live*. [1967]

...teaching a number of courses there on alternate weekends. At first we rented a classroom on the University of Toronto campus on Saturday mornings. I shall never forget that first session when I was introduced to my first class there by Bernard Zylstra. There must have been close to 100 persons present. Now I am a Fellow of the Institute, which for a young struggling institution has proven thus far largely to be an honourary position.

Meanwhile, the outlook for a greater penetration of North American culture and civilization by the Gospel as understood in the spirit of Calvin's Reformation has grown significantly brighter in recent years. For besides the Institute for Christian Studies in Toronto, we have the King's College opening in western Canada (Alberta), and in the state of Iowa Dordt College continues to take on distinctive coloring. In addition to all that, a renewed effort to find distinctive Biblically-reformed answers to crucial questions of our time, both theoretical and practical (and these in their relation to each other) is seen in a number of new undertakings at my own college – for example, the Calvin Center for Christian Scholarship. And then there is, in the political sector, what appears to me to be a most significant movement in the United States, the Association for Public Justice (A.P.J.).

You know what we need in Christian circles? Leaders, courageous and daring leaders for new and untried areas of scholarship, men who have been given very careful guidance and training for a period of some ten years or more. Thus also the means for such training. What you have to do is get promising young people who are wholly committed to serving Jesus Christ, get them when they are about 18 or 19 years of age, and start them on various programs of education. We sorely need some kind of a private program to see to this training of leaders in crucial and new areas of scholarship. It is a question, first, of religion, just as a commitment to life service as a missionary to a particular country is. For the young person may be asked to commit himself to an area of scholarship for which the need is not even generally recognized in his circles yet, which means, among other things, that he cannot foresee job possibilities. I have myself been involved in such situations, as when I advised Bernard Zylstra not to go on, as was the custom in those days, to prepare for the gospel ministry but to become an opening wedge in a reformational study of the law sciences, and when I suggested to Richard Van Houten that he make use of his Vietnam language experience to at last enter upon a study of the history of Chinese thought from a reformational point of view. In neither case were there jobs that could be promised. We had to expect everything from our Lord, but we *had* to venture out. The Lord, we knew, is always faithful and will open up the possibilities just in the nick of time, often to our own surprise.

I have been very much concerned about our realizing our world mission. We are very far from doing what Reformed Christians *ought* to be doing in this regard. What I would *like* to do is get hold of such a committed, bright young man with a feeling for languages and say to him, "Learn Arabic and (modern) Hebrew, or Russian and Slavic languages, or Chinese and Japanese, or Sanskrit and a couple of modern languages of India. Become as authoritative as you can in the language, literature, history, and thought of the people who are united in their language, and when you are, we'll set you up in a chair or department somewhere."

You see, in our large universities there has grown up, around the traditional center, that is, the various departments, another kind of life, that of institutes. And that is my idea, that around a traditional center we erect an Institute for Slavic Language Area Studies, an Institute for Sinic Language Area Studies, an Institute for the study of Hebrew and Arabic and Middle Eastern Studies, a Center for Hispanic Language Area Studies, and a Center of the study of India and its languages. And then you have covered most of the great cultural areas of the globe. (Indonesia and Africa are missing.) If, to begin with, we could get just one well-trained man in each institute, why, within ten years, think of the tens of people that would be in the process of being trained in that way, out of which further teaching staff would surely come.

This is of the essence if we are going to realize our world mission. If we do not develop that *world* calling, I think that what will happen to us is that we will become increasingly restricted and we'll say we only must try to hold on to what we have got (whatever that is) in our Anglo-Saxon civilization or in our Western European civilization, and then we will lose even this. One must always be pushing outward into the variety of cultures and peoples that have providentially emerged in history. Because revelation comes to all of them: the world that envelops them is revelational – *their own very beings are*, but they suppress that truth in their unrighteousness, and only the Gospel can break through that.

> And what of the philosophies of China and ancient India in this ecumenical age, when not only dialogue among adherents of the world's "higher" religions is being sought but we are at the same time being confronted with the irrelevance, and consequent impotence, of our Christian Mission to the proud cultures of Asia? [1965]

I have known enough missionaries, missionaries to Asia, for example, to feel that we aren't doing at all what ought to be done. I think that we ought to take those peoples very seriously, and the cultural and historical influences that molded them and made them what they are, and in the midst of which they live as individuals, and by which they are being influenced all their lives. We ought to try to understand from a Scriptural standpoint what fundamental distortions of creational revelation on the part of their predecessors have given form to their lifestyle and their institutions. But we aren't training our missionaries to do that sort of thing. What we need are places where they could be prepared for that. I really do think that we should begin with the major centers of culture and make an effort to understand their history and their literatures, the images with which they think and after which they model themselves, and their institutions. We should try, by the light of the Scriptures, to understand in what way men were giving response (however faulty) to that ultimate revelation of God to which they must respond, and in what way all that, in obedience to Christ, has got to be reformed by the light of the Word of God. In that sense you deal integrally with them. You allow them to stand in their full dignity, as they say, but a dignity which takes account of the fact that they are radically fallen from fellowship with God. Only then are you able, in a meaningful way, to lead to the reformation of what is there without destroying the sense, the religious sense, that they were, in what Paul calls the blindness of their hearts, responding to the ultimate religious conditions of our whole existence.

You know, I once had a Navaho student in my class in Greek philosophy. He told me over a cup of coffee: "Your missionaries came to my people and they – they're known as the People with the Book – they came and just threw the book into our laps, as it were, and told us that this was the Book of God and that we had to believe this. They never asked a question about how we thought, or what our religious ideas were, or why we lived as we did." I could tell that he resented it. Then he said to me: "I never knew that there was another way of relationship between us and you people until I sat in this class. But when you talked of all these concepts – universalism and partial universalism and individualism, about the theme of macrocosm and microcosm, about Realism and objectivism and dualism and monism – then I began to realize that here were many of the themes of my own people. And then I began to see how those things could be related to what the Scriptures present. I had never seen that before – how the real thoughts of my people were related to the fundamental themes of the Scriptures as [aberrational] responses to revelation."

So that is what I mean, you see, that revelation is a reality and that man everywhere must respond and that that is why we can talk together. Once you have seen that all the scientific and pre-scientific work is given direction by a person's religious stance in the heart with respect to God's revelation, then you really begin to work with people in the creational fullness of their life and your life and the life of culture. Then you get a true encounter, then you have true dialogue. *Even if there is an antithesis of direction with respect to that ultimate revelation, you meet each other in the notion that these positions, these views, are both there because we have got to answer some kind of a revelational impingement on our lives.* And both of us are called to order in that situation by the Word of God. God has given an order for human life, and that order is revelation which addresses us inescapably and calls us to obedience, to acceptance, to walking in its light, and so to blessedness.

In suggesting the incompatibility of Christianity and humanism I do not wish to be misunderstood. Not for a moment do I believe that... Christian and humanist have nothing to say to each other or must have no dealings with each other. The two can always in this life talk together, and they may repeatedly find ways of working together. But that talk and that practical cooperation will surely not be possible, as has so often been claimed, because the two faiths down deep somewhere share a common foundation before they diverge to two distinct and opposed movements... but solely – I speak from the Christian point of view (one must speak from a definite point of view) – solely because of the overwhelming, convincing testimony of the revelational creation-ordinances of God. The humanist, like the Christian, lives in the world God created, the world that is upheld and driven onward by His Word and by His Spirit... *All* men respond to the *one* law-order. Right here every man, just in this central capacity of *homo respondens*, is more than his own subjective systematizing of the moment. There is an element of *resisting*, which speaks of more than is contained in the positive systematic position that is being developed. Men do, after all, have to account for the structure of the creation as it is taken up in their experience, and until they adequately account for it they are restless, driven on to new modifications or to still deeper turnings of thought. [1960]

Well, I can see why you got me to say some of these things again here, because it has been central to what I have tried to say all these years to my students: it is the Word of God that orders our thinking and makes things fall into place. No, I wouldn't want to say just the Bible. The Bible is part of revelation: we can no longer understand creational revelation apart from God's gracious redeeming revelation of Jesus Christ – that is the coming of the Mediator. And Scripture – what has been inscripturated – is part of that, part of the whole coming of the renewing Word of God.

But we – we guard Article 2 of the Belgic Confession,[2] and we

---

2. Article 2 of the Belgic Confession reads as follows: "We know Him by two means: First, by the creation, preservation, and government of the universe; which is before our eyes as a most elegant book, wherein all creatures, great and small, are as so many characters leading us to see clearly the invisible things of God, even His everlasting power and divinity, as the apostle Paul

say the words, but we are not living as though revelation is real. I do not mean a *doctrine* of revelation, or a *theory* of revelation; I do not even mean a statement of fact about revelation. I mean that we live in a world whose very reality is revelation. We are living constantly in revelational light. I do not think we live and work in that realization. *And at this crucial point things are getting worse!* I think we are losing, under several influences. In the hands of men around Barth – *Zwischen den Zeiten*, Gogarten – creational revelation or general revelation got to be *Schöpfungsordnungen*, a kind of theoretical vindication of existing society. So there came a reaction against any talk about creation ordinances. And then there is historicism, which has been developing for a long time, and the influence of which I find is overwhelming now, just overwhelming. And then finally you have the traditional scholasticism – scriptural revelation gets to be propositional statements – and that is very strong at many of our seminaries today.

Thus a good deal of distrust arises whenever you talk about God's Word as Power. Yet, that is simple Scripture, and it is at this point that we have got to start if we are going to recover a vital Christian faith. All I have been concerned to do is to preserve the idea of revelation as God's sovereign Address to us, His Word that goes forth from His mouth into the world to do His will. I think, for instance, of Isaiah 55:11: "So is my word that goes out from my mouth: it will not return to me empty but will accomplish what I desire and achieve the purpose for which I sent it." And then there is Hebrews 4:12-13. The Word of God – whether that means the preached Word or that portion which came to be inscripturated makes no difference – is, as the very Address to us of the sovereign God, living, full of activity and power to accomplish. God is active in it to bring salvation or judgment. It penetrates with divine efficacy to the innermost being of man, commanding a response. Thus we can understand 1 Peter

---

says (Rom. 1:20). All which things are sufficient to convince men and leave them without excuse. Second, He makes Himself more clearly and fully known to us by His holy and divine Word, that is to say, as far as is necessary for us to know in this life, to His glory and our salvation."

1:23, that we "have been born anew... through the living and abiding word of God."

In its codified form, that Word, like the incarnate Son of God, becomes the object of our perception and analysis, but the Word of God itself is never object (and never subject, for that matter) but always LAW-WORD, a word that commands our life. It is usually the working in the background of the thinker's mind of a philosophy that does not comport with Scriptural revelation, a philosophy which leads Christians to think of Biblical revelation in terms of "propositions" to which the "mind" gives "assent." The anti-Christian philosophy of positivism has given us a view of "facts" which underlies much of the present discussion on the subject of Scriptural infallibility. And it is usually the anti-Christian philosophy known as phenomenology, or perhaps existentialistic phenomenology (Heidegger), that has brought historicism to the fore.

The solution is to allow the Scriptures themselves to speak to us again. The Word of God pierces to the very heart with its truth. That is why my wife and I have been translating S.G. de Graaf's *Verbondsgeschiedenis* (Eng. trans.: *Promise and Deliverance*, 4 vols. Paideia Press. 1977-1981). We really have great hopes that these four volumes will penetrate the whole Evangelical world, will draw worldwide attention, and will accompany our outreach to all the world's cultures. Already more than 25,000 copies have been sold, and now the work is being translated into Spanish and Chinese. We hope to see the day when it will be translated into Japanese, Korean, Arabic, French, and German. I just hope everyone will *read* this work, and that the covenanted structure of Biblical religion will get across. With Bavinck, I believe that the covenant relationship is the essence of the Christian religion, and that it explains the phenomenon of the world's religions.

There is another thing that concerns me very much, namely, that Christians must face up to the obvious collapse of our political system, and to the meaninglessness of the two-party system we now have in the United States, or even of the party structure as it is in Canada. What I think about this can be found in my little book *Scriptural Religion and Political Task*, and partly in the lecture "The Radical Christian Facing Today's Political Malaise" [see p. 377 of this volume]. I am encouraged by the direction taken recently by the Association for Public Justice (A.P.J.) in the United States. What about the political forming of the minds of the people in between the presidential election years? There is, you might say, none. And that is because the parties do not really stand for anything. In the mad rush for votes they tend to become parties of the center, or comprehensive parties that welcome all viewpoints, thus standing for none. How can we form the minds of the people politically in a Christian way? How will we handle the political education of our Christian youth? Until you have a party that *stands* for something, and candidates of such a party, you cannot tell what kind of political forming of the mind you have got to engage in. Our present system is nihilistic. We *need* Christian political organization and action.

> ...the real powers in life, the mainsprings and directors of cultural life and development, are convictions of faith. If the American parties wish to become significant as directors of *political* life, they will have to embrace clear-cut *political* points of view, a *political* creed. [1961]

> Dealing with this little fact or that little sin, kicking out the liquor bosses, ridding the streets of men engaged in illegal businesses, voting to keep a divorced person out of the White House – these matters, pressure groups, which have to work within existing organizations and concentrate only on individual problems – none of these get at the root of the matter. None of them deal with the problem. For the problem is *to array principle over against principle.* Liberalism is a religious *direction* in political matters. The two-party system, putting conservatism over against liberalism, or liberalism over against socialism, does not *realize* in American life the real struggle between the Gospel, the direction of life, and all these movements together as representing the humanistic direction of death. [1956]

So there is lots of work to be done! I still hope to do some of that work myself. I want to write especially for my Evangelical people – about the task in philosophy and why *this* type of Christian philosophy, and what *we mean* by a Christian philosophy. I want to explain all that very simply – prolegomena. And then I would like to write on Greek philosophy, and on phenomenology...

Grand Rapids, Michigan, June 18, 1976
Badhoevedorp, The Netherlands, September 6, 1976
Interview and notes by Harry Van Dyke and Al Wolters

Part Seven: Writings from 1979 to 1994

On Being Anti-Revolutionary and Christian-Historical at the Cutting Edge of History, 1979-80

An address given on the occasion of the centennial celebration of the founding of the Anti-Revolutionary Party, held in Noordwijk-aan-Zee, The Netherlands, 2-7 April, 1979

MR. CHAIRMAN, invited guests and friends:

First, a few words by way of introduction. And then permit me, first of all, to extend to leaders and membership of the AR Party of the Netherlands my most cordial personal congratulations on this joyous occasion of your "eeuwfeest," your centennial celebration, and to express the honour I have experienced, but also the joy I feel, at being privileged to be present here and to be a speaker at this International Symposium with which you are marking this event.

I cannot refrain from expressing my feeling of satisfaction that you have chosen to celebrate the occasion in just this way. I am reminded of how the great "Father" of the western church, Augustine, chose to celebrate his thirty-second birthday, his first after his conversion to Christianity, by discussing in the circle of his friends gathered in the rural retreat at Cassiciacum, near Milan, a central philosophical, nay, religious subject, man's inherent craving for happiness. It is the first of his preserved writings, the *De beata vita*. And what more fitting for a Christian political party than to draw aside to discuss in a week-long symposium the topic "A Christian Political Option."

I particularly want to commend you on making it an international symposium. AR Party, I have been waiting a long time for you to share more fully your political insight and experience, the wonderful vision of your founders and great leaders, with us Christians in other lands, who, starting a century late, and with such urgent business to attend to, have so much catching up to do. In its beginnings, the reformation associated with the name of John Calvin was a strikingly international movement. There are signs that such a phenomenon is reviving in a new generation, in many very young and exceedingly fragile groups of recently Reformed Christians in the United States and Canada, in England, Australia and New Zealand, and I can assure you that in that far-flung English-speaking world – I limit my remarks to that world – there is an as yet limited, but noticeably growing interest in what your party has stood for and accomplished in these last 100 years. I believe that I speak for all of these, largely young people in extending my congratulations and best wishes to you this morning. I should like to express the hope that your act of going international on this occasion is a harbinger of your reaching out a helping hand to us other Reformed Christians frequently in the future. Or have I come too late for that? Is your existence, like the philosophy of Merleau-Ponty, not characterized by a certain ambiguity?

For it is a fact, it seems, that in these days you are not only marking and taking note of God's great deeds in your midst this past century, but you are also having to face up to its being your last birthday as a separate political party inasmuch as you are looking forward to becoming absorbed into the *Christian Democratic Muster* or *Call to Action* (my attempt at translating Appèl) next year. Two things – and the question is as to their complete compatibility – are requiring your concentrated attention: God's glory in your history and your abandonment of your separate existence next year. That makes this not just a joyous moment but also a sobering and poignant one. I did not say "a saddening one." I said "a sobering one." And "sobering" is perhaps the very best kind of "joyous" occasion for a political party that is 100 years old and still making serious Christian claims in our time. To one like me who comes in from the outside, the really crucial question is, Just what is it that is really taking place? Obviously there are many excellent advantages, in a day when everything, including evil, tends to become a world-wide movement, to becoming part of a broad international movement of Christian Democracy. And for this reason too it is fitting that this symposium be international and that Dr. Papini, representing that broad movement of Catholics gathered in the Christian democratic movement worldwide, share this morning's session with me. What a witness and what a benefit it would be to the whole world if just here in Holland believers from the Catholic tradition and believers from the Reformed tradition could, *in answer to the call of God in His Gospel,* together take political action that would get to the root of the awakening world's misery and its sense of being exploited and oppressed by just the Christian nations of western Europe? At the same time I do want to ask, what does absorption into the CDA[1] mean? Does it mean that after 1980 there will be no on-going Reformed political reflection and witness and international support in the future? Will it prevent you, at least in any practical sense, from assuming, in a way and to a degree you have not done until now, the task of instructing new and enthusiastic groups of Reformed Christians out of your rich past? Or will it mean full and grateful acknowledgment of what has historically been brought about, and a strengthening of resolve to carry on and live out of the insight – singular, not plural – that has been gained in that experience? This is just one of the things I had in mind when I entitled these remarks I am making here today "On Being Anti-revolutionary and Christian-historical at the Cutting-edge of History, 1979–80."

I must ask your indulgence for one last introductory comment, a very personal word that I simply cannot omit. When a moment ago I extended to you my most cordial personal congratulations and spoke of the joy I feel at being privileged to be here, that was not just being done out of a speaker's sense of obligation at such a moment as this. It was not a perfunctory act, something, in other words, that I did just *pro forma.* Quite the contrary, I meant it to be my way of showing the deeply felt gratitude of my heart for what your party, its histo-

---

1.   Christen-Democratisch Appèl (Christian Democratic Appeal).

ry, the witness of its leading spokesmen and thinkers have meant to me, and have meant increasingly, throughout my life. I believe there is almost no one here who will know this, but at a certain crucial point in my developing life the bursting in upon my consciousness of an awareness of the existence of the Anti-Revolutionary Party, and a first acquaintance with it at the Kuyperhuis on an unforgettable day in early 1947, came almost as a moment of revelation. Out of an American church background that was not Reformed I had first embraced the Reformed faith while studying theology, and "Reformed" then meant for me largely my scientific-theological work. By 1947 my studies at the Free University in Amsterdam had convinced me of the importance of a Christian philosophy and the great need for philosophy to be reformed in the light of God's word-revelation. But it was through my contact with the AR Party, first on that spring day of 1947 when I met, among others, Prof. Gerbrandy, Dr. Rutgers and a daughter of Abraham Kuyper, that it began to dawn on me in a new way how all of a piece our life on earth is, and that God's call to man in the Gospel bears on *that life*, and that the issues of life are not, in *the first place*, scientific at all. Then I began to see the men of Patrimonium and the CNV, the men of the Christian school movement, and particularly the founders and builders of the AR Party, as the ones out in the front of that one battle of spirits to which theological and philosophical struggles also belong. The God of life, I came more and more to see, calls us in the undivided unity of our lives to live by every word that proceeds from His mouth, to love Him with everything we have got and are, to walk in His way. Strange that I should have had to learn that, since it is the very heart of the Christian religion. To have had one's view of "Reformed" restricted to scientific theology and philosophy shows how far our scientific arrogance had gone in the West. But enough of that. I have come here to thank God with you for spiritual men of the caliber of Groen and Kuyper and the first "adjunct-directeur" of the Dr. Abraham Kuyper Institute, Herman Dooyeweerd, who saw the need of a think-tank long before the word came into common use, and so many more, who through faith "conquered kingdoms, administered justice, obtained promises, stopped the mouths of lions, quenched the fury of the flames, escaped the edge of the sword, *out of weakness were made strong*, waxed valiant in fight, turned to flight foreign armies" (Heb. 11:33-34).

The saga of the remarkably rapid development of AR thinking in the second half of the 19th century and well into the twentieth has been a very important influence in my life. I could not help but pass on to my students, and to any others who would listen, what your Party has meant to me. As some of you know, for seventeen years I had a rather large club of students at my college, and I persuaded them, back in 1953, to call it the Groen Club, to hold in honour one who, in generations before us, had come to see that faith, far from being moralism or some introverted other-worldliness, is obedience to Revelation, a willing listening to the Word of God *which results in acts of faith that relate to our time and situation*, something that involves a probing or testing of the spirits that are in the "phenomena" and movements of our time. I believe that that Groen Club, combined with the immigration of Reformed families, has had much to do with the newly emerging interest in the AR Party in all those places I have already mentioned.

I wanted to tell you this about myself so that if someone should think me presumptuous in speaking as freely as I do, he would be inclined to forgive me and understand that it is only because of my great love for the builders of your Party and the interests of the Christian cause in the entire world that I speak. And of course you ought to have the interests of all these young groups in mind in your work here. Wherever, on the other hand, I speak out of ignorance, which is not only possible but highly likely, well, I have come here also to listen, to discuss and to learn.

~ ~ ~

At the beginning of the 19th century any significant development of distinctly Christian thought or of Christian social or political action must have seemed highly unlikely. The Enlightenment and German *Aufklärung*, for all their relative good, had shifted men's attention from revelation and faith to autonomous human knowledge and the benefits of culture (*Bildung*) and the sciences. There was a general weakening of Christian faith. Great inroads were made on the Reformation spirit. But the same rationalism and naturalism that affected Protestantism also made its influence felt in Roman Catholic life. George Hermes, a Roman Catholic professor at Bonn (he died in 1831, the same year as Hegel), who taught that man must doubt everything and then accept only that which is acceptable to his reason, that man himself is the last instance of truth and that obedience to God is nothing else than obedience to reason, had a large following. In his *Handbuch der katholischen Dogmatik*, M.J. Scheeben calls the period from 1760-1830 the "Epoche des Verfalles."

All this, however, was not just the effect of Enlightenment and *Aufklärung*. The flight from the God Who has revealed Himself and Who calls us back from our rebellion and disorder to His service and the Order of His creation work had long been going on. And although I may seem to be making an unnecessarily long excursus, I must, in connection with my theme, say just a word about it. In the end, I hope, this procedure will work clarifyingly.

In the Enlightenment we can see the continuation of two movements with which the modern era had begun in Europe, both of which enervated the Christian movement. Those two movements are: (1) Classical Humanism, in connection with the revival of the study of classical letters, and (2) the Renaissance proper. Since the Enlightenment is usually related only to the Renaissance, and is indeed closer to it, I shall, briefly, have only this to say. Central to the Renaissance is the idea of reliance upon one's own resources and inherent powers for the renewing of our life. It was a satanic attitude, utterly destructive of the life of Christian obedience. For the other side of the coin was the drive to be free from all external authority and restraint, be it of Church or State or Law of God.

The movement of Classical Humanism ultimately has had the same effect. Let me refer to its beginnings in the men around Petrarch and the later Florentine Academy. In an attempt to get behind the medieval world (the spirit of which was on the wane) to the grandeur of ancient Rome, Petrarch, who had been deeply impressed as a young man by his reading of Augustine's *Confessions*, oriented his thought to an Augustine in whom he saw both Church Father and Roman citizen. It was the freshness and immediacy of the synthesis of ancient classical and Christian thought in Augustine that attracted him. Just imagine a Church Father who had been at home in that great Roman Empire! (Centuries of *acceptance* on the part of the Church of the life and thought and ideals of the classical world are playing their part here.) Is it not significant, therefore, that later in Petrarch's life the place of Augustine was taken by Cicero, an outright pagan, and that Petrarch's most famous pupil, Boccaccio, the next head of the group, still, after the Rienzi episode, concerned to restore Rome to her pristine grandeur, listed those things which had been foreign importations upon Italian soil and thus prevented contemporary Italy from recovering her ancient splendor, placing the Christian religion from the backcountry of Judaea at the top of the list? Indeed, a spirit was emerging which, having initially failed to discern the opposition (antithesis) of direction between the classical world and the world of Christian faith, led quickly to the swallowing up of the Christian spirit in talk of virtue.

The revival of classical letters took place within the movement of Classical Humanism, and wherever this movement spread the same thing happened. In the North, who will ever be able to estimate the damage the Erasmian *gymnasium* and the *gymnasium* of John Sturm at Bucer's Strasbourg – the model, in general, for Calvin's academy – have wreaked positively, in the training of the clergy in classical letters and, negatively, in the failure to nurture the sound development of an educated Christian mind?

Because of positions that have been maintained in the history of education I fear that my remarks – and my reason for making them here – will surely be mistaken if I do not add a personal comment. In my country, at least, the study of the classical world and of classical thought is not held in high regard generally; only for specialist careerists and even then in but a very few of our best universities. I do not wish what I am saying to be associated with such an attitude. Not only am I *not opposed* to the study of the ancient classics; I am *an ar-*

dent proponent of their study. God in His providence rooted our civilization in the civilizations of Greece and Rome, and any education
which neglects these is scarcely worthy of the name. What is needed
is not less, but more – in my country far more – general education of
a solid quality in the meaning of the classical world. For several years
I was closely connected with Professor Werner Jaeger's Institute for
Advanced Classical Studies at Harvard University, which was engaged
in preparing a critical edition of the collected works of the fourth
century Cappadocian Father, Gregory of Nyssa. No; what is wrong is
not the study of the ancient classical world, but *the attitude of classical
humanism*, which looks upon the Greeks as the fecund source and
dynamic of all that is good and noble and just in our western culture;
cultivates an admiration for the Greeks in the minds of the young;
and fails to see the alienation from the God of historical covenantal
dealing with men and the erection of a world-picture which securely
locks that God, the only true God, out of His world, fails to see the
mis-taking of the divine LAW–for–HIS–creation, finding it instead
somewhere within this world, mis-identifying God's covenant part-
ner, man, with a rational mind left to its own devices in the present
world.

We are talking, you will remember, about the state of exhaustion
of the Church, Catholic and Protestant, around the beginning of the
19th century. I said that this was not to be credited solely to the Enlightenment, which only continued the emphasis of the Renaissance
on man's autonomous freedom, but found itself strengthened by the
discovery of a method, the method of mathematical physics. Classical Humanism contributed much more than has been realized. But
the story is as old as the emergence of Christianity as a power in the
Roman world. Let me say the rest in a couple of highly condensed
sentences.

When the Church entered the Empire it did not perceive the Call
(*Appèl*) of God in His Gospel as a calling of the monster-state of that
time back to the Order God had established in the beginning by His
Word. Obviously, such a state was in open conflict with the revelation
of the Rule (*basileia*) of Christ in His Kingdom. Instead, the Church

adapted itself to that form of the state, *except* where it came in conflict with the obligation to confess Christ, and the adaptation was justified by quoting Jesus' words: "Render unto Caesar the things that are Caesar's, and unto God the things that are God's," overlooking the fact that the second member of that sentence spoke not of the pope or of some other ecclesiastical head, but of God, the sovereign over *all* His works.

Likewise, the Fathers of the Church never arrived at a critical theoretical accounting of the Christian's relation to the world of culture they found at hand in the Roman Empire. The classical patristic solution of this problem, arrived at towards the end of the fourth century by men like Basil of Caesarea and Jerome, was more an immediate reaction, a working arrangement pressed from these Christians by the exigencies of their life in the Roman Empire. They were not yet able to come to real grips with the problem. They adapted themselves to a situation instead of critically appraising it in the light of God's *Appèl*. The analogy they used of the Israelites' taking the jewels of the Egyptians when they fled Egypt breaks down as soon as one realizes that jewels are not ideas that arise out of their hearts, but belong to God Who made the earth, and *were only found in the possession of the Egyptians*, who, like men at all times, are charged to be responsible stewards of God's earth.

It was this essentially uncritical *modus vivendi* of the *patres* which formed the nucleus of scholastic thought on the problem: classical letters ancillary to the study of theology, and any Christianly-discerning, in the light of Scripture, of just what it was they had before them lacking. This attitude of adaptation continued in the Erasmian and Sturmian gym*nasia*, and, I fear, in Calvin's academy in Geneva. Failure to push analysis of the problem Augustine raises in books V (11–21) and XIX (24–26) of *The City of God* to a point of greater clarity accounts, in my opinion, for the eroding effect of the movement of Classical Humanism on Christian life and thought. For, as a matter of irrefutable fact, the life of the Greeks and the Romans, including the thought of their great thinkers, was thoroughly paganistic.

We have to go back still another step. Actually, the failure we have been alluding to antedates the Christian era. That should not surprise us. There was a people of God before Christ came to earth, whom God had chosen to be His special people, in whose midst He chose to dwell, with whom He chose to have fellowship. Implied in that set-up was the Summons (*Appèl*) of the Gospel of God to the sons of Abraham to separate themselves from the world and to live lives characterized by reconciliation and shalom in the enlightening and renewing light of the revelation God gave, and continued to give, of Himself. Outside that circle of special revelation men lived in the darkness of their (alienated) understanding. But the Jewish community in Alexandria in the last century or so before Christ, surrounded by the Greco-Roman world and its culture, again, as now, adapted themselves to it, accepting it in a sense, arguing that Divine Wisdom (*Chokmah*) had illumined *both* the Hebrew prophets and the Greek philosophers, and thus turned a religious antithesis of direction (Light and Darkness) *into a mere difference of degree of clarity of insight.*

In early Christian circles Justin Martyr did the same thing, attributing the universal enlightenment to the work of the divine *Logos* "which lighteth every man that cometh into the world." The "natural world" was not satanically directed against the reign of God and His Christ; it was simply not complete. It needed to be supplemented by grace.

For just a moment in history the secular spirit of the Renaissance was powerfully stemmed in great areas of Europe by either the Reformation or the Counter-Reformation. And the Reformation began, though only here and there, to develop a sounder view of the world of thought and action found in classical letters. But the new divisions in Christendom ended in ceaseless theological and ecclesiastical disputings and in the Wars of Religion, and when the spiritual *élan* began to wane and Europeans generally turned in disgust from all the wrangling, the old spirit of the Renaissance re-emerged, but now reinforced by a marriage with the new, upcoming science and scientific method of Galileo and Newton, in the movement we know as the Enlightenment.

Who, then, in the early decades of the 19th century could have looked forward with any expectancy to a revival of Christian thought and action? And yet it came. A stirring in both Protestant and Catholic wings of Christendom. God's Spirit was striving with man. There yet had to be fulfilled the words of a very ancient prophecy: "that God enlarge Japheth, and let him dwell in the tents of Shem." The loss of Christian faith that is to be witnessed already in the 17th century was accompanied by a rising interest in curious non-European cultures and a downplaying of the uniqueness of European civilization. The loss of confidence in the direction and significance of European civilization in our time is nothing new, only its scale. Europe's importance remains, however. For it is not something inherent in us who are the West, but it lies concealed in that prophecy of Noah that Japheth would dwell in Shem's tents and thus share in the blessing of Shem, that is, in the salvation of the Christ. Its importance lies, in short, in God's gracious providence. Europe became the main theater of the fundamental battle of spirits. In Europe we see the bottom-line wrestling of the Spirit of Christ with the spirit of the world for the cultural unfolding of creation's possibilities. This struggle is what European history discloses, and in the beginning of the 19th century that struggle was not over.

Who, as late as 1845, could have foreseen the glorious history and remarkable achievements of the Anti-Revolutionary Party in these past 100 years, and that we would be gathered here this week in Noordwijk-aan-Zee celebrating the "eeuwfeest" of the first political party in Holland to be organized on a national scale?

I choose the year 1845 advisedly. It was the year Groen began giving the lectures *Ongeloof en Revolutie* to a circle of friends in his home. But also, in those lectures he carried his analysis of the Revolution down to the year 1845, Revolution conceived as the casting aside of the divine ordinances. This was also the year that saw the completion of Auguste Comte's major work, *Cours de philosophie positive*, which, with its "Law of the Three Stages," was to become so influential a power in European culture, especially for the next 75 years. This positivism, with its idea of progress from the (1) theological stage of societal development to the (2) metaphysical to the (3) positive scientific, three stages of organization of society arising from three ways in which men explained to themselves the experiences they had, was itself a systematic and aggressive presentation of Revolution in Groen's deeply religious sense of the word.

L'Ecole Polytechnique in Paris, where Comte had been a student for a couple of years, stood as the symbol of this third – and final! – stage in the development of human society in which men had finally learned how to use their rational powers maturely and responsibly, the stage of society which scientists and engineers would organize for the improvement of the human condition. Facts, scientific facts, were to guide men, and laws were looked upon as simply more general facts relating particular facts to one another. No, it was not especially a time in which to look for the rise of Christian reflection and action.

Yet there remained a people of God in the world, however unsettled and confused and weakened they might have become as a result of world events and the spirit of the times, and as early as the late 1820s there were significant stirrings in the Christian world. In 1830, when Comte was just setting out to write his *Cours,* Groen was in the midst of a profound change of position. He was becoming an evangelical confessor of the Gospel. In his *Autobiography* he says that his new Christian-historical ideas were formed and developed in the years 1827–29. According to a letter he wrote in 1831 his publication of *Nederlandsche Gedachten* brought him to see clearly the main cause of the evil in society, i.e., the systematic apostasy from Christianity. The evangelical awakening, which began with the sudden conversion of the Calvinist César Malan in Geneva in 1816, had reached Amsterdam and a group of prominent men of learning was forming around the converted Portuguese Jew, Isaac da Costa. Bible study and prayer constituted the heart of their gatherings, but articles by Koenen, van Hall and de Clercq in the magazine *Nederlandsche Stemmen* began to arouse Protestant believers to see the connection between their religious faith and political affairs. For 40 long years Groen developed AR principles and withstood the revolutionary ideas, and by his correspondence gathered a Reformed community, teaching them to think principally about political activity in the light of Revelation.

The *Réveil* in Amsterdam had led to the erection of the Anti-Revolutionary electoral association "Nederland en Oranje" and as other AR electoral associations arose, even though they were independent, they all looked to Groen van Prinsterer as their leader. In this way Groen prepared the way for the organized AR Party.

While all this was going on a similar development was taking place in French Catholic circles. The remarkable career of Hugues-Félicité Robert de Lamennais shows us French Catholics attempting to come to grips with Rousseau and the French Revolution. Although his career suggests, besides his consistent belief that a society cannot recover spiritual and moral health without a sure and well-founded faith in God, something of a capricious lurching in this direction and that, Lamennais represents a whole generation's attempt to come to grips as Catholic Christians with the changed conditions in Europe. One writer has said that the life of Lamennais is a drama in which the history of a whole century is concentrated. He "always stood... on the frontiers where church and state, church and society, meet and interact." In one respect he was like Groen: he was "a man capable of attracting intense loyalty from some of the leading figures of the period." Groen refers to him numerous times in his *Unbelief and Revolution* and even says that his book *Des progrès de la Révolution et de la guerre contre l'Eglise*, influential also in Belgium, had helped him to see that liberalism was nothing other than the revolutionary theory. That book was published in 1829, and the magazine *L'Avenir* began its short but intense life the following year (1830-31).

By the 1870s these new stirrings, both Reformed and Catholic, had become clearly discernible movements of the people. In Holland, the Reformed movement had seen the emergence of Abraham Kuyper as a great intellectual leader possessed at the same time with unusual organizational talents, and the establishment of the Anti-Revolutionary Party (April 3, 1879) in Utrecht. *Patrimonium*, the oldest Christian social organization, an association of workingmen, was organized a couple of years before then, in 1876.

In the interval, a most important event occurred in the Catholic world, one that had its repercussions in Dutch Catholic circles and prepared the way for the future Reformed-Catholic political coalition in Holland: Cardinal Pecci was elected pope and took the name Leo XIII. He reigned 25 years, dying in 1903 at the age of ninety-three. His eighty-six encyclicals, dealing with a variety of modern problems, constitute the most important single contribution to Catholic teaching since the Middle Ages. In the very first of his encyclicals, *Inscrutabili*, Leo XIII had said that "the cause of civilization lacks a solid foundation if it does not rest on the eternal principles of truth and on the unchangeable laws of right and justice." And speaking of his famous encyclical *Aeterni Patris* (1879), which deals with "the restoring in Christian schools of Christian philosophy according to the mind of the angelic doctor St. Thomas Aquinas," Leo wrote that he could see no safer way to end the war waged against both Church and society itself, than "everywhere to restore, by the teaching of philosophy, the right principles of thought and action." Etienne Gilson writes in this connection that "the teaching of the Christian philosophy of the Scholastics, especially that of St. Thomas Aquinas, is considered by the Pope a necessary prerequisite to any practical scheme in view of restoring the social order... Catholics should not hope to restore any Christian political and social order on any other foundation."

To get back to the situation in Holland, the elections of 1880 showed a marked strengthening of the AR faction. They also brought into the Second Chamber from Breda the 36-year-old Professor Dr. H.J.A.M. Schaepman, who belonged to the more socially progressive Roman Catholics. Professor Schaepman played an important role in the development of a Catholic political party and worked hard in the forming of a coalition of Catholics with the Anti-Revolutionary Party. In 1883 he published in *De Wachter* an article that has become famous: "Een Katholieke Partij: Proeve van een Program." Schaepman did not envision that this party should be ecclesiastical. "What Catholics want to avoid, what they want to make impossible in the future is just this: that they count in politics as nothing more than followers of the Roman Catholic faith. That is why they want a political platform that does not place them over against protestants but against liberals and conservatives... a platform that is anti-revolutionary to the core, but which yet betrays its own origin, reveals its own color and bears a character of its own."

The year 1880, besides being in these two ways an important election year, had witnessed a most historic event: the Free Reformed University of Amsterdam had been opened with an address, itself historic, on the subject "Sphere Sovereignty."

A decade later, the year 1891 witnessed the First Christian Social Congress, at the opening session of which Kuyper delivered his famous address *Het Sociale Vraagstuk en de Christelijke Religie*. Michael Fogarty, in his book *Christian Democracy in Western Europe, 1820-1953*, calls this "the most remarkable event of its kind in Dutch history. The speech with which [Kuyper] opened it is read and re-read to this day. As a statement of Christian social principles and policy," he writes, "it is worthy of the year which also saw the appearance of *Rerum Novarum*." This latter is, in the minds of many people, the most important of all the important encyclicals of Pope Leo XIII, and it strengthened in the Dutch Roman Catholic group the desire to seek for social legislation, a development which greatly helped make possible the political coalition with the strongly socially oriented Abraham Kuyper.

In 1901 we get the Coalition cabinet of which Kuyper was prime minister, composed of three AR ministers, three Roman Catholics and two others.

What a change in the cultural climate since the 1820s! Catholic and Protestant political parties, guarding their independence, but also a political coalition brought about by the great leadership abilities and the prudent wisdom of Schaepman, Lohman, and Kuyper. A coalition against the modern spirit of unbelief and the assertion of radical autonomy, but not a fusion.

Since then, in the 20th century, there have been at least two more outstanding developments I should mention: one, the founding of the Roman Catholic University at Nijmegen; the other, the bold plan Dr. Colijn submitted to the national convention of the AR Party in the spring of 1920, the last year of Kuyper's life, which led to the establishing of a party national headquarters, where Herman

Dooyeweerd became the first adjunct-directeur, with the intention of working out in a systematic and scientific way the foundations of a Reformed Christian political position.

Out of these historical developments there gradually emerged a Reformed Christian outlook or "mind" alongside the Catholic "mind" which Pope Leo XIII's *Aeterni Patris* had again encouraged. Both these "minds" became the basis also for the political activities of those who held them. But it is important to say at once that the life of politics is only one dimension of our life. God's Summons to be reconciled to His Order comes to us at that point in the undivided unity of our lives where I am I, and where you are you.

There is – and every generation will have to confess that anew from the heart – only one reason for Christian political activity and organization, and that is that the Christ of God, according to the promise, came into the world and brought to us men new life out of heaven, the life of the Spirit to replace the life of the flesh. Of course, this new life involves a whole new man, a new attitude, a new "mind," a new insight into the nature of the world, of man and his place and role in it, of law in the universal sense of that word, of human society, its pluriformity and its unity, of authority and freedom, of the dynamic of civilization. This new life in Christ is the ultimate ground of Christian political activity. To take hold of that life and to live of it – that is our salvation: "Work out your salvation with fear and trembling, for it is God who works in you to will and to act according to his good pleasure... that you may be blameless and pure, children of God without fault in a crooked and depraved generation, in which you shine like stars in the universe as you hold out the word of life" (Phil. 2:12, 13, 15, 16a). Let me put in juxtaposition with that one more place in the New Testament, namely Matthew 11:12-13: "For all the Prophets and the Law prophesied until John. From the days of John the Baptist until now, the kingdom of heaven has been forcefully advancing, and forceful men lay hold of it."

That is, from John's days until now the kingdom of God reveals its presence, and this activity is described strikingly as a display of power in which we men powerfully engage. Political life is only one of the dimensions of our life in its undivided unity which is a manifestation of that kingdom which is forcefully advancing. The moment we come to regard politics as something in itself, cut off from the life of that kingdom, the moment, for example, that we as Reformed men and women begin to think of a particular political party which has been bequeathed to us by our fathers as our own little bailiwick, a place where we can pursue, realize our own little political careers, judge strategies by counting numbers, at that moment Christian politics has come to an end.

For the Christian, therefore, the appearance of the word "Appèl" in a political context can only have meaning in the light of the Call that comes to us in the unity of our personal lives and our corporate life to forsake the ways of "the flesh" and to learn a new obedience, the way of the Spirit, Who is guiding our society and our history to their appointed end in Jesus Christ. To the person who has thought about the spiritual struggle of our time it should be immediately clear that the battle is none other than to determine which spirit is to give direction to our civilization as a whole. Christ said, "Man does not live by bread alone, but by every word that comes from the mouth of God." I once wrote, with reference to evangelicals in my country who were not waging this *total* battle of the human spirit: "A church organization, or a world of Christian theological activity, standing alone within a culture of which all its other activities are directed by an anti-Christian spirit, must remain impotent, and has become irrelevant, and will in time fade away. Even to preserve the organized church, therefore," I wrote at the time, "we must fight for an integral Christian society." The same could, on this occasion, be said of the AR Party. Either there will be a quickening of faith in us as persons and as a collectivity, a quickening which senses the unity of life as religion, or there will be a quiet accommodation, in almost imperceptible stages, to a way of life which is no longer responding to the Word of our God, which alone is life-giving.

It is important to observe that the beginnings of the AR Party lie concealed in the conversion of Groen, a conversion within the community we speak of as the evangelical awakening, with its rediscovered sense of the universality and radicalness of sin and its desire to develop an alternate Christian life-style. If it had not been for Groen's conversion in that setting, and his subsequent coming to see in the Revolution (not just the French Revolution, but the liberalism that issued from the Napoleonic period, and the revolution of 1830, and the revolutionary year 1848) the satanic will to contest the Reign of the sovereign God in His appointed Office-bearer, Jesus Christ, there would be no AR Party. If it had not been for Kuyper's conversion and rediscovery of Calvin and his emphasis on the sovereignty of God over all His creation, and on the glory of His Law, there would be no AR Party. If there had not been, however quiescent, a Reformed people in the land, Kuyper's beloved "kleine luyden," there would be no AR Party. If there had not been Reformed congregations of worship in the Netherlands where the gospel of salvation by sovereign grace was being preached, there would be no AR Party. The life of men is one, and the life of the Party can only be a reflection of the wider life, which it expresses in a particular way. That is true at any time; it will be true today. Where the life generally is strong, firm, resolute, so will be the life in the Party; where it is uprooted, dislocated, confused, uncertain, so will be the life in the Party.

What now is that specifically Reformed Christian "mind" that developed in the course of the 19th and 20th centuries here in Holland and became the basis of Reformed Christian political activity? In one sense that mind was completely present already in Groen. It was, simply, the desire to "read" reality – all of it, its natural as well as its cultural dimensions, the "world" of things and the "world" of human acts in all their complex interrelationships – and to live life in its entirety, by the light of God's word-revelation. But in another sense there was development, from Groen to Kuyper to Dooyeweerd, to mention just the main line. From the Groen who rediscovered the central and radical place in life of religion, that is, of faith and unbelief, which implies an integral creation, to the Kuyper who stressed the divine ordinances and achieved an intuitive grasp of the structures of society grounded in an Order of creation and the Law-word of God (the principle of sphere-sovereignty), to Dooyeweerd, in whose work we find that intuitive grasp theoretically-analytically grounded in our experience. Development that brought implications out clearly, and brought the whole into sharper focus. But also a development that was characterized by a tremendous and sustained effort at self-correction, a struggle to continue to cast off "the flesh" that is always clinging to us all and to our tradition and to become more completely subject to the revealed will of God in both His word-revelation and His act-revelation (acts of creation). For that is how the kingdom or rule of God forcefully advances, and how forceful men lay hold of it. It is not by force of arms, but by faith in the Word of the living God, itself begotten by that Word, that a discerning insight into the Order of Creation, the creation acts of God (themselves revelation) is engendered that so accords with reality's structure that it persuades. Always, "the vocation of the biblical people of God is prophetic discernment," an American Christian recently wrote; and he added, "What we need to engage in are acts of imagination that penetrate the apparent opacity and aimlessness of the historical present, and reveal how persons and institutions are accomplishing their destinies in relation to the sovereign God of history."

The intensity of my feeling requires that I break off my story for a moment to introduce another element into the picture. In my country the first sentence of Charles Dickens' *A Tale of Two Cities* is often quoted: "It was the best of times, it was the worst of times." But I must say that these words, and the time they are describing (1775), bad as it was, when judged by present realities seem so "bourgeois," almost trivial. For we live today in hellish times, and I do not mean just Solzhenitsyn's Gulag Archipelago, or the Cultural Revolution in China, or the genocide that recently took place in Cambodia, or the Holocaust, or the elemental barbarism that seems to lurk just beneath the surface of events in Iran, or the sudden disappearance of integrity from large sectors of both public and private life in my own country. Solzhenitsyn was getting closer to it in his Harvard commencement address of last June when he spoke of a disaster "that has been under way for quite some time. I am referring," he said, "to the calamity of a despiritualized and irreligious humanistic consciousness... On the way from the Renaissance to our day we have enriched our experience, but we have lost the concept of a Supreme Complete Entity, which used to restrain our passions and our irresponsibility. We have placed too much hope in political and social reforms, only to find that we were being deprived of our most precious possession: our spiritual life. In the East, it is destroyed by the dealings and machinations of the ruling party. In the West, commercial interests tend to suffocate it. This is the real crisis. The split in the world is less terrible than the similarity of the disease plaguing its main sections."

Part of my assignment here today was to say something, in the light of a Reformed Christian view of the ground of Christian political action, about the possibilities of cooperation between persons from the Protestant and Catholic traditions, and I want to get started on that part of my assignment right now. Our Senator Moynihan recently called attention to a lingering anti-catholicism in American religious circles, and while I must admit that what he says is true in wide areas of the more sectarian evangelical world, it is not true, I think, of the leadership of Reformed Christianity in America, and I personally wish to distantiate myself completely from such an attitude. I look upon Catholic believers as fellow-Christians in the first place, which, of course, and unfortunately, does not mean that all our problems are solved. When Pope John Paul II delivered his investiture sermon I happened to be sitting in a room alone, and I will confess to you that tears of joy rolled down my cheeks to hear his clear and ringing presentation of the Gospel of Christ (though admixed with some distinctively Catholic features).

I recognize the significant changes the Catholic Church has been undergoing, especially as to its posture in the world and the position it takes on social issues. I know something of the serious study of the Bible that is taking place and of the growth of a biblical spirituality, though not in all sections of that Church. We Reformed Christians accept at its full value the recent statement of an outstanding Catholic theologian, that as we grow closer to Christ we grow closer to each other (Küng).

In the light of the hellishness of so much of our present experience and the loss of a sense of direction in the dominant humanist movements, but also in the light of all the issues that are crowding in upon us in our one world screaming for attention, how could any Christian wish for anything more fervently than that all who know themselves to be Christ's and that the new life they have is a gift of God's grace (carrying with it a new "mind" that enables us to work redemptively in society) be *as united as they can be* in offering mankind an alternative to the dominant trends in our society?

For that reason, I can sympathize with your desire to have Catholic and Protestant political traditions here merge next year in the CDA. First of all I can understand it as a domestic strategy, a determination to offer the electorate in Holland a strong and significant Christian alternative to the growing power of the parties which even in your land, in spite of Groen's fundamental insight, are called the parties of the Left. Shall the rapid and parallel rise in the second half of the 19th century of Reformed Protestant and Roman Catholic political movements have been for any other purpose than to come, after our common humiliation and defeat experienced so often in the modern centuries, to just such a unified witness as our sick and troubled world cries out for? Must we not speak out on the basis of our common acceptance of a redeeming Word that has come from God? Or am I utterly beside the point, and is this not what drives you to your contemplated action?

But it becomes even more understandable when we consider how far the process of world integration has advanced and how worldwide all the important issues have become. For by allying yourself with the world-wide movement of Christian Democracy you have a means of addressing those issues in a manner commensurate with their range. The battle of spirits for the direction of human society is itself becoming ecumenical, to use the word in its original meaning.

Let me just list a few of these issues. High on the list would surely be the continuing struggle for human rights, and here Christians have things of momentous significance to say, generally against any form of collectivism and individualism – for in spite of what Maritain wrote Protestants may not legitimately be individualists – but particularly on behalf of the political self-determination of peoples, and this is of the greatest importance since the international community of states we know as the United Nations would appear to tolerate no other domestic political arrangement than majority rule on the basis of one person, one vote. Rousseau seems still to be the energizing spirit there, the spirit of rationalism, be it of a practicalistic kind, which by its view of the commonness of Reason in all men has caused the great "spiritual families" of the past to disappear, to use the language of Stanley Hoffman in a most significant article in the Winter 1979 issue of *Daedalus*, the journal of the American Academy of Arts and Sciences, or to weaken them to the point where they have no relevant future to propose. Mr. Hoffmann is professor of government and chairman of the Center for European Studies at Harvard University. He was born in Vienna in 1928. It is what he says next that bothers me. "What do Christian Democrats offer, except a plea for law and order, a spectacle of decay, or a touching faith in European integration as the *deus ex machina*?" For if his assessment has any truth to it, what strength could the AR Party possibly derive from the proposed merger?

There are all the other problems: nuclear energy; the weapons race; world poverty; the control of multinational corporations; the polluting of the air, the oceans, and the inland waterways and the effect of the use of fossil fuels on climate; developments in molecular biology, where we are confronted, it is said, with the eventual possibility of genetic engineering, such a thing as cloning, the development of radically new forms of life, all of them things that cause the most serious and enthusiastic scientists to hesitate and ask themselves whether limits should be set to technological development; computers and computer science, with the suggestion being made by some that if computers can be constructed that think much more accurately and to the purpose than we do, would it not be the part of wisdom for national governments, perhaps even the U.N., to build some and then let the computers make the important policy decisions. Drugs, crime, and violence have all gone international and begin to pervade systemically our society and as such require governmental control.

But there is also the *systemic* violence that is built into the capitalist system with its "survival of the fittest." There is the tendency, in my country, at least, for farmers to go in for specialization (huge feedlots) because, as Earl Butz, former secretary of the U.S. Department of Agriculture, said, "Farming is not a way of life; it is a way to make a living" (a view of man's life, reducing it to economic meaning). This raises the question of justice not only for the farmers, but for the cows and pigs and chickens as well. The justice of biblical shalom relates to an *integral* creation.

There is, further, the question of women's liberation – we have just seen its international repercussions in Iran; the breakdown of the family as a basic structure of human society (a recent alarming report in my country shows welfare agencies ignoring the larger family when for some reason it becomes necessary to separate a child from his parents, or preferring to separate a child from his mother to fixing a defective furnace, which would have been cheaper); the question of abortion on demand.

Enough of that. Certainly it requires no argument that a strong Christian political voice sorely needs to be heard. And for that reason, I am assuming, the AR and CH parties propose to merge with the KVP[2] in the CDA in 1980.

Difficulties and, especially, uncertainties abound with regard to that proposed merger and they have no doubt been agonized over for a long time. But the organizers of this international seminar have asked me, as a man of Reformed conviction coming in from the out-side, to say something about them nevertheless, as they have also asked Dr. Papini. As I understand it, that is exactly the purpose of our deliberations this morning. I am of the opinion that that was a very appropriate thing to do. Celebrating one hundred years of re-markable history in this atmosphere both of uncertainty and of great expectation calls for international consultation. For international in-terests are very much involved. This is a moment of historic decision, and at every new historical juncture our Christian stewardship must be marked by dependence on the Word and Spirit of Christ. We must not allow fear and the desire to hold on to old securities to govern

2.   *Katholieke Volkspartij*, i.e., Catholic Popular Party.

us if the Spirit is leading into a new and broader upland of Kingdom service. On the other hand, neither must we be swept away by desire alone. We must, at decisive moments of such historic importance, be guided by a sober analysis of the possibilities and by the knowledge that we are to work in a Christian-historical way. What this latter means will become clearer in a moment.

The Reformed "mind" that developed in the course of the 19th and 20th centuries in this land was the result, I have said, among other things of a tremendous and sustained effort at self-correction and of correction of tradition by listening to the Word of God, the result of the struggle, a constant in the Christian life, to cast off "the flesh" that is always clinging to us all, and pervasively to the tradition in which we have been nurtured and in which we function, in order to become more completely subject to the revealed will of God in both His word-and-act-revelation. Looking back, we can see that there were two traditions from which especially the Reformed "mind" was in the process of liberating itself, first from the dominant historicist thinking of the 19th century (Groen's "er staat geschreven, er is geschied"), where historical actuality was too easily taken for creation structure, but, second, from the much older tradition of scholastic philosophy, and particularly from its theme of Nature and Grace, the way to an acceptance of which had been long prepared by the Church Fathers' acceptance of ancient classical culture as a positive preparation for Christianity.

I suppose that there is a sense in which we may speak of the line Groen-Kuyper-Dooyeweerd also as a tradition, but then only in the sense of a tradition of *continuing reformation* of life and thought, not in the sense of a received tradition that is generally closed to such reformation. No one can escape tradition. The important thing is that in the midst of one's tradition one be willing to hear the Appèl of the divine Word and respond positively to it. Jesus Himself dealt with the matter of tradition, i.e., the rabbinical tradition, and in Him we see what the Word of God does with tradition. For what He did was to call the Jews back to the Word of God, to how things were "in the beginning," to creation and covenant. When He dealt with the

Law-traditionalists, i.e., the Pharisees, in the parable of the Pharisee and the Publican, He went behind the tradition to the fundamental religious (covenantal) meaning of life, to the matter of sin, estrangement, forgiveness and of humble whole-hearted life-service.

The line that unfolds from Groen to Kuyper to Dooyeweerd is a growing acknowledgment that the traditional pattern of Christian thinking was a very inadequate framework for Christian thought and action. This is not a remark directed against our Roman Catholic brethren. It is a judgment on the previous history of Christian experience, including much of the previous history of the Reformation. For it is a known fact that the scholastic synthesis – or *attempted* synthesis, since it is impossible of attainment, that is the very ambiguity of such a synthetic evaluation of culture – of the Christian faith with Aristotelian philosophy became increasingly characteristic of Reformed thinkers after Calvin. But in the line Groen-Kuyper-Dooyeweerd we see a more adequate response to the *Appèl* of the Word of God which comes from beyond our tradition. Here is an example of the principle *Ecclesia reformata reformanda est*, a principle which is generally applied to the life of the instituted church and regarded as something peculiarly Reformed, but is simply the norm of the Christian's life in this world. It points up the importance of the problem of the relation of Scripture and Tradition, to which I shall return in a moment.

I make some point of this because as I look out on the world of Christian Democracy I see everything being discussed in terms of Thomistic philosophy, or in terms of Maritain's philosophy, which, I think, does not differ from Thomas in any fundamental way, that is, in any way that relates to the general framework and its meaning. If I read about the movement in Dr. Frey's *Chile*, for example, I encounter the pervasive influence of Maritain and of Thomas Aquinas. And likewise elsewhere. This is not to be wondered at in view of the repeated papal statements regarding the philosophy of Thomas. And no one need convince me of the deep Christian *intention* of Thomas, or of Maritain, for that matter, in joining Aristotelian philosophy to the Christian faith so that all wisdom might be made serviceable to Christ the King. I can also understand how in the Europe of the 13th century there was such a strong desire to recover and make Christian use of the work of the last of the ancient Greek philosophers, who reportedly had summed up all of ancient wisdom.

What I do have trouble with is how it was possible for a Christian to believe that a pagan, without the renewing work of the redeeming Word upon his heart, could say the truth, albeit only up to a point, about man, the order of the world and the structure of human society. Or how Thomas failed to perceive in the Greek concept of "mind" or "intellect" a pagan distortion of the analytical mode of our experiencing, which came to be substituted for the biblical revelation of man as a religious being, denoted by the term "heart." I also have difficulty in understanding how a Christian could accept a Greek view of the state, which is really a totalitarian view, limited now in the synthesis only by the Church as belonging to a supranatural order, or hylomorphism's teleological arrangement of lower and higher, with the lower only being realized in the higher.

It simply cannot be denied that there is a tremendous clash between this Thomism and the Reformed mind that was developed by the founders and builders of the AR Party. Nothing could possibly be gained by ignoring this fact.

Groen's determining that there was a natural and necessary connection between unbelief and revolution involved a much larger fund of ideas, some of which were only clearly articulated later. Among other things, it involved that unbelief is less a loss or lack of faith, or a defect, than an active belief that has been misplaced or misdirected, as in the worship of the baalim in ancient Palestine, that we must distinguish therefore between faith in the sense of a structural component of our nature and faith in the sense of the direction it displays. Human nature is a created nature, dependent on the Word and Spirit of God, and religion, the established relation of covenant, is our most fundamental condition, expressed in all our individual and collective acts. The religious or spiritual, in other words, is not something next to, or coordinate with, man's other functions, but is rather a directionality in which they participate, of which they are manifestations, a force which animates and activates them in a given direction. That man was created to live "before God – *coram Deo* – *by cleaving* with his whole being – in singleness of heart" – to every word that proceeds from the mouth of God, the Reliable One, and that if he does not cleave to God he *will* cleave to something or someone else, is being amply demonstrated in our day in the resurgence, for instance, of Islam, and in many other ways. Man is a believing creature, and he either believes the Word of God or something he himself substitutes for that. His thinking activity also expresses the religious direction of his heart. Indeed, it is only within the sphere of commitment that he is able to do thorough analytical work.

Thus it gradually became clearer – in Kuyper a bit, and much more so in Dooyeweerd – that "heart" is the way scripture describes man in the integral religious root of all his *life-expression*, including his life of thought and that thus there is a religious-directional element to his analytical processes of conceptualization. How else explain adequately how men arrived at the concept of Zeus, the chief of the Olympian family of gods representing the culture-religion, or how the Greeks arrived at the notion that the rational soul, superior to the body, tends to the good while the body tends to the evil, except for their commitment to that same culture-religion?

Groen's position involves distinguishing a creation-*order*, centered in God's covenant with man and the whole earth, and the two religious directions denominated by the words Fall or Apostasy and Redemption or Restoration or Renewal (in Christ). Fall and Renewal can both be *radical* only because the creation itself is *integral*, has a religious root-unity. Secularization is not to be understood as a perfectly legitimate attempt on the part of man to assert his humanity in the face of an oppressive authoritarianism; it is, on the contrary, a result of man's sinful alienation from God. It is an expression of man's attempt to understand himself and to develop himself and his world independently of God and His revelation. Renewal or Restoration does not mean a turning back of the clock to Eden, but is a work that is accomplished in the creation in *its present stage of historical development*. It honours the unfolding of creation through culture, and is therefore not reactionary. Scholarship, for example, as part of man's creational life, must be renewed, not by a return to the theories of a bygone age, but by an inner reformation of 20th century learning. And central to such an inner reformation must be an explicit orientation to two realities which the Scriptures consistently teach and which 20th century humanism consistently ignores: the reality of constant creational ordinances (structure) and the dynamic reality of a spiritual antithesis (direction).

The recognition of the structure of creation as a God-given law-order was certainly present in Groen, but it becomes much more pronounced in Kuyper, who had rediscovered Calvin. I cannot refrain from quoting the lines from Kuyper that were so appropriately placed at the front of the De Wilde-Smeenk history of the AR Party, *Het Volk ten Baat*.

> Voor mij, één zucht beheerscht mijn leven,
> Eén hooger drang drijft zin en ziel.
> En moog' mij d' adem eer begeven,
> Eer 'k aan dien heil'gen drang ontviel.
> 't Is om Gods heil'ge ordinantiën
> In huis en kerk, in school en staat,
> Ten spijt van 's werelds remonstrantiën,
> Weer vast te stellen, *'t volk ten baat,*
> 't Is om die ord'ningen des Heeren,
> Waar Woord en Schepping van getuigt,
> In 't volk zóó helder te graveeren,
> Tot weer dat volk voor God zich buigt.

> (As for me, one holy passion rules my life,
> One supreme impulse prompts my mind and soul,
> And may breath fail me
> E'er I lose this sacred urgency.
> It is this: to establish once again,
> For the people's good, God's holy ordinances,
> In home and church, in school and state,
> Despite the world's remonstrances;
> It is this: to engrave the Lord's ordinances,

Which Scripture and creation witness to,
So sharply in the people's conscience
That they once more pay homage to their God.)

The importance of Kuyper is that he saw the connection between the biblical revelation of creation and the great diversity of kinds of association and relationship that we find in human society. The difficulty with constructing a Christian political or social program is that we must find a structural meaning in the central biblical revelation of creation, religion, covenant, office. A worked out conception of the structures of society is required if biblical revelation is to issue in specifically social and political content. Kuyper saw that we must look upon society and its structures as being rooted (despite human distortions) in creation. He saw that since ultimate sovereignty can belong only to God as Creator of everything that exists outside of Himself, nothing within creation, including the various spheres of society, can claim an absolute sovereignty for itself. A social sphere is at most characterized by a "limited sovereignty." The social structures, he claimed, are founded in the creation order but reflect that order only in one dimension. A plurality of social spheres mirrors the plurality of dimensions in the creation order. On this basis he taught that each distinct social sphere is characterized by a unique inner "life-principle" which conditions it, limits it, and sets it apart from other spheres. This inner principle accords to the respective social bond a measure of power and authority, but only in a limited manner.

What Kuyper saw, and in a grand intuitive grasp formulated in his doctrine of "soevereiniteit in eigen kring" (S.I.E.K.) was often not understood very well by his followers, and the phrase sometimes degenerated into being nothing more than an identifying slogan of the AR's. But Herman Dooyeweerd was able to give the principle a much more precise theoretical-analytical grounding in our experience. This enabled him to develop a philosophical sociology that is eminently subject to empirical controls. It enabled him, for example, to fix precisely the nature of the state as an all-embracing public community which ought to integrate all of the non-political communities as well as individuals and interpersonal relationships within its territory into a legal relationship of even-handed public justice for all. Christian political action is not to be directed to transforming the state into a church for God by force, but to taking on the form of a servant, so that God may transform our politics into true justice for men through Christian obedience. Christ is the One Who is redeeming and transforming politics by the power of His resurrection, and every group of Christians in every nation ought to act in Christian community for the transformation of public injustice into public justice in the several political communities.

In this Reformed line that we have sketched much too hastily, I have not yet mentioned the important subject of Office. "Office" suggests the allocation of a particular task by a Sovereign. "Office" speaks of service in the first place, but with the idea of preserving order in the developing of these creational potentials. It is service of God through an administering of God's love and solicitude to the creature. Kuyper saw it this way: Christ the second Person of the Godhead possesses absolute sovereignty, but to Him as Mediator has been *given* complete (delegated) sovereignty. He is *the* full and complete Office-bearer. And because His mediatorial sovereignty is total, such total sovereignty is to be found nowhere else in our earthly life. Total sovereignty cannot exist in two places. Christ, out of the fullness of His delegated authority, has delegated only partial sovereignties to men. In Christ all these sovereignties are united in an undivided service of God that involves no less than the redemption of all of life. Government is one of those partial sovereignties. It sins not only by usurping authority but also when it does not make use of all the authority given to it. The power and authority of the state is constantly limited by that of all other offices; the state does not stand by itself, but is only one of the links in the great chain which holds all the Creation intrinsically together. It cannot interfere in that life which properly belongs to another sphere because God has not delegated it competence therefor. The father, for instance, exercises his proper authority also by divine commission. Government as office is an institution of divine origin, quite independently of whether the persons of the government fear God. The grace of God lies in the existence of the governmental authority itself and therefore we must obey it, but only within the God-ordained limits of its powers. Thus the state takes its place not *above* but *alongside* all the other spheres. And as for us who are office-bearers in the political arena, Christian politics is our humble effort to obey the divine norm of public justice in the historically unfolding political circumstances of our time, circumstances for the ordered guidance of which we are responsible and accountable to God. Calling is our sensing the need for reformation of a mis-guided creation. We Christians cannot just enjoy the creation as it is. One of the things that is wrong with a liberal arts education is just that peace which it engenders with the creation as it is, without preparing the student for the battle of spirits in which, as a Christian, he will find himself engaged at every point.

Political life is concerned with *the direction taken in the life of the State*, and the State, though only one dimension of the Rule of God, is nevertheless invested with the power of the sword. It has, as Althusius remarks, a certain "*majestas.*" This power was bestowed by God, but it can be used wrongly. The power of the sword is indeed something to be feared. It comes into your and my family life, into our church life (think of the *Afscheiding* of 1834), into all areas of our life. And this power is used. It will be used responsibly or irresponsibly, obediently or disobediently, but *it will be used*. For that is part of the structure of the life God created. Thus the way this power will be used, the *direction* the life of the State will take in our time, will depend on the nature of the political action that emerges in the State. In the making, the interpreting and the administering of laws the direction of the life of the State influences us all daily. The element of direction is simply the basic or central religious Drive that is at work in all human cultural life. This is why as Christians together we should be concerned about political life.

~ ~ ~

Ladies and gentlemen, some of you may be wondering what all this has to do with today's proceedings. Well, in a word, everything. For every concrete political goal that is even conceived, but then, further, pursued; every political program that men set themselves to realize; every body of positive law arises from an idea about the nature of man; and his place and task in the world arises from an idea about the order of the world and structure of society. It may be that as Christians we have many common concerns, that together we sense the need of a powerful common Christian witness in regard to these concerns. But these concerns are turned into formulated issues; tactics and strategies are determined by reference to a basic grid or schema, and the difference in our fundamental schemas is what always impresses me, though, I must add, it causes me great agony and pain.

It is not to the point to argue that the Catholic political parties have become de-confessionalized. It is not Catholic *dogma* here, but the *philosophical schema* of Thomism or of Maritain that is the problem. It would be very good to know just what the status is of Thomistic philosophy in the Catholic Church and the Catholic community. For to the Reformed mind there simply is no such realm of Nature as the Thomistic philosophy talks about, no realm of natural or civil good which grace then supplements, strengthens, perfects, elevates. There is no natural mind that in a normal way, i.e., a properly normal way, relates to an intelligible world. These things to the Reformed man simply do not exist. But we do not take that to be the private view of Reformed communities. We do not hold to another view because we have need of distinctives to maintain our independence. We believe that what we believe is what the Word of God calls us to believe, that there is only the one Creation of God, revelatory of His own integral oneness, concentrated in a covenantal-religious relation to Him, which outside of Christ, because of the entrance of sin into the world, is not in a normal condition but in a very abnormal one, in a state of rebellious alienation from God, a world which it is necessary for grace to restore to a new communion with the Father, as Adam originally walked, in the fellowship of the Holy Spirit. This is of fundamental importance for political action, for the drawing up of political programs, for political strategy and tactics. What does one see as one looks out upon the world of men?: Natural virtues, which association with Christian persons can strengthen and elevate and perfect, or a spirit of anti-Christ, that is, of lawlessness, of apostasy or will-worship, of unwisdom, things that manifest themselves in an unholy standard of conduct (the Playboy-Penthouse mentality, which appeals to the principle of separation of Church and State but says nothing of the universal *Appèl* of the Word of God to all human hearts), in a misguided Reason and in corrupt desires (e.g., the Me First mentality).

Catholic and Protestant theologians have debated much recently about whether the Catholic Church accepts the doctrine of the *sola gratia*, but again, that is not the problem for us here. The problem here is the place of grace in the Thomistic framework, the Thomistic view of special grace as a super-endowment or enrichment and perfection of an already existing natural grace, and behind this is an awful lot of history that goes back to the Synod of Orange of AD 529 at least.

The problem concentrates itself in the view one entertains of "natural law." Professor Berkouwer, in his book *General Revelation* (*De Algemene Openbaring*), points up the radical difference between Calvin's concept of natural law and the schoolmen's. While their theory is grounded in the rational nature of man, which, according to Rome, must always – with the necessity that attaches to being – *strive after the good*, nothing of that is found in the former's. Calvin sees as central the corruption of human nature directed against the good will of God in hostility and disobedience. I hope you can forgive a somewhat extended quotation from Berkouwer's book.

> For Calvin [he writes] the natural man does not live from what remains of real, ontological goodness within the ordinances of God, but he moves within the *witnessing* force and the *evidence* of the divinely ordained good as revelation of His holy will. The predominating aspect in Calvin is not the goodness of human nature, but *the goodness of the law and the ordinances of God*... The total depravity of man is indeed present, according to Calvin, but that is, for him, not equivalent to the *absence* of all God's gifts to human nature. For Calvin is convinced that man can manifest his total depravity *with* his gifts and in the functioning of those gifts. A profound view of sin is the background of Cal-

vin's thought: one could say, a total-existential view which is *religious* in character and is governed by the question of the attitude of the *heart* of man towards God... We find ourselves here in the area of the activity of God in preserving and governing. Therein lies the possibility of the connection between so-called 'natural law' and... *corruptio naturae*... It is indeed a strange thing that in the radical aversion of human life from God and His holy will, in its inability to subject itself to the law of God, there is nevertheless still present a championing of right and justice, a punishing of evil and a rewarding of good, a valuing of community with one another and of limits set for man in that community, a seeking of truth and science... Every man stirs and moves within the superior power of the works of God and of the preservation of His blessing-bestowing law... and *in his actions, in his conscience, in his judgment with regard to others and in his protest against complete anarchy he manifests the superior power of the work and the law of God...* To acknowledge this does not therefore involve an optimistic estimate of man. For this man, in the total direction of his existence, is turned away from God, and moreover can also in his concrete deeds progress continually farther along the road of manifest degeneration. In Romans 2, Paul is not speaking of a constant quality of the heathen (the doing of that which is contained in the law). The process of sin can also so burst forth that there remain only minimal remnants of the power to distinguish. The eye of man can be increasingly darkened with respect to the goodness of God's ordinances, so that he finally has an eye only for the 'law' that is pleasing to himself and that protects his own life. Life can develop as Paul predicts it for the last days, in almost complete and uncompromising opposition to what the law of God still makes valuable in life. Those are days in which man will even be without natural love. Therein can be manifested the judgment of God, as it already was revealed in the divine 'giving over' of which Paul makes mention in Romans 1... one cannot describe the history of humanity from the point of view of human 'nature' and its 'natural light'. The relation between the general revelation of God, common restraining grace and human life is not a static one, but a dynamic relation, which is completely and utterly tied up with the development of history and with the process of sin.

Whew! That was quite a quotation, but I have included it because it is so much to the point. Berkouwer is discussing what I talked about when I referred to Structure and Direction. Since the creation structure is integral, that is, has a root-unity that is religion or our covenant-walk before God, the direction of life, be it the rebellion of sin or a newly learned obedience to the Word of God in the Spirit, will be radical, that is, will be evidenced in *every* aspect of life.

The patristic and medieval natural law tradition quickly revived after the first stages of the Protestant Reformation, and it quickly led the Protestant world to an accommodation with the rising rationalism. I have described the process in my paper "The Development of Calvinism in North America in the Light of Its Development in Europe" (see above, p. 201). The result was a Modernism which is another religion than Christianity.

Frankly, I was troubled by the comment of Stanley Hoffmann in his *Daedalus* article. And as I look out on the world of Christian Democracy I am impressed with the "secular" appearance of it in so many places. I hear Dr. Eduardo Frey say that Christian Democracy is inspired by its trust in man. Christian Democracy talks a great deal about Christian humanism (vs. autonomous humanism) and about personalism, both of which terms receive their definition from the Thomistic scheme of Nature and Grace. I read in a commentator on the encyclical of Leo XIII which defined Christian Democracy (*Graves de Communi Re*, 1901) that the movement is simply social Catholicism. Fogarty closes his book by defining it as

> that aspect of the ecumenical movement in modern Christianity which is concerned with the application of Christian principles in the areas of political, economic, and social life for which the Christian laity has independent responsibility.

In a similar statement early in his book he again speaks of it as "a movement of laymen, engaged on their own responsibility in the solution of problems in the light of Christian principles..." But then, after quoting 1 Corinthians 1, of all places, he goes on, "in the main stream of Christian thought it has always been clear that revelation completes natural knowledge but does not replace it." And in another place he writes: "...in the face of new developments in natural reasoning... the Church failed to show clearly and forcibly how these developments were relevant to revelation, and revelation to them. It was not quick enough to take up the new threads and weave them into its own pattern of thought. As a result, these developments tended to proceed independently of, and to some extent in opposition to, Christianity."

Sometimes I get the impression that Catholics and we, somewhere behind the world where the schema is operative, are talking about the same thing: God's good creation and the sinfulness of man that has affected that world. But I always feel that the boundness of the Catholic mind to the Thomistic schema stops him short of seeing the radical integralness of man the creature's life before God, and of discerning and appreciating the real sinfulness of secular movements.

But is not all this related to that fundamental Thomistic schema of Nature and Grace? And, as I tried to show earlier, that schema is not unrelated to the Church Father's acceptance of classical humanism's assessment of Greek and Latin thought and even to the position developed among Alexandrian Jewry towards the world of Greek culture. It sits deep in Christian historical experience, whether or not it adequately accords with the enlightenment of scriptural revelation. It is significant that Leo XIII, who defined Christian Democracy, is also the pope who, in a letter to Cardinal Parocchi of 1885 wrote:

> Perceiving, then, the usefulness of the literature of Greece and Rome, the Catholic Church, which always has fostered whatsoever things are of good report, has always given to the study of the humanities the favor that it deserves, and in promoting it has expended no slight portion of its best endeavor.

My Harvard instructor, the famous Edward Kennard Rand, in his *Founders of the Middle Ages*, after mentioning the pope's Ciceronian cadences, makes the wry comment: "Nor does His Holiness fail to quote St. Paul, though not the passage about that wisdom of this world which is foolishness with God."

Was not this traditional view of a normal natural world part of Lamennais' problem? In the end he accommodated himself to the very liberalism which Groen viewed as the continuation of the Revolution (though Lamennais did make distinctions) – as though the popular democracy of the day could be read as a technical way of satisfying the legitimate longings of the people. Lamennais did not think of the separation of Church and State as something in itself desirable, but as safest for both under modern conditions. In other words, it was a thoroughly pragmatic act that really involved the abandonment of his conviction. A Reformed mind might have found the emergence of the idea of popular democracy to be the finally attained stage of historical development that marks the New Testament believer's maturity in Christ in the communion of the Spirit while the direction in which this structural opening up process occurred was antithetical to the direction of Christian obedience. This was what made Groen an antirevolutionary and set him against the contra-revolutionary ideas of his predecessors Bilderdijk and the Da Costa of the earlier years.

In various papal utterances too there appears to be an attempt to separate the "technical" in liberalism or socialism, from the more philosophical drives in those movements. Certain priests, at least in Latin America, approach communism in the same way. The technical, however, I would suggest, exists only as an integral element of the human intention and purpose, which is really a prophetic (religious) statement about man, religion, law, the structure of human society. A good example is the "technique" of one man, one vote and majority election (Rousseau) as opposed to the "technique" of proportional representation. The former "technique" carries with it a whole philosophy, indeed a religious reading of experience. So does the latter.

Lamennais' lunging first in the direction of the State, then of the Church, and then of liberalism suggests another weakness in the Catholic view of nature. He appears to miss any firm view of a creation-order, the result of the divine will in the work of creation. The Aristotelian view was that the lesser associations, such as marriage and family and village spring from the instincts of propagation and self-preservation, and that their "end" was life, whereas the "end" of the city-state was the "good life," the life of the mind, and (according to the Olympian religion of rational form) was thus superior. In the immanent teleology of this hylomorphism the lower is subsumed under the higher as part to whole. The subordination of the realm of Nature to the realm of Grace in Thomas does not appreciably alter the fact that in the Roman Catholic view of the structure of society the state is the final organizer and the director of the common good in the domain of nature (*Rerum Novarum* and *Quadragesimo Anno*, 1931). Fogarty sees similarities between the Catholic principle of subsidiarity, as it is called, and the Reformed principle of sphere-sovereignty, but that simply is not the case; there is, unfortunately, significant difference between the two views. In Lamennais there is no clear notion of creation ordinances for the various societal associations, and he shows no real appreciation for the variety of offices God has placed in life. Roman Catholic thinking is dominated by the Nature-Grace scheme, and further makes no fundamental biblical corrections of the Aristotelian view of the natural world. But in our increasingly complex society, there is more need all the time for insight into the God-ordained limits of government. Dooyeweerd's view of sphere-sovereignty or modal irreducibility makes room for a proper and open "horizontalism," as opposed to a verticalized view of society in terms of a principle of subsidiarity, or to any conception of reality in terms of hierarchical subordination.

So really the question of the status of the Thomistic philosophy, and of Maritain's, in Roman Catholic thinking and particularly the role it plays in the thinking in Christian Democratic circles is very important. The possibility of meaningful cooperation in any fundamental way between Roman Catholic and Reformed Christians, even in concrete political projects (unless they are vaguely and superficially conceived) will at least require, from the very outset, a frank, open-hearted and thorough canvassing of this question. How bound is a Catholic involved in social action to the Thomistic philosophy?

There is the further, but closely related, point in Fogarty's definition of Christian Democracy that the laity have an independent responsibility. Just what does that mean in Roman Catholicism? Even

Fogarty's explanation of the three levels of action: that specific to the clergy, Catholic Action and social action appears to be blurred. He goes on to say that "the lines between the three levels of activity are often uncertain," that movements which, though directed to economic or social ends, have a particularly high educational content, lie on the margin between the third and the second, "and may even be absorbed into the level of Catholic Action altogether." The significance of that remark is that in Catholic Action the laity carry on some form of apostolate as auxiliaries of the ecclesiastical Hierarchy; and not merely with the approval of the Hierarchy, but *under its special mandate, in direct dependence on it, and under rules called for and sanctioned by it*" (italics mine). The strictly hierarchical structure of the Catholic Church compels us to raise this question as to the independent responsibility of the laity.

The encyclical *Mater et Magistra* of 1961 (sec. 239) states that

Catholics must bear themselves as Catholics and do nothing to compromise religion and morality. When the Hierarchy has made a decision on any point Catholics are bound to obey their directives. The church has the right and obligation not merely to guard ethical and religious principles, but also to declare its authoritative judgment in the matter of putting these principles into practice.

Fogarty himself, while saying that in social action "the laity take over entirely and act on their own initiative and responsibility," adds "though within the normal framework of the beliefs, rules and practice of their church."

Of course, I do not expect a Catholic to be something else than a Catholic. But it is the Catholic Church itself that constitutes the problem. Where the Reformed "mind" sees a difference between the sovereign working of grace on the heart, which changes the direction of all of a man's life-activities (= the *ecclesia invisibilis)*, the evidence of a man's hearing the Word of God in the changed direction of his various life-activities (= the *ecclesia visibilis)*, and the particular activity of worship that has been redirected to God (the instituted church), the Roman Catholic Church is always an Institute, and every activity of a member of the Catholic Church is related to that Institute.

There is a finer point, one that almost brings me to the point of despair. The Catholic sees the relation of Scripture and Church quite differently from the Protestant. The Scriptures, in the Catholic view, arise out of the Church. The Jesuit scholar, Gustave Weigel, writes:

> The inspired books, which have God as their author in consequence of their inspiration, are ecclesiastical Instruments for teaching, guiding and exhorting. They are not over the Church, but rather a part of the Church's panoply to be used in her work of accomplishing the task of uniting man to God. It is the Church which teaches, the Church which sanctifies, the Church which builds and vitalizes. The Church is not a fruit of the Book but rather the Book is a fruit of the Church.

Related is the much-debated question of the relation of Scripture and Tradition. Again, what troubles me is the Roman Catholic idea of the Church of Christ, the single reality of the Body of Christ on earth with doctrinal authority, which under the direct presence of the Spirit is endowed with an infallible character (the Magisterium). If the Scriptures arise out of the bosom of the Church and the Church has an infallible ongoing teaching authority, then the Church in its historical presence and reality cannot be understood as a response to the Call of God in His Word. How then could appeal ever be made (except to the "pope better informed") to the Word of God as Norm to be obeyed in all our earthly life? How can reformation ever come about?

Our hope is in the fact that the Gospel, God's Call to man, while it has been incorporated into our creation life, is never exhausted in the form it assumed in common with all creatures. It remains always God's sovereign address, with Power to accomplish that for which God sent it into the world, and princes and ecclesiastical hierarchies are responsible for how they respond to that *Appèl*. That is the hope for fruitful contact between Catholic and Reformed Christians.

~ ~ ~

Dear AR friends, I have no intention of expressing an opinion directly on the desirability or undesirability of your proposed merger.

That would be inappropriate for one coming in from the outside, and I know that you do not expect that of me anyway. The fact is that I really do not know whether the merger should take place, because I am coming in from the outside. I have spoken of the crying need in our time, if it is feasible, of an enlarged and vigorous Christian political witness. Surely there is no other place in the world where Reformed and Catholic strengths together could make a greater contribution to meeting this need, domestically first, but never forget the possibilities internationally.

I have also attempted to point out what to me appear to be very formidable difficulties in the idea of a merger. It seems to me, as one coming to you from without, that for a time, until the changes that are taking place in the Catholic Church become clearer to us all, and until some of these fundamental issues are clarified, you would be working in a more Christian-historical way to set up a center to discuss these issues and to test the practical political possibilities, Catholics and Reformed retaining their independent identities. I still feel about cooperation and fusion very much as Abraham Kuyper did.

But I may be wrong. The proposed CDA may be more feasible at this point than I imagine. Actually, it all depends on what is going on here, what is taking place in your hearts. It could be that this move for union stems from very worldly considerations, i.e., to strengthen your power as "parties of the Right." Or the desire for merger in broad areas of the AR Party could be an instance of a phenomenon that is occurring in many places and forms in our time, the phenomenon, as Stanley Hoffman speaks of it, of disconnection with the past, of the past's no longer nurturing us. I will not easily believe that that is what is happening among you. And if your desire is, together with your Catholic colleagues, to let the *Appèl* of God come through to men concretely in the political life of this nation in the first place, to men in their awfully tormented lostness, who would dare to say that you do not stand at a new and wonderful frontier, a *terra incognita*. At the cutting-edge of history things are always uncertain. There are no recognizable landmarks. Risks have to be taken. But the God of history is always with His people in the fellowship of the Holy Spirit, and He has promised victory. The Spirit, driving the creation onward to its appointed End, works mysteriously, beyond the ways our traditional imaginations can conceive. It may be that we have to "fly on instruments," but if the instruments are the oracles of God, we know that the way to our destination is secure and the landing will be safe.

But given the hard and sobering reality of the deep differences between the Catholic "mind" and world and the Reformed, I urge you not to take lightly God's great deeds in your midst these past 100 years, but to honour them as the precious heritage (*kostbaar cultuurbezit*) they are. I urge you to recognize the world-historical importance of what Almighty God saw fit to accomplish in this small country of northwestern Europe, and to cherish what you have received, not as a museum piece, to be safely stored away and taken out only occasionally to be shown to foreign visitors, but as something to be appropriated, talents to be put to use and someday to be accounted for.

As representing those young groups of Reformed people scattered all over the globe, I take the freedom to beg you even in a merger to keep the Kuyperhuis as a think-tank for on-going Reformed thought. And do not forget, because of your great blessings here in the past, your responsibility to give of your experience and expertise in the future to us who so sorely need it.

And *whatever* you do, may it reinforce the cry of the ancient prophet:

"O Earth, Earth, hear the Word of God and live."

Anecdotal Notes:

a. Johannes Althusius (ca. 1557–1638), famous Herborn and Emden jurist and Calvinist thinker, who – this against Gierke – first formulated the principle of internal sphere-sovereignty in societal relationships. See H. Dooyeweerd, *A New Critique of Theoretical Thought*, III, 662f., but also *The Politics of Johannes Althusius*, abridged and translated by Frederick S. Carney, with a Preface by Carl J. Friedrich, Beacon Press, Boston, and S. J. Reginald Saunders & Co. Ltd., Toronto, 1964.

b. The "Afscheiding" or Secession of 1834 from the Dutch Reformed
    Church because of serious and widespread departure from the
    Reformed Confessions saw the seceders harassed, persecuted, and
    imprisoned under terms of articles of the Penal Code dating from
    the time of the Napoleonic regime.

The Christian Philosophical Enterprise in the Light of Biblical Prophecy

The following was the opening address which was given at the Second International Symposium sponsored by the Association for Calvinistic Philosophy held at Zeist, The Netherlands, August 23-27, 1982

Mr. Chairman, Colleagues and Friends,

I was glad to be a participant in the First International Symposium that was held in 1976 in Driebergen, and now it is very good to be here among you in the Netherlands once again. This is the land where, under men like Professor Klaas Schilder and Professor S. Greydanus at the Kampen Theologische Hogeschool in the academic year 1939–40, and especially under the genial guidance of Professor D. H. Th. Vollenhoven and – from a bit more of a distance – Professor H. Dooyeweerd in the years immediately after World War II, my grasp, my understanding of covenantal religion in the biblical sense greatly deepened and was very much enlarged while for the first time I really familiarized myself with the philosophy that the beloved founders of our Association were developing. Thus this land, through these experiences of mine here, is where the future course of my life was to a large extent determined. This also is the land that gave me my wife of 35 years, the place where our first child was born and spent the first year of his life and made himself ready to speak Dutch, which he still can do. So it is always good to be among Reformed Christians in the Netherlands, and I am delighted that your kind invitation has made yet another visit possible.

Much of what I came most to esteem in the Reformed circles of the Netherlands seems lately to have vanished into thin air or at least to have been muted or shunted onto the sidelines: the bold confession of the sovereignty of Almighty God, the Creator, the Lord of hosts; that He has subjected all things to His Law (ordinances); that Jesus Christ is the risen and ascended Lord of the creation; the straightforward acknowledgment that as a result of the gracious election of God in Christ, the Mediator of a new covenant, the battle of spirits is being waged, and *is to be waged*, constantly everywhere we find men in action; the recognition that in and through that battle the Kingdom of God is coming; the clear prophetic discernment of the simple and radical secularism of western civilization as it emerged from the Enlightenment and the French and subsequent revolutions and then boasted of an age of permanent revolution. *That* Reformed world is rapidly disappearing, it would seem, in family life as well as in schools and institutions training a new generation for leadership, having given way to a world characterized by the attitude of dialogue and dialectic. We live in a time that loves to erase boundaries, even the boundaries between truth and falsehood. There has been, in more than just a theoretical sense, a Hegel revival, and "falsehood" turns out to be partial truth. The result seems to be that in many places, what I knew as Reformed Nederland has lost a sense of its original aim and thus lost much of its power to give new direction to our faltering western society. For the power was in the aim: to allow the Word of God free course in our hearts and lives, thus in our acts, both individual and societal, confessing it to be the only Power capable of bringing new life and giving new and salutary direction to all our undertakings.

Such Reformed commitment to the living and active Word of God still exists here and there, but it now lacks – what it has got to have – effective institutional and organizational focus, first of all in the church. Accordingly, I am particularly happy to be here among my fellow-members of the Association for Calvinistic Philosophy, and particularly to note, as I believe, the following two fairly recent developments: (1) a more determined effort on your part here in the

Netherlands to reach out to the youth generation to form leadership cadres for a new generation of renewed Reformed life and action if God permit, and (2) – what I believe is extremely important – increasing zeal for reaching out with what our Association stands for to people in all the nations of the world who are pursuing academic vocations and confess Jesus as Lord. I am very glad to note what I believe is a new sense of international responsibility in this Association. How far we have traveled from our First International Symposium of 1976, with Drs. Son and Haruna, respectively Korean and Japanese representatives of our movement listed among our speakers at this Symposium! Personally, I have worked to strengthen this effort towards greater international involvement by bringing along a former student of mine, the son of Mennonite missionary parents in Japan, himself raised and schooled with Japanese children, who is, I assure you, stalwartly Reformed and greatly concerned to relate the work of our Association to the Japanese mind and experience. I am grateful that Mr. Philip Blosser has been given a part in this Symposium.

I am, I must say, very pleased indeed with the theme that was chosen for this symposium: "Christian Philosophy in the Light of Biblical Prophecy." And I would like to express my gratitude to the organizers of the symposium for not further burdening me as to what I should deal with in my paper. I feel that this is a critical moment in the life of our Association and I do want to be entirely free to speak to you from my heart. At the same time, please remember that I probably speak with something of a North American accent. At any rate, I speak from the distance of another continent, and there is always something precarious in that. I hesitate to speak my thoughts so freely; yet in the weeks that I have reflected on what I should say here I have continually and even increasingly felt myself moved in one certain direction. If in any way I should speak amiss or prove to be beside the point, please excuse me, ascribe it to human fallibility and limitations. But know that I only wish my words to be helpful to this Association in the carrying out of its important work for our common Lord.

For my own paper, at least, I would like to change the wording of the theme slightly to read: "The Christian Philosophical Enterprise in the Light of Biblical Prophecy." I'm not even sure the organizers of the symposium would consider that a change or an expansion of their intention; for I am confident all of us have learned from our founders to think of the philosophical result as proceeding from the preceding activity of philosophical thinking, and too, to think of the philosophical task as integral with the whole of mankind's covenantal walk before God and in particular with our obligation to pass on to future generations by means of the nurturing and paedagogical processes what we ourselves inherit and accomplish.[1]

So, in short, I am delighted to be one of your invited speakers because it allows me to say here some things that have been very much on my mind of late. And I am happy with the theme of our symposium because it confronts us, head-on, at this critical juncture in our history, with what I am persuaded we most need to think about: who we are and what we are about. With the precious gift of firm biblical insight our founders bequeathed to us and the example they have given us in their work, we must not make ourselves guilty of the phenomenon which Professor Santayana called fanaticism, the phenomenon of "redoubling our effort when we've forgotten our aim." Our theme is a fitting one to remind us, in rapidly changing and perilous times on a global scale, but also in the immediately surrounding environment, of our aim as an Association.

First, then, I should like to say some things about the phrase "biblical prophecy" in our theme. I have taken that phrase, as I am sure the organizers of this symposium meant it, not in the narrower, merely eschatological sense, as many evangelicals in my country would undoubtedly do, even though the foretelling of future events does indeed constitute an element of prophecy in the biblical sense, but rather in the radical and full sense that the word "prophecy" has in Scripture: a speaking for, a speaking on behalf of, a speaking in

---

1.   In its educational system and program, as in family nurturing, any culture or society discloses, in its conscious and deliberate preserving and transmitting of its character, its deepest sense of its identity in its awareness of a standard. See Werner Jaeger, *Paideia* I, xiii–xiv.

the name of God. A prophet is God-possessed, is possessed by the Spirit of prophecy, as John, the author of the last Bible book, was "in the Spirit" (Revelation 1:10) when he received his revelation. Thus a prophet, as the speaker for Jehovah, or the mouth of the Lord, declares the Lord's will ("I take no pleasure in the death of anyone... repent and live" – e.g., Ezekiel 18:25-32) and the Lord's intention or plan for wrathful judgment on covenantal disobedience, victory over sin, the establishment of Jehovah's supremacy, blessing on covenantal obedience, the fulfillment of the creation design. He is under compulsion to speak (Amos 3:8); the words of God are in his soul as a burning fire until he utters them (Jeremiah 20:7, 9).

Old Testament prophecy aims to establish the supremacy of Jehovah, binding man and all creation to the Law-word of God. It views detailed events in their relation to the divine plan, which has for its purpose the absolute establishment of the supremacy and glory of Jehovah in Israel and eventually on the entire earth. This involves the Messianic prophecies: the person of the Messiah and the coming of the Kingdom of God.

The two outstanding figures among the Old Testament prophets are Moses and Elijah—Moses, the lawgiver (cf. Deut. 18:15,18 with Num. 12:6-8 and Heb. 3:1-6) and Elijah, representative of the prophet's calling to bind the covenant people to the law of the Lord. The last prophetic word of the Old Testament mentions them together (Mal. 4:4-6), and in the last New Testament book the vision of the two witnesses (Rev. 11), having reference to the Church of God in its prophetic capacity, uses language (verse 6) reminiscent of the prophetic work of Moses and Elijah. Christians think at once of the scene of heavenly glory on the Mount of Transfiguration, where these two men, Moses and Elijah, talked with the transfigured Jesus, prophetically still, about His decease which He should accomplish at Jerusalem.

The ultimate meaning and ground of possibility of prophecy becomes clear in the coming in the flesh of the Son of God, the Messiah. The incarnation, the life and public ministry, the trial and death, the resurrection and ascension of Jesus Christ is the culmination of prophecy because of the unique relation between Him and God. Matthew 11:27 reads:

> All things have been committed to me by my Father. No one knows the Son except the Father, and no one knows the Father except the Son and those to whom the Son chooses to reveal him.

Geerhardus Vos, commenting on verses 25-27, says that this passage "expresses that God has devolved upon Jesus what is His own special prerogative: the task to reveal the whole truth in all its wide extent." The term Father, Vos writes,

> serves to account for the absoluteness and comprehensiveness of the task of revelation entrusted to Jesus. Because God is His Father and He the Son of God, such a delivering of all things in the realm of revelation was possible. Here, therefore, the Messiahship on its revealing side ('all things were delivered') is put on the basis of sonship ('by my Father')... the Messiahship is of such a nature, even so far as its revealing function is concerned, that it demands for its prerequisite a wholly unique relationship to God. That the Son possesses this is guaranteed by His name and dignity as Son. The intimacy is such that God alone can know Him, and that He alone can know God. God knows Him and He knows God with an exclusive knowledge... Jesus has this exclusive knowledge of God in virtue of His being the Son; God has this exclusive knowledge of Jesus in virtue of His being the Father... It scarcely needs pointing out,

Vos continues,

> that in this great deliverance Messiahship and sonship are distinguished. The Messiahship appears in the reception on Jesus' part of the commission to *reveal* all things. But the sonship underlies this as the only basis on which it could happen, and on which it can be understood. And the sonship of this Messianic person [– *the* Prophet of Old Testament prophecy (Deut. 18:15, 18) –] altogether transcends His historic appearance... He is called 'the Son' not simply because of His being the Messiah, but because His Messiahship is determined by an anterior

sonship lying back of it.[2]

Here, then, at the point of culmination, the phenomenon of prophecy we see running through the Old Testament and culminating in the coming of the promised Prophet becomes identical with the process of God's self-revelation in His covenant. And revelation is, essentially, God coming down to our level – think of the Old Testament theophanies – through the Word, the Logos, by whom all things were created and in whom they all hang together; and in the Spirit, Who is the Spirit of God and of His Christ, the Spirit of Christ Who, the apostle Peter tells us (I Pet. 1:10,11), was in the Old Testament prophets, pointing forward to "the sufferings of Christ and the glories that would follow." It is interesting to note that in the first three verses of the last Bible book the words "revelation," "word of God," "testimony of Jesus Christ," and "prophecy" occur in close proximity and approximate juxtaposition. Thus too the author of the Epistle to the Hebrews: "In the past God spoke to our forefathers through the prophets at many times and in various ways, but in these last days He has spoken to us by His Son, whom He appointed heir of all things, and through whom He made the universe. The Son is the radiance of God's glory and the exact representation of His being, sustaining all things by His powerful word." And the Epistle to the Colossians tells us that "He is the image of the invisible God... For God was pleased to have all His fullness dwell in Him... in Christ all the fullness of the Deity (godhead) lives in bodily form" (Col. 1:15, 19; 2:9).

That brings me to what remains as a key passage for our present consideration. In Revelation 19:10b we read: "for the testimony of Jesus is the spirit of prophecy." Of it Professor S. Greydanus has written in his commentary on the book of Revelation in the *Korte Verklaring* series, 3e druk, Kok, Kampen, 1955, p. 287): "For the testimony of Jesus, that is, what Christ the Lord says and witnesses about God, about Himself, about the Kingdom of heaven is the Spirit of prophecy, its content, the working of the Holy Spirit, that Spirit Himself!"

2. Geerhardus Vos, *The Self Disclosure of Jesus*, George H. Doran Co., New York, N.Y., 1926, see esp. pp. 147-151.

We might think in this connection of what the apostle John wrote in his gospel (15:26): "When the counselor comes, whom I *will* send to you from the Father, the Spirit of truth who goes out from the Father, He will testify about me." In his larger commentary on the Revelation passage in the *Kommentaar op het Nieuwe Testament* series (Amsterdam: Van Bottenburg, 1925, p. 391) he says this:

> These too are the angel's words, by means of which he indicates the exalted station of them who have the testimony of the Lord Christ. In or with this testimony they have the spirit of prophecy. Thus they all are prophets and therefore are all equals with John and with the angel himself. Though there may be some difference of degree, there is no essential difference. The angel said that he is a fellow-servant with John and his brethren who have the testimony of Jesus. To this he adds an illuminating remark to stress the exaltedness which is contained therein, namely, prophetic dignity and service, a worth equal to his own work. If the angel first came down, as it were, to all true believers by placing himself on one line with them, he now leads them up, so to speak, to the height of his own service: they are what he is, just as he is what they are: each other's fellow-servants, all of them equally inspired and qualified by God for the same exalted service of being His prophets.

> ...The genitive 'of Jesus' in this connection is first of all a subjective genitive, indicating that the Lord Christ gave that testimony, cf. 1:2,9; 6:9 etc.; 22:16. But since the Lord's testimony was also a witnessing about Himself, Who and what He Himself was (Luke 4:17–21; Matt. 12:41, 42; John 8:23–26 and others) that genitive is at the same time also an objective genitive, which speaks of a witnessing about or regarding the Lord. To possess in faith the testimony of Christ the Lord regarding Himself in such a way that it governs your inner being and very existence, all that you do and say, is to have the Spirit of prophecy. He of whom this can be said is a prophet. Since the spirit of prophecy manifests itself in causing one to have and to speak about the Lord Jesus' testimony regarding Himself, ..."all true prophets are witnesses of Jesus, and all who have the witness of Jesus in the highest sense are prophets," – H. B. Swete.

All who have the Spirit will be witnesses of Jesus, and all who have the witness of Jesus are possessed by the Spirit of Prophecy. Since Pentecost, the Spirit of God is poured out on all Christ's people, on each one of us, qualifying and enabling us to be prophets, to be witnesses of Jesus, that is, to have the witness respecting Jesus that Jesus had regarding Himself, a witness, as Greydanus remarked, about God, about Himself, about the Kingdom of heaven. On Pentecost, Peter, standing up and quoting the prophet Joel (2:28-32), said of the wondrous events of that day:

> In the last days, God says, I will pour out my Spirit on all people. Your sons and daughters will prophesy, your young men will see visions, your old men will dream dreams. Even on my servants, both men and women, I will pour out my Spirit in those days, and they will prophesy (Acts 2:17,18).

We come now a step closer to the theme of our symposium: Christian Philosophy in the Light of Biblical Prophecy, or, as I have modified it for the purposes of my paper: The Christian Philosophical Enterprise in the Light of Biblical Prophecy. For we who wish to work at our philosophical task in the light of the witness of Jesus – we are prophets. Let me now, then, outline very summarily what we find in the Scripture about prophet and prophecy, in order then finally to relate it to the work of our Association.

A prophet is a spokesman; he is God's chosen spokesman *(nabhi)*. The spirit of the prophet is taken possession of by the Spirit of God and he feels *compelled* to speak. He cannot help but speak the things that he has seen and heard (Acts 4:20). There is passionate commitment, firmness of will, the fear of the Lord. The prophet, in his prophecy, is God-possessed, God-driven. And it is the witness of Jesus that is the Spirit of prophecy. What, in summary, is the prophet authorized to speak about?

First, he is a witness to God's being exalted and glorious above all that He has created, to His holiness, as when Isaiah (57:15) speaks of "the high and lofty One, who inhabits eternity, whose name is holy." Second, he is a witness to the sovereignty and glory of God in all His created works. That is what the Kingdom of God is all about. It is what the first section of Genesis is all about. As S.G. de Graaf writes *(Promise and Deliverance* I, 29, 30 = V*erbondsgeschiedenis* I, 15, 16), "In this first section of Genesis we are not just told that God created all things. What is revealed to us first and foremost is the Kingdom of God... The Kingdom of God can be described as that Kingdom in which all things have been subjected to man while man is subjected to God in voluntary obedience. It is not enough," De Graaf writes,

> to tell the children that the world was created by God. They must learn more than that. If a child's heart has been touched by the Spirit of the Lord, he will also long to hear more; he will want to hear about God living in constant communion with the entire creation. This communion was present in the Kingdom of God: man, exercising his dominion, served God... Central to this section, therefore, is the institution of the Kingdom of God. The surrounding and supportive context of this central point is the revelation that all things are from God, through God and unto God. This is exactly why God was able to institute His perfect Kingdom. Man, as king, was to direct all things unto God, that is, to God's glory. Man could do so only because all things, himself included, are from and through God.

Since man fell, Christ, the God-man, had to come and give us God's communion again and through that communion revive our life. (See S. G. De Graaf, *Promise and Deliverance* IV 11-13 = *Verbondsgeschiedenis* II 311-313). This is what is meant by the coming of the Kingdom. God's grace, God's Spirit reigns over us again because of Christ's obedient life and atoning death, and we are once more made glad to serve God in our lives, for His glory. But because of the presence of sin in the world there is also judgment. In this way, then, the prophet, in witnessing to the sovereignty and glory of God in all His created works, is a witness to the coming of the Kingdom (Herman Ridderbos, *De Komst van het Koninkrijk,* p. 36 [italics at bottom], 39 [last 9 lines] = *The Coming* of *the Kingdom,* p. 19 [last 7 lines], p. 23 [middle]).

Third, the prophet is a witness to man's sinful condition of being in a state of rebellion within the sphere of God's Law and Covenant, thus in a state of alienation from God and of hatred not only of His sovereignty and glory, but also of himself and his fellow-man seen as (the) imager and servant of God, a condition which has darkened his understanding of his nature and situation and of the nature of the encompassing world in which he finds himself. In this way the prophet is a witness to covenant wrath. God is high and exalted; He is holy. He is the sovereign Lord of hosts. Accordingly, He holds all men to the conditions of His Law and He does this through His spokesmen, the prophets. Again, Elijah is the great example of this, as he is also of the following two points. (See Van't Veer, *My God Is Jahweh,* Paideia/Premier, 1980, esp. pp. 39-58.) Elijah, and every true prophet, ministers to the *real needs* of the people. These real needs involve the economic, social, and political injustice in their lives, but the true prophet recognizes that in and through all those dislocations their real need is to be reconciled and bound to the Law of God. That is why the true prophet always points to Christ, who in His active and passive obedience has reconciled to God all those who are in Him, justifying them and giving to them the Spirit of sanctification. I am reminded of Karl Barth's famous address to the first assembly of the World Council of Churches in Amsterdam. Professor Berkouwer writes of it that "in one of his side remarks, Barth said he had been dismayed to discover in the preparatory papers so little awareness of the fundamental significance of that which had happened, once for all, in the cross and resurrection of Jesus Christ."[3] Reinhold Niebuhr criticized Barth's speech for its quietism, for encouraging flight from struggle and cultural obscurantism. "For Barth," though, Berkouwer contends, "the significance of God's salvation for this world was not really at issue. He called for the sort of activity in the world that would get at what was most essential in the gospel: freedom and righteousness, fellowship and responsibility. Barth had no quietistic impulse. His was not a quietism as opposed to concrete obedience. *But he did want a Christological analysis* of *authentic obedience"* (emph. mine).

Fourth, prophets, in bringing the Word they receive from God,

---

3.   G. C. Berkouwer, *A Half Century of Theology,* p. 184ff.

are to distinguish the spirits that are in the world. Possessed by the Spirit of God, we recognize that Spirit in the world in the testimonies of men, in their actions, in their lives. 1 John 4:1, 6 says:

> Beloved, do not believe every spirit, but test the spirits to see whether they are from God, because many false prophets have gone out into the world... We are from God, and whoever knows God listens to us, but whoever is not from God does not listen to us. This is how we recognize the Spirit of truth and the spirit of falsehood.

Of this last verse Professor Greydanus writes (in his commentary in the *Korte Verklaring* series, p. 96):

> There are two kinds of people; they are completely different and the exact opposites of each other, and they show that in their whole way of life. The way a man speaks, and his attitude towards the Christ of God and the word of the Gospel that preaches Him as He is and as God sent and gave Him, reveal what spirit possesses him, out of what spirit he lives. The spirit of the truth is the Spirit of God's revelation in Jesus Christ.

In short, the true prophet – and that is now a description of all of God's people – is engaged in a fundamental battle of spirits with false prophets by witnessing to the truth. Again, Elijah is the prime example: "As the Lord God of Israel liveth, before whom I stand..." He is qualified and enabled to do this by the indwelling Spirit of God, the Spirit of truth (John 14:16,17). This involves witnessing to, pointing to the presence of the Church of Jesus Christ in the world, the community of those whom the Spirit of truth gathers out of the world. For we whom the Spirit has brought to the light are united in one Christ (John 15) and by one Spirit, and "if we walk in the light we have fellowship (community, communion: κοινωνία) with one another (I John 1:7; cf. I John 4:13). The Church, as Paul is concerned to communicate to Timothy, is the pillar/support and foundation/bulwark of the truth (1 Tim. 3:15). The truth is all that God has revealed in prophecy, i.e., in His Gospel. There follow in 1 Tim. 3 words that suggest an early creedal hymn that speaks of the pre-existence (by implication) and incarnation, resurrection, ascension, and glorification of Christ, and of a gospel to be proclaimed to the nations. Again we see that "the witness of Jesus is the Spirit of prophecy."

One last thing must be mentioned in speaking of this battle of spirits in which, as true prophets, we are of necessity engaged. I mean the note of triumph that characterizes Jesus' own witness and all biblical prophecy. God's plan *will* be carried out. His Kingdom *will triumph*. Christ, the second Adam, overcame the temptations of Satan. "In the world you have tribulation; but be of good cheer, I have overcome the world" (John 16:33). Christ arose from the dead, and became the firstfruits (ἀπαρχή) of them that have fallen asleep (I Cor. 15:20-23). That beautiful 'firstfruits' is a most important revealed truth the prophet is always to keep before him. In Romans 8:23-25 we see it applied to the blessings which we receive now through the Spirit, the earnest of greater blessings to come, namely, the redemption of our bodies and the deliverance of the whole creation. After disarming the powers and authorities and triumphing over them (Col. 2:15), Christ leads *us* in triumph (II Cor. 2:14). So Paul speaks of hope, which produces patience. With this triumphal note, which characterizes all true prophecy, we are simply making a return to the sovereignty of God and the prophet's task to witness to that sovereignty and the absolute establishment of the supremacy and glory of Jehovah in the entire earth. "He who is in you is greater than he who is in the world" (I John 4:4). But this brings us to our fifth and final point.

Beginning with Christ (John 10:16; Matt. 28:19; Luke 24:47,48; Acts 1:8), the consummation of all that it is to be Prophet – though there are intimations of this in all biblical prophecy (in the Old Testament) – prophets are to extend their witness outward to the ends of the earth. Original prophecy had an ecumenical – in that word's original meaning of "the inhabited world" – range; only subsequently was it narrowed down to Israel, though with the promise that with the coming of the Lord's Anointed One prophecy would extend again to all mankind, and hence again have ecumenical range. Paul, the untimely-born apostle, was God's chosen instrument to bring His

Gospel to the gentile world and its kings (Acts 9:15). The Spirit possessing the prophets drives them farther and farther afield. God's plan will not be thwarted. His Kingdom has come, is coming, will come throughout the length and breadth of His creation.

~ ~ ~

Well, why have I taken all this time to develop these thoughts, and how had I thought to relate them to us of the Association for Calvinistic Philosophy? I wanted to bring out clearly that we who are members of this Association and are Christ's men – we are called to be prophets, we are *meant* to be prophets, in our thinking, critiquing, writing, publishing, in our instruction of the new generation, in the way we organize and finance (budget) our Association's efforts. That means that we are to be God-possessed, possessed by the Spirit of God, God-driven in our personal lives and work as members, and in our organized activities. Remember Professor Greydanus' words,

> To possess in faith the testimony of Christ the Lord regarding Himself in such a way that it governs your inner being and very existence, all that you do and say, is to have the Spirit of prophecy. He of whom this can be said is a prophet.

We members of this Association are prophets. That means – let us make bold to say it – that we are *not* in the first-place philosophers, that is, that is not the ultimate truth about our lives and work, either as individual members of this Association or in our collective work as an Association. We are *prophets,* and our being philosophers, or, to put it more modestly, our being engaged in philosophical work, must be understood as a moment of our lives as prophets. We may not, we cannot, actually separate our philosophical task from our prophetic calling as men, and it is the prophetic calling which works through in our philosophizing, not vice versa.

Our task as Christian men who are engaged in philosophical work is to be witnesses to God's glory, to glorify God in His exaltedness far above all His created works, in His holiness.

Further, our task, again as Christian men engaged in philosophical work, is to be witnesses to the sovereignty and glory of God in all His works of creation, to the reconciliation of all things to God's sovereign Rule through Jesus Christ, to the coming of the Kingdom.

Again, as Christian men who are engaged in the work of philosophy, we are to point men to their lostness, their alienation in the creation, to their having lost the meaning of their lives in the world, the meaning of experience, to point them to the fact that the real nature of the transcendental and transcendent horizons of human experience – the continued revelational witness of God's Order – escapes them.

Once more, in the philosophical work that we as Christians engage in, we are prophetically – thus not by our own wisdom or in our own strength, but in the power of the Holy Spirit – to bring to the light in our critical analyses the spirit of the lie, of suppression and distortion that is at work in the world, however many traces of the truth may be found therein, and at the same time to point to the gracious revelation of the Way, the Truth and the Life and the age-old community of the Truth and fellowship in the Way and the Life, the Church of Jesus Christ, already known in the Old Testament light out of which our analysis springs. It is in the Church of God that the community of scholars is born and flourishes, nowhere else.

Finally, as Christians engaged in our philosophical task, we are to go on the offensive to extend God's prophecy to the ends of the earth, to all the nations of the world, and, in pushing outward, always to be busy proving, that is, putting to the test, the spirits that are at work everywhere in the world, confident that He who is in us, and who by His Spirit binds us together in the bonds of love, is greater than he that is in the world, and that our Lord's intention is, as He has told us, the establishment of His supremacy over all His creation and the fulfillment of the creation design. All, however, in His own time and in His own way.

The Spirit of truth, dwelling in the hearts of believers and there bearing witness to the testimony of Jesus (John 15:26), urging them forth into the *oikoumené* to witness to the testimony of Jesus – He it is who effects in us the fervency of a genuine faith, the passionate commitment, the determination of will, the enthusiasm, the zeal, the spiritual power of witness that is associated with the fear of Jehovah. The only enlightening, convincing power there is in the whole wide world is the working of God by His Word and Spirit in the community of reborn mankind. I think first of all of the dynamism you feel in the Acts of the Apostles. But I think also of the life work of an Augustine, a Huss, a Bradwardine, of a Calvin, of 19th century pioneer missionaries, of so many others whom we honour in the history of the church!

Is our Association marked by these characteristics? Do *we* have this prophetic power? The power, the will to extend our witness to the nations of the world, to set aside and overcome other spirits (again not in our strength, but in the power of the Spirit), to exult (by faith) in God's sovereign working in the world, to glorify God and enjoy Him – always? Does this not all arise from what the Scripture calls "the fear of the Lord"? Is this prophetic power clear in our work? Is it sensed by our students? Is it felt in our working environments? Or are we, in our philosophical work, cool and detached men of *Wissenschaft*, impressing upon our students and colleagues all the true insights there are in the non-Christian cults of the world and the philosophies of unbelievers?

I put these questions with this amount of emphasis, first because, in general, I am, and have long been, troubled by the image of itself that the Dutch Reformed world, whether here in the home country or in Dutch communities overseas, seems to project to the broad Anglo-American evangelical world. Often it seems to be the image of an ethnically introverted, too cerebral, "cool" group of Christians enjoying their heritage of Dutch art, for example, and their "gezellige" family life, but lacking in prophetic intensity. I know that a number of misunderstandings enter into this image that Anglo-American evangelicals throughout the world so frequently have. Some of the misunderstandings are fundamental, as, for instance, the failure to understand the nature of our covenantal life with God in the family relationship. But these misunderstandings, I am sure, are not the chief reason for the image that is received. And now, of course, the situation is complicated by the extreme and pervasive secularization of all classes of the society, and even of traditionally Christian communities, and the rapid falling away from a biblically grounded lifestyle and way of thinking that appears to characterize the Dutch Reformed world, especially noticeable since the 1960s, but in reality detectable in significant ways at least since the passing of Kuyper (1920) and H. Bavinck (1921).

Since the rise of the neo-evangelical movement in the U.S.A. I have heard spokesmen of that movement refer a number of times to the U.S. Christian Reformed Church as a "sleeping giant." Undoubtedly the World War I experiences of a young generation, combined with a generational reaction against the older immigrant "narrowness" and "isolatedness" led, in that Reformed community, to an overemphasis on certain passages of A. Kuyper's *De Gemeene Gratie* (Common Grace) and a misreading of his intention with the reviving and development of that doctrine. The result was a muting of the prophetic voice of this Reformed community in our North American society just at a time of gross self-indulgence (the 1920s). Many of our most gifted students from that time drifted off into the secular universities, humanist political parties and labour unions, and the New York world of the arts and media just in an age when all the restraints a Christian witnessing community had preserved in our North American society were being broken down and a hellishly destructive egocentrism was breaking out all over, too rapidly for us to get any hold on it in order to deal with it, to attempt to redirect it.

Recently, Richard Lovelace, making a plea for evangelical renewal in his book *The Dynamics of Spiritual Life* (published by Inter-Varsity, 1979), wrote that,

> ...one of the few parts of the church which was still intelligently seeking the biblical-cultural synthesis dreamed of by Comenius and Edwards was one which was still feeling the impact of the Reveil... At the end of the 19th century, the great Dutch theologian and statesman, Abraham Kuyper, inaugurated a tradition of theological integration which took seriously both the... antithesis between redeemed and unredeemed thinking and common grace... God's blessing of all men, converted and

unconverted alike, with gifts of truth and beauty and ethical value...
While Kuyper himself incorporated a powerful experiential core in his
theological outlook, the later Amsterdam school has sometimes been
hampered by an incipient aversion to Christian experience, the effect
of the reaction in Dutch Christianity against the excesses of Dutch Puritanism. This may explain why the movement has so far failed to have
the impact and the growth associated with intellectual leaders in the
Awakening tradition... (but) it is not hard to imagine what a powerful
intellectual force would be released in Western culture if the Reformed
orthodox community... would recover the dynamics of renewal which
characterized the earlier awakenings (p. 181f.).

Now I know there are misunderstandings involved here; I am
not interested at this point in discussing them. I am concerned about
the projected image. About that, it seems very clear, there can be no
doubt.

As for the Dutch Reformed community in the Netherlands itself, I read recently that in an interview in *Nederlands Dagblad* Dr.
Willem Glashouwer spoke of plans that were crystallizing for a new
International Christian University in the Netherlands, to be opened
possibly in 1983. The reason, Glashouwer was quoted as saying, is
the humanistic materialistic spirit of the present universities. No exception was mentioned. Abraham Kuyper's instinct in founding the
Free University was good, he is reported as saying, yet Kuyper was too
much a cultural optimist. (Is that again a reference to his exposition
of the doctrine of common grace?) Though the Free University still
has professors who are positively Christian in their scientific work,
the school, in the judgment of Glashouwer, can no more be called a
Christian university.

Now – let me say it again – I do not bring up these matters in
order to argue with anyone about any one of them. I want simply to
indicate the image the Dutch Reformed world too often – whether
rightly or not – seems to project. And of course, the rapid changes
in the traditionally Reformed world, here in the Netherlands, in the
course of the past decade or so, simply complicate and intensify the
picture.

I bring these things up in this paper only because the Dutch Reformed world is, after all, the matrix and home-base of our Association's life. What happens there, or is true of it, is bound to have an immediate effect on the life of this Association.

At the same time, it must be recalled not only that the movement represented by this Association, from the beginning, voiced certain biblically supported criticisms of what was then the prevailing Reformed mind, but also that a lack of prophetic intensity, of evangelical fervor, of the fear of the Lord as the fundamental guiding principle of Calvinistic living in no way characterized the lives and the work of the founders of our Association – and, indeed, of many others with them, but I shall limit myself to them. While recognizing that they too were sinful men, we remember, especially on this occasion because of the theme of this symposium, the religious intensity that there was in their work that was clearly derived from their strong desire, their will, to live wholly by the light of God's holy Word.

They were the inheritors of such a biblically-directed way of life. I think of Guillaume Groen van Prinsterer's "The Gospel against the Revolution," and his identification of European liberalism as a muted advocacy of the principle of the Revolution and its continuation, and especially of this seminal assessment he once made of 19th century society: "Modern society, *with all its excellences* [emphasis mine, the development of creational potential and recognition of traces of truth in the Lie], having fallen into bondage to the theory of unbelief, is being enticed more and more to a *systematic repudiation of the living God*" (the Antithesis, the Battle of Spirits). I think of Abraham Kuyper's *Pro Rege,* which, published just a few years after *De Gemeene Gratie,* seems to indicate that a different interpretation of the latter work will be required than has generally been given to it hitherto in my North American Reformed circles (though not only there).

But their own witness – I am talking about our founders – was unambiguous and emphatic, and they cannot justly be made the butt of the evangelicals' criticisms.

I remember it as though it were yesterday, and I can never forget how my whole being thrilled when I read for the first time Professor

C. Veenhof's moving description of his experience as a theological student in the 1920s and early '30s of the time in which our Association was organized in Amsterdam.[4] Veenhof described that low-point in Reformed life as:

> A heyday of criticism and relativism in theology and philosophy. The best spirits struggled against the flood; they felt it to be a question of life and death, for the church and for themselves. But in their work, in their study, they were unable to cope with the situation. The leaders did not fathom the danger; they were, though entirely unawares, deeply entangled themselves in the snares of all kinds of accommodation to the ideas of their mortal enemies. A paralyzing defeatism took possession of large groups. A subtle psychologism destroyed in many the power and glory of a childlike faith... The ethicistic religiosity of the N.C.S.V. [Nederlandse Christelijke Studenten Vereniging, Dutch Christian Student Union] infected the entire student world. A man was almost ashamed of being Reformed... Moreover, already an emerging bourgeois spirit, a spirit of rigidity, a growing spirit of worldliness in political activity in leading circles of the Reformed world had become offensive to men of a fine and keen spirit.

It was in the midst of this crisis, as Veenhof tells the story, that S.G. de Graaf, A. Janse, K. Schilder, Vollenhoven, Dooyeweerd and others appeared upon the scene. Of Vollenhoven and Dooyeweerd, Veenhof writes that the Kampen students – he was one of them – heard them and were convinced by them in the student congresses held at Lunteren. "A new world," as he recalls it, "was opened up to us."

> Everywhere God's Spirit was at work. Oh, no, nothing special happened actually. It was just that for a great many people the Scripture suddenly became clear. It was as though God's loving hand brushed away the dust that scholasticism and mysticism, pietism and every other kind of subjectivism and individualism had heaped upon His Word,

---

4.   C. Veenhof, *Om de 'Unica Catholica'*, Oosterbaan en Le Cointre N.V., Goes, 1949. See esp. pp. 51-58.

in order that that Word might once again send forth its clear sound and shine forth as a lighthouse to give direction in a dark night.

When this Association for a scripturally grounded and directed philosophical enterprise was established in 1935, Professor D.H.Th. Vollenhoven, the man who was to be its president for the next 28 years, spoke the following telling words. We do well to ponder them often in private and to remind ourselves of them regularly in public. "It is a glorious and blessed thing," he said on that auspicious occasion,

> that brings us together here. It is not philosophy; for that is not the first thing in our life. It is rather the attachment to God's Word, because we have learned by grace to want to live only out of the Christ, and religion, as a matter of the heart, has become the root-center of our life in its totality; because we have learned that only in attending to the commandments of the Lord are peace and life to be found, not only for the individual, but, to be sure, also for all those associations of life in which we find ourselves. This is why philosophy does not occupy the first place here. It has never held that position in our circles, and if the Association which we now propose to erect *remains faithful* [emph. mine] to its task, it will not be its fault if philosophy should ever become the prime consideration. We wish only to take that which is the main thing seriously in the philosophical work that we do... That is something we badly need; for the philosophy that is current knows nothing of all this that is so dear to us: nothing of God, if you understand by that the God of the Scriptures; nothing of a heart that can find rest only in Him; nothing of a world-history that is bound up with the first and the second Adam; even very little of any difference between the spheres, the distinguishing of which in the practice of life proves to be so very essential.

Although Professor Dooyeweerd's utterances are often found in the midst of a philosophical discussion, often one of great complexity and abstractness, their meaning is not one bit less unambiguous. Very simply, they all the more strikingly illustrate the point I am trying to establish.

In the Foreword to the *New Critique of Theoretical Thought*, there is the passage celebrated everywhere the name of Dooyeweerd is known:

> The great turning point in my thought was marked by the discovery of the religious root of thought itself, whereby a new light was shed on the failure of all attempts, including my own, to bring about an inner synthesis between the Christian faith and a philosophy which is rooted in the self-sufficiency of human reason. I came to understand the central significance of the "heart," repeatedly proclaimed by Holy Scripture to be the religious root of human existence. On the basis of this central Christian point of view I saw the need of a revolution in philosophical thought of a very radical character. Confronted with the religious root of the creation, nothing less is in question than a relating of the whole temporal cosmos, in both its so-called 'natural' and 'spiritual' aspects, to this point of reference.

Dooyeweerd then goes on to declare the Kantian "Copernican" revolution in philosophy to be "unacceptable" because, in merely making "the 'natural-aspects' of temporal reality relative to a theoretical abstraction such as Kant's 'transcendental subject,'" it "proclaims the self-sufficiency of the latter" and "withdraws human thought from the divine revelation in Christ Jesus."

For Dooyeweerd, the work into which he was thus newly projected as a result of this scriptural enlightenment was not just a personal project, by working at which he might gain wide recognition and secure for himself a successful career. "The question," he writes at the very beginning of the *New Critique* (I viii), "is not a matter of a 'system' (subject to all the faults and errors of human thought), but rather it concerns the *foundation* and the root of scientific thought as such." Then, at the end of the Foreword, this (I ix): "I do not consider it to be a disadvantage if this philosophy does not enjoy a rapid and easy success." After quoting to the same effect Kant in the Foreword to his *Prolegomena to Any Future Metaphysic,* Dooyeweerd proceeds:

If the elaboration of the Kantian philosophy was deemed worthy of this self-denial, it is certainly obvious that those interested in the Christian foundation of theoretical thought should not be concerned with personal success, which is after all of no value. Rather, they should be willing to carry on a long and difficult labour, firmly believing that something permanent can be achieved with respect to the actualization of the idea concerning an inner reformation of philosophy.

For, as a matter of fact, the precarious and changing opinion of our fellow–men is not even comparable with the inner happiness and peace that accompanies scientific labour when it is based upon Christ, Who is the Way, the Truth and the Life!

There is the magnificent passage (*N.C.* II, 362-5) entitled "Final Remarks on the Christian Idea of Cultural Development." I wish I could take the time to read every word of it to you.

Holy and without any inner contradiction is the world-order, even when it binds the possibility of a defective positivizing of Christian principles to a historical basis of power and to the guidance of true Christian faith... Holy and without inner contradiction is the world-order when it avenges itself on the process of disclosure in which the *civitas terrena* has gained the power to direct the formation of history.

But let me quote just his very last observations.

The Christian Idea of cultural development continues to observe the inner tension between sinful reality and the full demand of the Divine Law... This demand is terrifying when we consider how much the temporal ordinances labour under the destructive power of the fall into sin. Terrifying also, when it puts before us our task as Christians in the struggle for the power of cultural formation. For it makes a demand on us which as sinful human beings we cannot satisfy in any way. And it urges us, in the misery of our hearts, to seek refuge with Christ from Whose fullness *nevertheless* a Christian can derive the confidence of faith to carry on the ceaseless struggle for the control of cultural development. This is the remarkable 'nevertheless' of Christian faith... Christian philosophic thought has to fight shy of self-exaltation, because it is directed in its root to Christ. The whole struggle that positive Christianity has to carry on for the direction of the opening-process is not directed against our fellow-men, in whose sin we partake and whose guilt is ours and whom we should love as our neighbors. That struggle is directed against the spirit of darkness who dragged us all down with him in the apostasy from God, and who can only be resisted in the power of Christ... As Christians we shall hate that spirit because of the love of God's creation in Christ Jesus.

There is one more passage in the *New Critique* that I simply have to mention even though I cannot take much more of your time in order to quote from it. It is the sublime passage on "the perspective structure of the horizon of experience" (*N.C.* II, 560-598) with which Dooyeweerd concludes his masterful analysis of the epistemological problem. I quote a brief passage:

> But man cannot attain to true self-knowledge without true knowledge of God, which cannot be gained outside of the Divine Revelation in Christ... At this point, many a reader who has taken the trouble to follow our argument will perhaps turn away annoyed. He will ask: Must epistemology end in a Christian sermon or in a dogmatic statement? I can only answer by means of the question as to whether the dogmatic statement with which the supposed autonomous epistemology opens, i.e., the proclamation of the self-sufficiency of the human cognitive functions, has a better claim to our confidence as far as epistemology is concerned... Our philosophy makes bold to accept the 'stumbling block of the cross of Christ' as the corner stone of epistemology. [Here Dooyeweerd refers in a footnote to 1 Cor. 1:23.] And thus it also accepts the cross of scandal, neglect, and dogmatic *rejection*. In the limitation and weakness of the flesh, we grasp the absolute truth in our knowledge of God derived from His revelation, in prayer and worship. This knowledge in the full sense of the word contains the religious principle and foundation of all true knowledge, and primarily has a religious *enstatic* character. It no more rests primarily on a theoretical meaning-synthesis than does the cosmic self-consciousness... The knowledge about God in which religious self-knowledge is implied is not primarily gained in

a so-called theological way. That which is very inadequately called 'theology' is a theoretical knowledge obtained in a synthesis of the logical function of thought and the temporal function of faith. It is a knowledge which itself is entirely dependent on the cosmonomic Idea from which the thinker starts. The true knowledge of God and of ourselves is concerned with the horizon of human experience and therefore also with that of theoretical knowledge. It rests on our trustful acceptance of Divine revelation in the indissoluble unity of both its cosmic-immanent sense and its transcendent-religious meaning; an acceptance with our full personality and with all our heart.

Why, now, all those quotations from Dooyeweerd for a group very much at home in his work? Because here we see Dooyeweerd's passionate prophetic witness in the very midst of his philosophizing. From such passages as these we hear Dooyeweerd saying, with Vollenhoven, that not philosophy but religion – in its biblical sense of our life in its totality as our walk before the high and holy and jealous God in terms of His covenant Law – is first with us and is what brings us together, not just in this room, but in this Association and its work.

Indeed, to return to the point, the need for a revolution – better, reformation – in philosophical thought of a very radical character derived from an antecedent passion for the supremacy of the Word of God, in the lives of individuals, of nation-states and societies and of the world community, a phenomenon in our time reminiscent again of the prophetic mission of Elijah in the days of Ahab and Jezebel. A passion for the Word of God as the only Power to sustain us, to heal us, to renew us, to liberate us, to bring the whole of the creation to its intended fulfillment. That Word, we know, had again been mightily at work in the Netherlands since early in the 19th century to call men and churches and a nation back to a whole-hearted service of God according to His ordinances. Recently I have heard some pretty strange accounts of Abraham Kuyper's life by men of a social scientific bent within the *Gereformeerde* community, which stressed, somewhat cynically, it seemed to me, Kuyper's flair for the political manipulation of the "Gereformeerd volksdeel" (the Reformed segment of the populace) just before every election. I will not argue the question of Kuyper's political tactics, but it must in all honesty be acknowledged that pointing to that kind of a talent is not the way to understand the gigantic figure of Abraham Kuyper, or the power he commanded to control affairs in his lifetime, or to appreciate God's work in him. Nor is it possible to see him as in any way the precursor of present-day liberation theologies.

Recall what was said about a true prophet's meeting the people's real needs. Kuyper himself revealed the deepest secret of his life when he wrote:

> As for me, one holy passion rules my life,
> One supreme impulse prompts my mind and soul,
> And may breath fail me
> E'er I lose this sacred urgency.
> It is this: to establish once again,
> For *the people's good,* God's holy ordinances,
> In home and church, in school and state,
> Despite the world's remonstrances;
> It is this: to engrave the Lord's ordinances,
> Which Scripture and creation witness to,
> So sharply in the people's conscience
> That they once more pay homage to their God.[5]

It is in that line of reformation and of biblical prophecy that the

---

5.   "Voor mij, één zucht beheerst mijn leven,
   Eén hoger drang drijft zin en ziel,
   En moog' mij d'adem eer begeven,
   Eer 'k aan dien heil'gen drang ontviel.
   En 't is om Gods heil'ge ordinantien,
   In huis en kerk, in school en staat,
   Ten spijt van 's werelds remonstrantien,
   Weer vast te stellen, 't volk ten baat,
   't Is om die ord'ningen des Heren.
   Waar Woord en Schepping van getuigt,
   In 't volk zóó helder te graveren,
   Tot weer dat volk voor God zich buigt."

philosophical efforts of our founders are to be placed and understood. "The men of the Philosophy of the Cosmonic Idea," Veenhof writes (*op. cit.*, p. 56),

> aimed very high. They undertook the formidable task of not coming to the Scripture with a philosophy, but with the Scripture to philosophy. They laboured at the construction of a truly Scriptural philosophy. What motivated them, as they themselves declared, was not in any sense an intellectual passion, a mere craving for knowledge and facts. On the contrary, they confessed it openly as their conviction that *the scientific enterprise also had to be a moment of true religion and thus a service of God in a distinct way* [emph. mine, H.E.R.].

Thus the *ecumenical* nature of their work had to come more and more clearly to light. This work was not properly the project of just one particular association, even though, given the history and divisive consequence of synthesis thinking in the world Christian community, one particular association such as ours might in the present situation first be required in order to bring the world community of Christians finally to address itself to it. Our founders were not out just to develop a philosophy for Calvinist circles (much less for *Dutch* Calvinist circles), as opposed to Lutheran or Anglican or Roman Catholic or Eastern Orthodox circles. While recognizing (*N.C.,* I 523-4) that their philosophical work could "only be understood as the fruit of the Calvinistic awakening in Holland since the last decades of the 19th century, a movement which had been led by Abraham Kuyper," Dooyeweerd was very clear on the point that their

> philosophy is not to be understood as the exclusive thought of a small clique of Calvinists. On the contrary, according to its basis, by reason of its transcendental ground-idea, it includes within its range all of Christian thought as such... No Christian can escape the dilemma that it sets forth if he really takes seriously the universality of the Kingship of Christ and the central confession of God's sovereignty over the whole cosmos as Creator.

In the eyes of our founders, then, the work of this Association concerned, besides the Dutch Calvinists from whom they were sprung, Scottish and North American Presbyterians – of Vollenhoven I knew this from an intense personal relationship over a number of years – Lutherans, Baptists, Anabaptists and Mennonites, Anglicans, Roman Catholics of all sorts and orders, the Orthodox of the Eastern churches and all for whom Christ is God come in the flesh – that to begin with. And then, beyond that, it concerns the other great world cults, such as Judaism, Islam, Hinduism, and Buddhism in their many varieties of expression, Taoism, and all the various man-ifestations of religious experience that have been designated by the word "animism," etc. In this connection I should like to remind the members of our Association of Professor Berkouwer's discussion (in his volume *General Revelation*, pp. 165-172 = *De Algemene Openbar-ing*, pp. 138-145, with references to A. Kuyper's *Encyclopaedie* [the *Encyclopedia of Sacred Theology*] and other writings and to Dooye-weerd's *Wijsbegeerte der Wetsidee*) of Kuyper's way of viewing and dealing with pseudo-religion and the great variety of non-Christian religious expression. This matter will require our most serious atten-tion in the coming days of our increasingly village-like globe, and the attack which some of us have been associating with the name of John Hick has just come again in the publication last year, by – just imag-ine! – Westminster Press, of the book *Toward a World Theology: Faith and the Comparative History of Religion,* by Wilfred Cantwell Smith, a professor at Harvard University, who is described as "a Harvard authority on world religions." But for the founders of our Association recovering the principle, that is, the foundation and root, of Chris-tian thinking involved the prophetic-missionary task of confronting men the world over with the light and enlightenment of the revela-tion of the God who in Jesus Christ became man for us men and for our salvation.

It is now almost 50 years, almost half a century, since the day Professor Vollenhoven spoke those words of such great moment – I quoted them to you – in inaugurating the work of this Association. I want to repeat them now.

It is a glorious and blessed thing that brings us together here. It is not philosophy, for that is not the first thing in our life. It is rather the attachment to God's Word, because we have learned by grace to want to live only out of the Christ, and religion, as a matter of the heart, has become the root-center of our life in its totality; because we have learned that only in attending to the commandments of the Lord are peace and life to be found, not only for the individual, but, to be sure, also for all those associations of life in which we find ourselves. This is why philosophy does not occupy the first place here. It has never held that position in our circles, and if the Association which we now propose to erect *remains faithful* [emphasis mine] to its task, it will not be its fault if philosophy should ever become the prime consideration. We wish only to take that which is the main thing seriously in the philosophical work that we do.

So now there is every reason for us of this Association, after 50 years, especially after these particular 50 years, so full of strife and of changing perspectives, both world-wide and very close to home, to ask ourselves how *we* stand with respect to this stated purpose of our Association. Could the projected image of the Dutch Reformed world in the minds of the evangelicals be more true of us now? Could the complaint of a Richard Lovelace be more truly lodged against us today than against our founders? Or are we just as conscious as our founders were that our first calling in our work is to be prophets of the living God? Do *we* all have the same passionate commitment, the fervency, the zeal, the urgent sense of calling, that "ecumenical" vision – in short, the sense of prophetic mission – in all the work we do daily as Christian philosophers, the work we do in and for this Association?

Of course, in one sense we do. Why else would we be members of *this* Association? And yet there is reason to ask ourselves this momentous question in this age of dialectical discussion, in a time that loves to erase boundaries.

I am fully aware that it is always very difficult to address a question like this. But I think that everyone will sense the need of doing it who understands what is at stake and who has known something of what the recently deceased great preacher at Westminster Chapel in London, England was getting at when, in the preface to his book *The Unsearchable Riches of Christ, an Exposition of Ephesians 3:1-21*, he writes:

> If I were asked to name the greatest trouble among Christians today, including those who are evangelical, I would say that it is our lack of spirituality and of a true knowledge of God. We have a certain knowledge about God, and we are experts in the 'Christian attitude' toward politics, social affairs, drama, art, literature, etc., but do we, with Paul, say that our deepest desire is to 'know Him'?

And, just speaking generally, it was not without reason grounded in experience that Professor Santayana warned against "redoubling our effort when we've forgotten our aim." That has been the experience repeatedly of organizations – even of the instituted church in human history. This is why I was so happy with the theme that was chosen for this symposium. It encourages us honestly and forthrightly to address ourselves to the question who we are as members of this Association, and what the nature is of the task we have undertaken to work at together.

And there are, as a matter of fact, a number of indications that something about us has changed, and that not everything is as it should be. At least, there is a spirit of disquiet and discontent. Let me just quickly point to a number of observations I have noted, and these are probably not even those most important perceptions which most of us receive through our spiritual antennae (*voelhoorns*) in the regular course of our daily living.

First, then, I would note that the letter of invitation that went out to us for this Symposium, signed by the members of the Board of the Association, included the words: "We are afraid that at present our Christian philosophizing has become introverted. Perhaps we have lost the spiritual awareness of being called by God to work, be it on a modest scale, on the reformation of a secular culture."

To this I would add, in the second place, a personal comment of my own regarding some impressions I received during our First International Symposium held at Driebergen six years ago. Without denying that good and solid contributions were made, I had a general very uncomfortable feeling that we were a very small bunch of extremely theoretically oriented Dutchmen and Afrikaners talking to ourselves, often about things long debated among us, as, for example, whether scientific thought is analytically or lingually qualified. I also felt that men had been asked to address us who did not share what is foundational, in our view, to Calvinistic or adequately scripturally grounded philosophy. I am referring, of course, to representatives of a more traditionally scholastic patterning of biblical revelation. Permit me to refer to something related to that patterning that I briefly remarked on years ago in my lectures collected under the title *The Relation of the Bible to Learning*. I shall refer to the recently published fifth revised edition since it will allow me at the same time to correct a serious mistake that has crept into this otherwise greatly improved edition. On page 143, just below the middle, where I am discussing a remark someone made to the effect that "our theological heritage is a rich mine *with educational implications,*" I refer, between parentheses, to the "familiar scholastic idea of theological *Lehnsaetze* [it reads wrongly: Lehrsaetze] for the educational theory of the Christian, instead of an integral scripturally directed paedagogics." And in that other collection of lectures of mine entitled *Scriptural Religion and Political Task* (p. 121 bottom), quoting Alsted, again I refer to "theological *Lehnsaetze*," "principial" deductions from a theological system, which are a kind of marginal correction setting limits within which, for a life that possesses its own laws of development and not a reformation of that life from its religious root. I would suggest that present-day discussion of control beliefs, from the point of view of the founders of this Association, is very similar to, if not identical with, this scholastic notion of *Lehnsaetze*, and that both are borrowed from an extraneous *theological* system to be applied to a world of rational thought having a life of its own, governed internally by its own (rational) laws.

Do not misunderstand me. I think it is both a fine thing and proper to encourage thinking Christians who entertain such traditional scholastic views to attend our gatherings and, in the course of our gatherings, to engage them in intense (prophetic) discussion. But I am asking how representatives of such views, as principal speakers at our gatherings, could possibly contribute to the promotion of what our founders saw as the aim or task of this particular Association? To that task in the light of biblical prophecy as I have outlined it? And *this* confusion I see not only as particularly characteristic of our day, but also as rendering the trumpet call to the battle – not against persons, but of principle against principle – unclear, something Paul, in a passage encouraging prophesying, warns against (1 Cor. 14:8).

Could it be that there is a spiritual relation between the phenomenon of talking to ourselves, where I felt prophetic passion lacking, and the other phenomenon of requesting the guidance of men who accept a separate world of rationality? I am only asking the question, because at this point I am simply enumerating certain observations.

Third, I noticed that in the September/October, 1981 (25th anniversary) issue of *Perspective,* the newsletter of the Association for the Advancement of Christian Scholarship (p. 22), Dr. Bernard Zylstra, the Principal of the AACS's Toronto-based Institute for Christian Studies, speaking of the Institute's academic future and particularly of its connection with the Free University, had this to say: "On a select basis, we will advise our philosophy students to complete their Ph.D. studies there... And we do so with our eyes open, recognizing that the Free University as a whole is caught up in the spiritual confusion of western Europe and *being fully aware of the fact that the 'Dooyeweerdian' school of thought is fragmented and has lost a great deal of its initial vibrance and vitality*" (emphasis mine). Here are two things: fragmentation, and loss of initial vibrancy and vitality. Could *they* be related? Now of course I realize that when Zylstra speaks here of the "'Dooyeweerdian' school of thought" he has in mind the *Centrale Interfaculteit* at the Free University and not our Association. Yet I hope legalistic sophistry has not penetrated *our* circles to such an extent that we would avoid seeing at once the close connection between what he *is* speaking of *and us.*

Finally, as a fourth indication, I would point to the January/February 1982 issue of *The Guide,* organ of the Christian Labour Association of Canada, where Dr. Hendrik Hart, in a requested exchange of views with Dr. Bernard Zylstra, makes this remarkable comment, significant, I think, for our present purpose (p. 10): "Two decades ago, individuals and organizations in the reformational movement seemed to speak with one voice. Today this is no longer the case." Again, "reformational movement" is not exactly the same as the Association for Calvinistic Philosophy. But no one acquainted with the developments of the last three decades will fail to recognize the very intimate connection between the so-called "reformational movement" and the philosophical movement represented by our Association. Here again there is the suggestion of fragmentation and also perhaps, by implication, of lost vitality.

These four indications of change and disquiet will suffice to suggest the possibility of some dislocation in our life as an Association.

The presence of some dislocation since 1935 should not at all be surprising when we consider the great and rapid changes that have taken place in our surroundings in this last half century, both in the world at large and here in the Netherlands, the "*bakermat*" or home-base of this Association, and, indeed, even in the Dutch Reformed community. And particularly when we consider the sense of foreboding, of impending doom, of threatening fundamental collapse that has accompanied so much of this change. The renowned Irish poet, William Butler Yeats, from his own perspective of epochal cycles, has captured the feeling well in these oft quoted dread lines from his poem "The Second Coming":

Things fall apart; the center cannot hold;
Mere anarchy is loosed upon the world,
The blood-dimmed tide is loosed, and everywhere
The ceremony of innocence is drowned; The best lack all conviction,
while the worst Are full of passionate intensity.

Indeed, we have lived through, we are living in "an age of hot ideologies and global crusades,"[6] of reviving nationalisms, of sporadic

---

6. See Ronald Steel, in the Prologue to his remarkable book, *Walter Lippmann and the American Century*, p. xvi.

advocacy of anarchism and increasing international terrorism. And while, on the one hand, the incredibly rapid development of current technologies, almost too rapid for us to keep abreast of them – think only of computers, of satellite communication and the latest military weapons – not only accelerates the advance towards a global village but at the same time holds most scientific technicians and generally educated people in the West or wherever the western mind has penetrated to the ideology and paradigm of progress first clearly articulated by Jacques Turgot at the Sorbonne in 1750 in two *Discourses* and afterwards elaborated by Auguste Comte in his "Law of the Three Stages;" on the other hand, not only do men like Jeremy Rifkin (in *Entropy: A New World View)* and Rifkin and Ted Howard (in *The Emerging Order: God in the Age of Scarcity)* say that the mechanical worldview, developed by Francis Bacon, René Descartes and Isaac Newton, is crumbling, to be replaced by the Entropy Law, but many of our contemporaries are becoming increasingly aware of "the disintegration of world public order and the consequent spread of anarchy, fear and panic in many parts of the world," as was stated by Eugene Rostow, director of the U.S. Arms Control and Disarmament Agency in his agency's recent annual report, an awareness that only intensifies the efforts, for example, of the World Order Models Project.[7]

Ronald Steel, speaking of Walter Lippmann's book, *Essays in the Public Philosophy*, reports that the notes for the book, published when Lippmann, clearly the greatest journalist and political commentator America has ever had, was 65 years old (in 1955), reflected a time when "totalitarian movements had captured the allegiance of what he [Lippmann] called the 'deracinated masses'... A civilization must have a *religion*... Communism and Nazism are religions of proletarianized

---

7.   See "On the Creation of a Just World Order: An Agenda for a Program of Inquiry and Praxis," by Saul Mendlovitz, in *Alternatives: A Journal of World Policy*, Vol. VII No. 3 (Winter 1981-82), pp. 355–373. The entire number of this journal, published by the *Centre for the Study of Developing Societies* in Delhi, India and the *Institute for World Order* in New York City, is most provocative reading.

masses."[8] By the 'public philosophy', Lippmann wrote his friend Bernard Berenson, he meant the "natural law on which Western institutions were originally founded"; it was a time in his life when Lippmann was strongly drawn to Catholic theology. Lippmann's analysis was that "the democracies had suffered paralysis and given way to authoritarianism because the people had imposed a veto 'upon the judgments of the informed and responsible officials.' As the people became sovereign, their governments lost authority and were unable to preserve the peace and uphold standards of 'civility.' The problem, in short, was that the people had 'acquired power they are incapable of exercising, and the governments they elect have lost powers which they must recover if they are to govern.'" Interesting sequel, in the mind of this "modern" man, to the natural law theory behind Rousseau's state absolutism, based on the *volonté générale,* and to radical forms of democracy!

In the wake of this breakdown of public order and the concomitant rise of psychology as a cult of self-worship[9] has come the fruit of all this self-centeredness, the breakdown of married life and family life and of all meaningful personal relationships. Divine institution has been replaced by the claims of "situation ethics" and the outcry for "maximum individual autonomy." Yet loneliness has become the agony of the century, to be repressed by drugs, for example, all kinds of experimentation in the "social" use of drugs, by sexual promiscuity and experimentation, by violent and unnatural sexual activity and by "social" or gang criminality.

I know that there have been many wonderful achievements in our time, and output of outstanding 'quality' in all the arts and sciences. [I have placed single quotes around that word 'quality' to indicate that my use of it here has abstracted it from one fundamental criterion of quality, an obedience, out of faith, to the Law-word of Almighty God, the Lord of hosts, as a condition for the salutary functioning of all created being. See my remarks on "Structure and Direction" below.]

---

8.   R. Steel, *op cit.*, p. 491.

9.   See Paul C. Vitz, *Psychology as Religion*, Eerdmans, 1977 (reprinted, 1980).

In fact, one of the problems of our time is just that there is so much. [But should that ever be a "problem" unless it is complicated by the issue of distortional direction, even the question of the focusing of all our energies upon the accumulation of "facts" in the special sciences?] The rapid development of all the special sciences, the sudden blossoming of a host of behavioral sciences, has often been commented on. But if I think of the field of philosophy itself, then it is the rapid succession of "schools" or, better perhaps, the short-span rise and fall of movements (with the great expectations attached to them), some striving for comprehensiveness but missing certainty, others determined to save certainty if not the phenomena (comprehensiveness), that produces in me a feeling of exhaustion. In a recent review in *The New York Review of Books*,[10] John R. Searle, speaking of what he calls "the great dream of the human sciences in the twentieth century," all the efforts towards realizing which, he says, "have been, in varying degrees, failures," goes on to declare: "The most spectacular failure was behaviorism, but in my intellectual lifetime I have lived through exaggerated hopes placed on and disappointed by games theory, cybernetics, information theory, generative grammar, structuralism and Freudian psychology, *among others*" (emphasis mine). At the moment I have in mind not the repeated failures so much as the flood of theoretical constructions in so short a time-span, the mere enumeration of which is wearying. And all the while there is a still more fundamental anxiety. For the other developments that I have only very briefly touched upon threaten to undo everything. Man, nay, rather mankind, recipient of covenant blessing or covenant wrath, is central to all created being.

The Netherlands, since 1935, besides suffering all the traumatic effects of these more global developments, experienced the ugly dividedness of its citizenry around the N.S.B. (National Socialist Movement) and finally – what it had escaped in 1914-18 – the horrors of becoming an active participant in a 20th-century total war, one that had a peculiarly divisive effect on the populace in that it sprang up, in part, from the rapidly spreading infection of a "hot ideology and

---

10. Issue of April 29, 1982, p. 3.

global crusade." Then the need for a "renewed" Netherlands gave rise to a discussion of the need for a "*doorbraak*," a breakthrough in the Dutch political climate. In the atmosphere of a growing acceptance of a synthesis of Christianity and humanism in a personalistic socialism which could make an appeal to a broad European tradition in both Protestant and Roman Catholic circles, the Dutch National Movement encouraged a widening discussion about the evils of "*verzuiling*" (pillarization), with the result that patterns of public behavior that by now had become widely accepted (due in large part to the Reformed Christian struggle for a rightful place in the public life for Christian schools and a university, for Christian social, political and economic action) were first called into question and then began to disintegrate, amid much bitter personal wrangling, family feuding, generational clashing – and everywhere: frustration, suspicion, alienation.

In the midst of all this distress the increasing attraction of the possibility of emigration to a new world lightened the lives of many families, but it also broke families up. Considering emigration often only increased the tensions. It also caused Dutchmen to turn their attention more outward and be influenced by conditions and developments in the non-Dutch world (which, incidentally, had generally not experienced the revival of Reformed religion of 19th-century Holland or the changes it had effected in the organization of Holland's national life – remember Romein's remark about Abraham Kuyper's influence in this regard), thus strengthening other influences from without that came with the end of the war, like the awareness of European Catholic socialist thought that Catholic men in the new post-war government brought with them and the ideas, attitudes and strategies that returning Dutch missionaries from the East Indies had gained from their association with British Anglicans/missionaries there.

Meanwhile, the rapid economic and industrial recovery of Europe under the Marshall Plan brought an understandable, perhaps scarcely noticed, obsession with material things, like the latest models of radios, stereos, nylons, TVs, refrigerators and freezers, and, of course, automobiles, a quite predictable reaction to years of terrible deprivation. But I said "obsession with," and I believe it is clear that only a Christian community already greatly weakened in its commitment to live in covenantal obedience according to the Word of God, and now exhausted and divided, could so easily, along with the rest of the nation, have fallen into such an engrossing concern with things and with fashion ("wit is 'in,'" i.e., "white" is in style).

At the end of the '60s there came the shock of the student rebellions and the growing assertive acceptance among the young of marxist and neo-marxist viewpoints and of so-called alternative lifestyles. There even developed, to my knowledge, a curious "playful" experimentation with Eastern and African cults, which spoke, I believe, of the emptiness of whatever Christian profession was left and of a scarcely conscious search in other directions for a source or locus of power.

The traditionally Reformed Christian community in the Netherlands, which since the early '20s had been experiencing a rapid weakening of Reformed consciousness, no doubt played its part in these national developments. The words of C. Veenhof which I read to you earlier spoke of how the founders of our Association, and others who were with them in the struggle, sought to address that crisis with a powerful biblically prophetic witness. Global and national developments, on the other hand, were having their own effect on the Reformed Christian community. By the end of the '60s many theologians and other intellectual leaders, it was clear, had consciously, deliberately rejected what they called the old "*Gereformeerdendom*" (i.e., Reformed community-bond and its life-style) and its "provincial" ways. Moreover, rather than maintain the Free University as an intensely and consistently Reformed Christian university, it was decided, as it is said, to fulfill Kuyper's vision of a complete, up to date university even if it meant filling out the staff with non-Reformed and even non-Christian instructors rather than having a smaller institute. (Here, with a vengeance, is emphasis on Structure with an ignoring or minimizing of Direction, for which see below. Undoubtedly the alleged "cultural optimism" reading of Kuyper is here coming to full practical fruition.)

In the meantime, this Reformed Christian community, for reasons not unrelated to all these developments, experienced the bitter, heartrending events that led to the ousting of Professor Schilder and the separate existence of the Liberated Churches, and their own riven history.

Into these terribly troubled, sorely divided and significantly uprooted Reformed communities of post-war Holland the big outside world penetrated increasingly, affecting long cherished family ways. Bible reading at the table often became something of a formality, an embarrassment to be over with quickly, or one of the "provincial" ways of that old "*Gereformeerdendom*" from which people were experiencing liberation, as it was said, and thus brought into the more enlightened and globe-wide accepted ways of modernity. Prayer at the family table, instead of being offered on behalf of the family by its responsible head, very often became the silent prayer of individuals, at times to be dispensed with altogether. Therewith, in growing families, an awareness in the young of the meaning of "office" (*ambt*), which is fed from such daily experiences, was greatly reduced and often to all intents and purposes lost. Individualistic practices became more visible in behavior at meals. From such little changes as these in the intimate family circle one could get a sense of the great spiritual changes that were taking place in society.

~ ~ ~

In one sense it may seem quite superfluous to rehearse all these developments here. Still, I think we ought not to deceive ourselves. They all have had their own way of exhausting us, not only emotionally, but especially spiritually. In that way they have been a factor affecting our work. Just how they may have affected our work I will say a word about in a moment. But right here I wish to repeat that the theme chosen for our symposium has indeed been happily chosen; for after these years we must recall to mind what our Association was organized to work at: the Christian philosophical enterprise in the light of biblical prophecy. I have therefore addressed myself to what it means to be a prophet, because the years of our lives demand all the spirituality we can muster. By spirituality, let me repeat, I mean our daily walk before God, in His covenant, according to all the words of His Law, in union with Christ, in the power of His Spirit, responding to His Word in unceasing prayer, meditation, witness and service as prophets,[11] living in the fear of the Lord and to His glory. Originally God's gift, this new life in Christ is ours to exercise and develop. And develop it we must, intensely, calling on the Spirit of God to help us, as individuals and in the world we undertake together.

I should like now, without losing sight of all the developments we have but lightly touched upon (in order to suggest something of the "rapidation," complication, intensification, and "ecumenical" nature of the events of this end–time), to get back to the more immediate context of our Association. For I suspect that whatever dislocations have been felt in the Association's work are much more likely to be due to factors closer to home and to our own philosophical heritage (even though strongly supported sometimes by developments in the wider world).

Earlier in my paper I spoke of the precious gift of firm biblical insight bequeathed to us by our founders, and for any consideration of the subject of the Christian philosophical enterprise in the light of biblical prophecy our founders provided us with many valuable insights that have stood the test of time. Originally, I had intended to comment on several of them, but now there is not time for that. For now, then, I wish to focus our attention on one such insight. After 35 years it assumes in my mind the importance of the principal precept for biblically grounded and directed thinking, and thus also for our philosophizing. Professor Vollenhoven formulated it somewhat aphoristically and constantly reiterated it in order to stamp it indelibly

---

11. In the light of biblical prophecy we are, in Christ, not only prophets, but also priests and kings unto God. We have, for example, if we are to live our lives unto God's glory, to render up our renewed philosophical work unto God as the sacrifice of our hearts. In this paper I have limited myself to developing something of what, in the light of biblical prophecy, it means to be a prophet. The rest will have to await some future occasion.

on the minds of his students. He did that because he was firmly convinced it was the way to keep our prophecy, also in our philosophical account of the world and man's life in it, comprehensive and balanced in a biblical way, and to keep us from falling back into the one-sidedness that have characterized so many movements in the history of Christianity. If the witness of Jesus is the Spirit of prophecy, and if the Power of our prophecy is in the Word, then the biblically balanced comprehensiveness of our prophecy is a matter of the utmost importance, certainly when it comes to our philosophical articulation of it. Vollenhoven's formula: Structure and Direction.

I suppose he came to it as he reflected on the somewhat different emphases of Abraham Kuyper (his so-called cultural optimism, arising from a perhaps too one-sided emphasis on the structures of creation in connection with his development of the theme of common grace) and Herman Bavinck (who, in addition, stressed the theme of the imitation of Christ), and then there were the later attacks on Kuyper's view, not only by Haitjema and van Ruler, but also by S.G. de Graaf and K. Schilder.[12]

By means of his little device Vollenhoven meant to indicate that God's creation, according to Scripture, involves not only the presence of a Law-order – not an agglomeration, mind you, but an *Order* – of different modes of functioning (kinds of lawfulness) in an indissoluble coherence that points beyond itself to an underlying unity (the structural component), but also of man in his relation to the God of the covenant – religion – and his heart-response to the Law of the covenant with the covenant-favor and -blessing that follows upon the newly learned obedience the Spirit instills and the covenant-wrath and -curse that is the consequence of rebellious disobedience (the Antithesis, or the directional component). The created reality about which we are to philosophize never presents us then with a merely structural or a merely directional given. The two components are everywhere intertwined. (For Dooyeweerd's similar position one need

---

12. For an excellent current discussion of the different emphases of Kuyper and Bavinck see John Bolt, *The Imitation of Christ Theme in the Cultural-Ethical Ideal of Herman Bavinck*, an (as yet) unpublished doctoral dissertation, St. Michael's College, University of Toronto, Canada, 1982.

only read *New Critique* I 114-124.)

In the short time remaining I should like to suggest that it would be very easy for us in this Association at any time, but particularly in these times, to lose our grip somewhat on this balance that biblical prophecy presents, and to do that in either of two ways.

The reawakening evangelical world of North America with its aroused sense of Christian responsibility for the direction of our culture is inclined to emphasize the Battle of spirits (Antithesis) in a way that is too simplistic because the structural component, for lack of analysis, gets ignored. Good in this response is the recognition of the fiercely anti-God dynamic that is at work in our society. Unfortunate is the failure to see effects of the impingement upon the unbelieving mind of the (revelational) Order of creation and thus to credit the scientific labours of unbelievers or the serious human reflection in the various non-Christian cults of the world with traces – I prefer that word to "elements" – of the truth even while seeing them as vitiated by the immanentistic and reductionist tendencies of unbelieving thought.

There's the rub: For the mind that has not been renewed in Christ, just because of the revelational reality of creation *sensing* the need for a place of unity but because of the alienation of sin no longer *knowing* the religious walk of man before his covenant God, is driven to locate the religious point of concentrated unity *within* the cosmic diversity as this presents itself to us all (immanentism), and that leads to a reducing of the diverse sides of creational activity to some putative unity (like Matter, or Mind). If the Battle of spirits is to be waged effectively, the involvement of the structural in the directional must be acknowledged and worked out. If this were done, for example, North American evangelicals would be less deceived into thinking of natural law theories as essentially Christian. (For this the invaluable historical work of Professor Vollenhoven must become better known.)

On one of his trips to the United States, Hans Rookmaaker took me aside at the close of one of his meetings to tell me – it was obviously very much on his mind and important to communicate to me – that the modal analysis he had attempted in his 1946-47 articles in

Philosophia Reformata was just too much and too heavy intellectual baggage for North American students and they would not accept it. Hans and I had been good friends since late 1946 or early 1947, and I have always had great respect for the work he undertook. But I confess I was a bit shaken by his "advice." My difficulty is that I do not know for sure whether his remark was just an impression of the moment or if perhaps he meant it only as a guideline for our easing ourselves into the North American situation. He cannot have meant it as absolutely as it sounded; for I note that in his article "De Constituerende Factoren ener Historische Daad" [*Philosophia Reformata,* Vol. 19 (1954)] he acknowledges that one's insight into an historical situation, while dependent on one's life-and worldview, must also surrender time and again to the world-order (p. 101; 120), and at the close of his *Modern Art and the Death of a Culture* (p. 234ff.) he discusses, though somewhat sketchily, decorum, righteousness and purity in art, a bare and belated suggestion of modal analysis.

The fact is that once we have broken with the immanentistic-reductionist way of dividing the world into "the material" and "the mental" or "the intelligible," having recognized the great diversity of lawfulness in the world and acknowledged that the creation must somehow in its diverse ways fundamentally reflect the unity of its Creator, modal analysis, sphere irreducibility and sphere universality thrust themselves upon us.[13] In this sense modal analysis is inescapable. And where we take it seriously good progress is made. Recent examples of such work are Stafleu's *Time and Again,* an article by André Troost in the May 22, 1981 issue of *Opbouw* and Doug Blomberg's Sydney (Australia) University dissertation.[14]

Nevertheless, I have heard voices now and then suggesting that we discard or at least play down modal analysis, and this I see, for the reason just given, as threatening the health and vigorous prophet-

---

13. Dooyeweerd, *N.C.* I 507: "The intermodal coherence of meaning is not a construction of philosophical thought but is rather sustained by the divine temporal world-order, which is also the condition of theoretical thought."

14. D. G. Blomberg, *The Development of Curriculum with Relation to the Philosophy of the Cosmonomic Idea,* Ph.D. diss., Univ. of Sydney, 1978.

ic witness of our Association, particularly as we penetrate more and more deeply into the Anglo-American world.

There is another very closely related matter. There have been here and there attempts at revising the modal scale as Vollenhoven and Dooyeweerd presented it. There is nothing wrong with that; in fact, these attempts suggest that serious efforts at modal analysis are continuing, and that is good. I begin to fear, however, when various attempted revisions are made the starting-point paedagogically for introducing a new generation of students to what God has so signally blessed us with. While we are seeking more of a consensus, let us have our students, just as a matter of paedagogical wisdom, be introduced to a common starting-point – certainly our North American evangelical students, for whom the whole theoretical enterprise and its relation to revelation is so completely strange. In other words, behind our struggle in systematics there is a revealed Order. Let us give our students *the time necessary to grasp the significance of that.* It is enough of a temptation for a student in his 20s to get too wrapped up in the systematics of his present professor. But this brings me to the second way we might tend to lose our grip on the comprehensive balance of biblical prophecy that Vollenhoven meant to encapsulate in the apothegm "Structure and Direction."

This second way involves our becoming too completely absorbed in our philosophical systematics. This possibility gives me, in a way, greater concern than the former one. For one thing, I think that for a number of reasons it is more likely to happen. But, far more important, it would tend to diminish our sense of the directive Power of the revelational *given* in our systematic investigations.

Most of us, I am sure, can recall Dooyeweerd's words in the Foreword to the *New Critique* (p. vii):

> I am strongly convinced that for the fruitful working out of this philosophy in a genuinely scientific manner there is needed a staff of fellow-labourers who would be in a position independently to think through its basic ideas in the special scientific fields. It is a matter of life and death for this young philosophy that Christian scholars in all fields

of science seek to put it to work in their own specialty.

And Professor Langemeijer, in his appreciation of Dooyeweerd's work marking Dooyeweerd's 70th birthday *(Trouw,* October 6, 1964), said this:

> It can be said, I believe, that the theories of Dooyeweerd lend themselves, to a greater degree than is normally the case, to an exchange of thought with persons of a different persuasion. The reason for saying this lies in the fact that he has drawn the implications of his doctrine concerning the supra-theoretical presupposition of philosophy very far – farther than other movements which at this point are akin to him – even into the special sciences. As a matter of fact, it is precisely in the problems and perplexities, in the impasses of the special sciences that he has demonstrated his thesis.

Indeed, the great gifts God's Spirit bestowed on Professor Dooyeweerd reveal themselves, in the *New Critique* and elsewhere, in the rich suggestions he made for a number of special sciences, and our present (potential) weakness, as I see it, may derive in part from these very riches he left to us. It may also derive partly from our own incapacity to keep such a mass of learning under control. No one of the second generation has, in my estimation, approached the level of performance of either Vollenhoven or Dooyeweerd. That ought not to surprise us, or discourage us, either, but it has taken a whole generation for us to learn the meaning of Professor Langemeijer's assessment of Dooyeweerd's great gifts.

As I was writing this I remembered something that Professor B.B. Warfield (Princeton; died 1921) wrote about his teacher, Dr. Charles Hodge, one of the "founders" of American Presbyterianism. "We think," he wrote, "that though learning is fuel to the mental fire, yet there is such a thing as smothering the flames with a superabundance of fuel. But 'so intense and ardent was the fire of his mind that it was not only not suffocated beneath this weight of fuel, but penetrated the whole superabundant mass with its own heat and radiance.'"[15]

---

15. *Selected Shorter Writings of Benjamin B. Warfield* – I, edited by John E. Meeter, Presbyterian and Reformed Publishing Company, Nutley, New Jersey, 1970, p. 440.

Not all of us will fit that description. The result that threatens is that our prophecy becomes suffocated in the details of scholarship. And we who are the heirs of a great tradition of prophecy must not let that happen to us. We must beseech our faithful God not to let it happen to us. But there are things we can do and must see to.

It was Dooyeweerd's *systematic* philosophy (modal analysis) which led to his call for workers in the several special scientific areas. Modal analysis requires for its realization the clearest possible conception and formulation of the structural states of affairs encountered in the various areas of scientific inquiry. The heed that was given to Dooyeweerd's appeal for help – let us thank our covenant-keeping God for that response – meant that now a considerable amount of attention would be given to systematic inquiries in every one of the special sciences. Add to that a number of problems in Dooyeweerd's own philosophical systematics, and differences between his and Vollenhoven's, and we see that work in systematics was quite naturally going to demand a very great deal of our time.

There is nothing at all wrong with that, and not for one moment am I so much as even suggesting that the doing of all this systematic work was or is improper in itself. It is not a question of quantity, but of the *qualitative* nature of our work in systematics. Systematics is a great part of the Christian philosopher's work, and of the Christian's work in the special sciences. It also constitutes a considerable amount of the work of an association organized to promote and propagate Christian philosophy. It is only when something happens that causes us to become too much, too exclusively absorbed in these systematic investigations, as if the systematic accounting for states of affairs existed by itself, that a radical shift in us as individual philosophers and as an association can very subtly, and perhaps almost imperceptibly at first, take place.

All the sciences direct their investigations to structural states of affairs grounded in the creation-order, structures which urge themselves upon everyone who is seriously confronted with them (*N.C.* II, 577). In this way, and to this extent, these structures are commonly experienced, and it is the task of all practitioners of a particular special science to attempt to account for the ones that belong to their field of investigation. This leads very naturally, in each field, to discussions, exchange of ideas with fellow-practitioners in an attempt to reach a statement all can agree on as to the nature of the states of affairs being investigated. Science aims at common agreement, publicity, possibility of repetition of experiment, or investigation by anyone properly qualified. Of course, the other side of Dooyeweerd's statement (II, 577) is as follows: "It may be that no true philosophical insight can be gained into the Divine world-order if our cognitive selfhood does not abide in the full religious Truth of Divine Word-revelation."[16] Here we have that play of the directional component in the structural accounting we give of the (revelational) creation-order.

Now I am convinced that no one in this Association would ever intentionally allow himself to get lost in structural analysis and thus no longer acknowledge the engagement in it of the directional component. That would be to abandon the very purpose that led to the setting up of our Association. Nevertheless, every one of us who belongs to Jesus Christ and has vowed to live by His Word must constantly give heed also to that admonition of Paul to the Corinthian Christians: "So, if you think you are standing firm, be careful that you don't fall!" (1 Cor. 10:12).

There are, indeed, a number of forces at work in our society which, sometimes in combination, tend to encourage a scientific analysis that concerns itself exclusively with what we speak of as structural matters. During our lifetime, for example, all the sciences, not just the natural ones, have developed so fast that one can properly speak of an "explosion" of scientific activity: a proliferation of "sub-sciences," i.e., subdivisions of the special sciences; masses of practitioners; a multiplication of centers of scientific inquiry; organization of scientific communication on a global scale; in all fields a staggering increase

---

16. The "may be" here, it should be clearly stated, suggests nothing of hesitation or doubt; it has simply to do with the structure of this and the following sentence. Also to be borne in mind here, in contrast to the still widely current largely positivist view of the matter, is the *intrinsic* relation of philosophy and the special sciences. Recall what is said in footnote 13 above.

of periodicals and abstracts. All this means that it takes as much of a man's time as he is willing (the will!) to give – it will promptly take all if he permits it to – just to try to keep on top of the continuous influx of data in his field. The limitations of many of us probably play a subtle and usually unacknowledged role here.

Closely related to this development – it is felt as a necessary consequence of it – is the trend, even pressure, towards earlier specialization in the training of students and the early determination of career-field, which frequently brings with it an earlier narrowing of the mind's focus, following which, after the achieving of doctoral status, the awful pressures to produce and publish in one's increasingly narrow area of specialization come with a prompt insistence. I have no doubt that especially the younger generation of members in this Association have experienced what I am talking about.

In these circumstances one inadvertently finds oneself using one's time and employing one's energies analyzing and describing relevant states of affairs and relations holding between them, discussing with one's fellow-practitioners differing opinions, suggested hypotheses and theories respecting these, and summarizing all that one thus finds. These days one travels, if one can find the funds, from one center of scientific activity to another to talk to one's colleagues and to observe their work – a time-consuming matter – and then tries to give as complete a survey as one can of the various opinions and of what is going on in one's field. Much of all this is proper if kept in restraint and governed by our vocation, in the light of biblical prophecy, to be prophets *first,* as Vollenhoven said, even in this Association, *to be prophetic voices in the philosophical work that we do.* To be philosophically engaged is a moment in our religion. The generation of Vollenhoven and Dooyeweerd struggled spiritually to recover the meaning of biblical prophecy for our philosophizing.[17] It is easier for the next generation, without experiencing this struggle to the same

---

17. Professor Kohnstamm in discussing Dooyeweerd remarks that recognition of the gap between biblical and Greek or "idealistic" thinking was the result of the thorough biblical studies of the past century. *Cultuur-geschiedenis van het Christendom* V, 426.

degree, to take the results of their experience for granted, so that the matter is removed a bit farther to the periphery of consciousness unless consciously and regularly renewed.

We must never lose sight of the fact that the vast humanistic world of scientific investigation is organized in the way I have just been describing, grounded as it is in that philosophical intellectualism which it tends to think of as axiomatic. It requires on our part an ever-present sense of our primary vocation as prophets not to begin to fall in with that world's way of doing things. A man accommodates himself in order not to stand out as so "peculiar" as to be ignored in scientific circles, and in order to become recognized there so as to obtain the grants, the opportunities, the professional appointments that are absolutely necessary if a scholar is to establish himself and gain a reputation. And isn't all this accommodation justifiable if we can gain recognition "for Christ's sake"?

There is, I am confident, something more. The deeply experienced insecurity and frightful rivenness of our time, which I referred to earlier in this paper, not only exhaust us both emotionally and particularly spiritually, but also work on us to induce us, all subconsciously, to seek in our theoretical work a security and a unanimity we cannot find in the world at large. The building of the tower of Babel is only a striking early example of men's determined effort to create security for themselves and to find community outside the safety and community which God in His grace has provided in His Son, Jesus Christ in the fellowship of the Holy Spirit. Basically, then, it is the dividedness of our hearts and the remaining sin that still always cleaves to every one of us which, when appealed to by the great majority of practicing scientists around us, and especially under the constant stress of the spiritually enervating developments of our time, distracts our attention from our prophetic task, in every aspect and at every stage of our work, to a purportedly purely structural engagement. In our particular case we may not fail to recognize the influence, in traditionally Dutch Reformed circles, of the virulent reaction that has been occurring, on the background of a reading of Kuyper's doctrine of common grace as emphasizing creation-structures and expressing cultural optimism, against an external, formal, perhaps not always sufficiently informed application of the doctrine of the Antithesis that has been identified with the "provincial" character of the so-called old "*Gereformeerdendom*."

It is not for me in this paper to say how much, or just where, these ungodly forces at work in our society may have begun to take hold among us, in our hearts. But I must say that it troubles me to hear mathematics or logic being described as independent or almost independent (of philosophy) sciences, to read of one's choosing one's point of departure *within* logic, for example, itself, and wondering out loud what one could possibly mean by the term "Christian logic."

It troubles me to read again in a letter I received some years ago from a student I sent to study in the *Centrale Interfaculteit* of the Free University that his instructor, although, as he writes, "undoubtedly presupposing the vision," was "himself caught in a *theoretical 'Grund-lagen-krisis,'* pointing constantly to unresolved problems in Dooyeweerd, hinting at remnants of synthesis and suggesting areas of capitulation to the problematics of immanentism, and rejecting any effect of a scripturally grounded *'wetsidee'* on the field of mathematics." It is not the critical systematic work that I have objection to. It is the degree to which emphasis on that had apparently all but drowned out the life-giving, life-sustaining Power of biblical prophecy in that student's classroom experience. "Undoubtedly presupposing the vision" is not enough.

Again, it troubles me that since the early '70s at the Institute for Christian Studies in Toronto, with the establishing of which, and setting the direction for which I had something to do, and of which I am still a Fellow, I have regularly been hearing from students how far some of their instructors have got beyond Dooyeweerd. Now quite apart from the truth of the claim – why shouldn't we get beyond Dooyeweerd if God bless our work? – if *this* is what students are going to be exclaiming about, and not the marvelous break, through the Power of the Word of God, from the stifling hold of scholastic and all synthesis thought regarding an autonomously operating Rationality, then systematics, and perhaps even our own career-building and image-building are looming too large and our prophetic witness (servanthood) grows relatively weaker, God being glorified less in the immediate classroom experience of each day. From the beginning of the Institute we have also frequently heard it said that the philosophy of Dooyeweerd would only be used as a "tool." That can only be said if we remove Dooyeweerd's "system" from what he himself called "the foundation and root of scientific thought as such," which it is impossible to do if we are to work in the spirit of his philosophy.

It also troubles me to read in *Moratorium* (published 1977) of a shift within the Committee on Justice and Liberty (C.J.L.) of Canada which emphasizes structural problems, solidarity and creaturehood and soft-pedals the biblical prophecy from which real justice and liberty spring.

I am greatly troubled by the article in *Calvinist Contact* (March 26, 1982) about the participation of the Curriculum Development Centre (C.D.C.) of Toronto in the Educational Task Force of the Grassy Narrows Band, which, according to the report, involves the C.D.C. in "designing an educational model which would be more in line with native spirituality and ways of life" and "in the workshops held on the reserve to reawaken the Band's sense of identity and spirituality." "Both the natives and the Christians on the Educational Task Force," I read there, "could agree on the importance of having an awareness of the unity of life and a respect for nature and for the dignity of each human being."

I say all these things, arising from the so-called "reformational" movement, trouble me. I do not wish to argue with anyone about any one of them here. My purpose is not to cause argumentative division, but to call for prayerful reflection on what has been brought forward.

The corrective for any dislocation that may have occurred or be occurring in the direction of becoming too much absorbed in philosophical systematics (or with the structures such systematics study) Dooyeweerd himself offers us in his Foreword to the *New Critique*. The words occur in that very section in which he calls for assistance from special scientists and then addresses those "who still resist the Christian idea of science." They are a prayer, a prayer that such persons "may be convinced that *the question is not a matter of a 'system' (subject to all the faults and errors of human thought) but rather it concerns the **foundation** and the root of scientific thought as such*" (*N.C.* I, viii, emph. mine). This is what elsewhere is called the revelational *given*. Dooyeweerd himself says expressly what he means by this foundation and root of scientific thought. It occurs in the longer passage I have quoted earlier, but let me repeat just these words: "In the limitation and weakness of the flesh, we grasp the absolute truth in our knowledge of God derived from His revelation, in prayer and worship. This knowledge in the full sense of the word contains the religious principle and foundation of all true knowledge..." (II, 562).

In the Christian philosophical enterprise, "system" has a very different place *and authority* than in a humanistic one. William James tells us *(Pragmatism,* ch. 1): "The actual universe is a thing wide open, but rationalism makes systems, and systems must be closed." After Hegel, many philosophers of name had only contempt for system-making. Robert Heiss *(Hegel, Kierkegaard, Marx,* Delta, p. 35) says, "Whether [systems] are completely over and done with... is open to doubt. Man's bent to see the whole from one visual angle is ineradicable." For the humanist there is need for a *closed* system to guarantee that there is system at all. The Christian believes that only God can tell us about the origin, unity and end of the heavens and earth He created and all the creatures that dwell in them to serve His glory. There is a revealed Order, and that puts in their proper place and relativizes, but also directs, all our efforts at systematization. In these systematic efforts of ours differences *will* continue to show up, but we must know how to assign these a relative importance within the total framework of our philosophizing, and how to witness to the unity of our prophecy, which our efforts in systematics are trying to exhibit and work out in a scientific way. To fall into a humanistic confinement to systematics in philosophy and in each of the special sciences is, for the Christian philosophical enterprise, an extremely pernicious form of myopia and can only lead, indeed, to fragmentation (the specialist in each science who cannot speak with any assurance about anything outside his special field), and also to a loss of vibrancy and of vitality. Only the Power of the Word can move us fruitfully to systematic work and vitalize our activity in the light of the Truth. The life we share in this Association is by the Word. Our fellowship is in the Spirit, in the fellowship of the Truth (q–h–l).

Constantly we must remind ourselves that it is a wonderful thing what God did in the generation of Dooyeweerd and Vollenhoven, a wonderful thing in the long history of Christ's church. The Spirit of prophecy (the witness of Jesus) was at work to sanctify and to protect the Church. The break with synthesis thinking, allowing the Word of God more completely to govern our thought, was a liberation from a tradition that takes us back to the so-called "Christian philosophy" of Justin Martyr in the middle of the second century. The famous Berlin church historian, Hans Lietzmann, says that "it is obvious that Justin's Christianity is divided into two halves; one is a philosophical religion which clothes Greek ideas and conceptions in a loose biblical garment, and which in the end issues in man's self-redemption by means of an ethical decision," and of this element in Justin he also writes (p. 241) that "Justin and his fellow-warriors introduced it into speculative theology, placed it immediately on the throne where it kept its place victoriously for many centuries."[18] When we know the long, sad history of the Christian churches in these matters, we can only continuously be filled with joy and thanksgiving at the liberation our founders experienced and passed on to us.

But we do have to know something about that tradition, and about the *meaning* of Greek philosophy. I am not talking about specialists in Greek philosophy or specialists in church history. I am talking about the need for every one of us, in a sense, to be *generalists* to a degree. Even if that means sacrifice in our "careers" as specialists. Christians may have to pay a price in this world in order to maintain their own community. We must all make more use of, and work more with, the extremely important work that Professor Vollenhoven did in revising the history of ancient philosophy, thus shedding light on the nature of the fundamental question the Greek philosophers were

---

18. Hans Lietzmann, *The Founding of the Church Universal* (= Vol II of *The Beginnings of the Christian Church*), Scribner's, N.Y., 1938, p. 244.

concerned about (LAW). And if, for example, our Christian classical high schools (gymnasia), with all their instruction in Greek and Latin often oriented too much to the classical humanist viewpoint, fail to let our young people see the pagan (immanentistic-reductionist) nature of Greek society and thought, let us work to change that instruction, and, if that should prove impossible, to find other means to educate our children in the fear of the Lord. In this age of computers and video-cassettes, schools no longer have the monopoly they once had on education. We have got to have a younger generation that has been educated out of the "foundation and root." We have got to train a leadership.

If we possess the Spirit of prophecy and the witness of Jesus, and have seen what Dooyeweerd calls the necessary inner connection between that and our theoretical work, then we will be qualified and empowered to work in the *oikoumené* as agents of reconciliation and redemption in our philosophical work. The Lord will push us outward, ever outward, in the great battle of the spirits, to the ends of the earth. Our number – let us always remember this – is not important. The Power is in the Word of God, which goes forth in victory, conquering and to conquer. We should not allow our personal reaction against a certain worldly triumphalism that crept into many cultural activities of Dutch Reformed Christians in the early part of this century to blind us to the signature of triumph inherent in biblical prophecy, although we must remember that it is God's triumph, to be accomplished in His way, at His time, but through His servants who ask Him to use them to that end. Let it be our constant and fervent prayer that we may so be used. Let us always be actively seeking opportunities where we can so be used. Let unhesitating obedience, ineradicable joy, unquenchable hope, invincible courage, irresistible longing to glorify God – and deep gratitude – be the spontaneous expression of our lives, until our Lord return.

Christendom in Crisis

Christian Renewal, February 21, 1983

READERS OF *Christian Renewal* in both Canada and the United States have recently been able, along with the rest of their compatriots, to witness some startling, and at the same time deeply troubling, evidence of the deep dividedness and, behind that, the awful confusion of thinking which today characterizes much of the Christian community worldwide.

1983 began in Canada with a New Year's message to the nation from the Canadian Catholic Conference of Bishops (CCCB), drawn up by the eight bishops of the Conference's Commission for Social Affairs and approved for release by the five-member executive committee of the Conference. The 10-page statement is entitled "Ethical Reflections on the Economic Crisis." Its publication on the last day of the old year made first page news in *The Toronto Star* and throughout the country. The *Star's* religion editor, calling it "the most controversial political statement ever made here by a prestigious religious body," was certain that it would provoke "a national furor."

And, indeed, the very next day Emmett Cardinal Carter, Archbishop of Toronto, was quick to point out "that the bishops of Canada have not made a statement on economic policy" (only eight bishops of Canada's 120, he is reported to have said), and he proposed that since the report has not been approved by all of Canada's bishops it has no weight in the church other than as a discussion paper. He suggested that Canada's 10 million Catholics "read it very critically," adding that he himself had "serious reservations concerning some of the material and attitudes contained therein..." Even one of the members of the Commission, Bishop Bernard Pappin, describing himself as a minority voice, called the report "too socialistic."

So much, to begin with, for the extreme dividedness and singular confusion of thought at the highest level of the Catholic hierarchy in Canada, at least on this matter of no mean importance.

Last November saw the release in the United States, just at a crucial moment in the 1982 election campaign, of a draft of a proposed pastoral letter to the nation's 51 million Roman Catholics. (After further revision it will be formally issued as a pastoral letter next May.) This draft statement, entitled "The Challenge of Peace," was likewise prepared by a committee of five bishops of the National Conference of Catholic Bishops (NCCB), and it too instantly called forth an anguished outcry of (Catholic) dissent. *Time* (Nov. 8, 1982, p. 16) said of it: "The detailed document marshals moral principles and strategic arguments in a counterstrike at the heart of U.S. military doctrine," and got directly at one of the points of heated debate with this comment: "By addressing not only the moral and theological dimensions of nuclear arms, but also the political and strategic complexities, the bishops have invited heated dissent from church members and Government leaders." "Despite its detailed prescriptions," *Time* went on to state, "the document is presented as a theological tract, suffused with 'the good news which has come to us in the person of Jesus.' It invokes a biblical vision of peace..."

The American bishops' attack concentrates, as one might expect, on the doctrine of nuclear deterrence. Acknowledging "that the U.S. threat to use nuclear arms in response to a Soviet assault might prevent the outbreak of war... they nonetheless conclude that the policy is unsatisfactory because it created, and keeps in place, a balance of terror that all too easily could lead to a holocaust. They are also offended by the cost of maintaining deterrence, which they say takes money away from programs for the poor" (*Time*, Nov. 29, 1982, p. 68).

That last sentence brings into the open a connection between the two statements, the one of the Canadian bishops on the state of the economy, adopting what it calls the preferential option for the poor, the afflicted, and the oppressed and choosing for the priority of labour over capital, and the American bishops' statement with regard to the morality of nuclear war. We are also told to expect in the near future a statement on the economy from the American bishops. Undoubtedly, a common mind is at work among the Catholic bishops of North America, a mind that is fiercely challenged by some other bishops and by a significant number of outstanding and very well informed Catholic lay scholars.

Strong protest against the American proposed pastoral letter was immediately voiced by one leading lay thinker in the U.S. Catholic Church and a leading intellectual in the neo-conservative movement, Michael Novak, a former seminarian, now Scholar in Residence at the American Enterprise Institute in Washington, D.C., who was quoted in *Time* as saying of the bishops' statement: "This is not the faith that nourished me." Novak found the argument to be "seriously flawed both as a political document and as a religious one." Of the bishops themselves he is quoted as saying: "They are overreaching. The desire to speak like prophets is sometimes only hubris." These are very strong words to be used by a Catholic of his bishops; we shall see below what brings Novak to employ them.

But Novak was not alone. An equally severe judgment was passed on the American bishops' statement by James Hitchcock, who since the '70s has become widely known through the publication of a number of very significant books, the most recent being *Catholicism and Modernity: Confrontation or Capitulation*, Seabury Press, N.Y., 1979. Hitchcock, now Professor of History at St. Louis University, was quoted in *Time* as follows: "They [the bishops] seem to say there is no real problem with the Soviets. And some of them have fallen into the habit of saying that a nuclear holocaust would be the greatest of all evils. Yet in religious terms physical destruction, no matter how horrible, can never be the worst evil. It makes me shiver when it is implied that we should allow ourselves if necessary to be conquered."

The older slogan "Better Red than dead" suggests itself. Only now we are dealing, not with the likes of Bertrand Russell, but with the spiritual leaders of the (American) Roman Catholic Church!

It was no mere coincidence that November, 1982 also saw the appearance of the first number of a new monthly magazine, *Catholicism in Crisis: A Journal of Lay Catholic Opinion*, from the Jacques Maritain Center, Notre Dame, Indiana. Michael Novak is the magazine's Executive Director, and in this first issue has written a searing criticism of the position the American bishops take. He argues that the

> ultimate logic of the bishops' second draft is unilateral disarmament... First, spiritual, moral disarmament. Then, the removal of weapons. They avoid the political consequences of this recommendation, but by a kind of doubletalk. This is casuistry at its worst.

Novak asks why the bishops "have not seen that their present position entails unilateral disarmament," and asserts that "the more thoroughly pacifist among them do grasp the logic. They celebrate this draft [pastoral letter] as the indispensable pillar of their ultimate goal: pacifist surrender before aggression, which they hold is to follow the example of Christ."

"How," Novak asks, "did the bishops get into this predicament?" And he continues:

> As John Langan, S.J., has recently pointed out in *The Washington Quarterly*, they did not do so because a flood-tide of theological writing in this area obliged them to. Quite the contrary! They have been moved by very recent popular opinion. This is a dangerous motor force. Everyone desires peace. That is why the Soviets since Lenin have always conducted campaigns for 'Peace' in public opinion as a main force in strategic warfare. The popular desire for peace is always genuine. To attain peace vis-à-vis the Soviets, however, vigilance in distinguishing false peace from true is always necessary.

A matter for rejoicing is Novak's sharp criticism of the document's view of the church and its offices ("far too much authority to clergymen in areas beyond their vocational calling") – a criticism which many have made also of the Canadian document – and especially what he calls its biblical theology. "It leaps," he writes, "from true peace as conversion of the heart to Christ... to political peace and nuclear peace." In the Nov. 8 issue of *Time* we read that "Novak faults the bishops for adopting a sentimental view of the Bible... I think it is an outrage," he says there, "to identify this sentimentality with faith in Jesus Christ. I do not think Jesus promises us that we are going to live in political peace. The Bible gives a much harder vision of reality. True Christianity is a religion made for hard times as well as shining dreams."

As for the biblical theology of the *Canadian* bishops, their statement reads: "As pastors, our concerns about the economy are not based on any specific political options. Instead, they are inspired by the Gospel message of Jesus Christ." However, the document immediately continues: "In particular, we cite two fundamental Gospel principles that underlie our concerns." Their first principle "has to do with the preferential option for the poor, the afflicted, and the oppressed." They say: "In the tradition of the prophets, Jesus dedicated His ministry to bringing 'good news to the poor' and 'liberty to the oppressed.'" "As Christians," they go on,

> we are called to follow Jesus by identifying with the victims of injustice, by analyzing the dominant attitudes and structures that cause human suffering, and by actively supporting the poor and oppressed in their struggles to transform society.

"The second principle" accepted by the Canadian bishops "concerns the special value and dignity of human work in God's plan for Creation." Fine, except that later in the document this becomes the "priority of labour" principle, and "labour" as opposed to "capital." That raises the question of what – that is, how much – is included in human work, and whether what divine revelation says about human work can be set in a human context of labour *versus* capital and technology. It also brings up the question of the proper translation of the 1981 encyclical of Pope John Paul II to which so much appeal is being made in the current discussions. Is *Labourem Exercens* to be translated *On Labour* or rather, *On Performing Work?*

There are, to be sure, many fine points in the statement of the Canadian bishops. It may be that in this global village of multinationals, businesses tend to move to those national economics where labour is cheapest and the greatest profits can be realized, without too much thought being given to their local responsibilities, and greed can surely play a role here. It may also be that the bigger bankers also lend more than they "ought" to Third World countries because they can get a better rate of interest, and, greedily unmindful of their social responsibilities, quote in their justification the "maxim" that money, or capital, always seeks its highest rate, as though that were a natural law. The sin of greed is at work here, though no less in the long history of the North American labour unions screaming for more money until they price themselves out of the international competitive market. One thing is certain: economic life is not an end in itself but must be made to serve man. Compare the middle paragraph on page 66 of Goudzwaard, *Capitalism and Progress,* Wedge/Eerdmans, 1979.

There is plenty in the Canadian bishops' statement that needs to be thoughtfully, not passionately, discussed, though it is a question whether the presentation of the bishops has brought such careful and thoughtful discussion a step closer, or whether it has simply strengthened the *adversary* mentality which has for so long soured labour-management discussions on this continent.

Certainly, we will agree with the Canadian bishops about "the special value and dignity of human work in God's plan for Creation" if by that the bishops are referring to what we usually speak of as the cultural mandate. However, that divine command, it ought not to be forgotten, was given in a covenantal setting, in which it was possible for man to work in a spirit of covenantal fellowship and obedience, guided by the multi-dimensional Law Order laid down by God or, while remaining subject to this Law of God for the creation, to carry on his daily work in a spirit of rebellion against the Reign of Almighty God, bringing down, according to the scriptural record, God's wrath and judgment. The almost two-millennia-old accommodation of Catholic thinkers to the thought of the ancient pagan world (Greek humanism) has made their talk about the dignity of human work ambiguous. Is this dignity something *per se*, that is, intrinsic, without reference to the human worker's covenantal relation to God? And if not, has the sin of our human race's religious rebellion against God and His Word (also against His Word for Creation) affected "the special value and dignity of human work in God's plan for Creation?"

Certainly, all Canadian Christians, Catholic and Protestant, and all men and women there who sense the seriousness of our present predicament, which the Bishops are seriously attempting to address, should do whatever they can to open a broad discussion in every community regarding the issues that have been raised. At the same time, biblically Reformed and reforming Christians might well ask themselves whether a social-gospel, or socialist, even Marxist reading of the Gospel message has not begun to intrude itself. (Social gospel, by the way, is something entirely different from acknowledging that the Gospel of Almighty God has its social dimension; it is something else than the Christian religion altogether; it is false religion, darkness of the soul.) In the Canadian document

> Christ is portrayed, not as the Son of God who came to atone for man's sin and thus to reconcile God and man, but merely as an exemplary figure whose identification with the poor, and the workers *per se* we are exhorted to imitate.

These are the words of Harry Antonides, long known to us for his excellent analyses in the Christian Labour Association of Canada (CLAC) and particularly for his book *Multinationals and the Peaceable Kingdom* (Clarke, Irwin & Co. Ltd., Toronto/Vancouver, 1978) – a topic not unrelated to the concern of the Canadian bishops – in the first issue of a new Canadian publication, *WRF Comment*.

As for the description of the gospel as the gospel of the poor, the reader can do no better than to read the brief, but particularly illuminating section of Herman Ridderbos' *The Coming of the Kingdom* under the heading "The gospel of the poor," pp. 185-192, to see that the social-gospel understanding of this phrase is not the meaning the phrase has in Scripture. I tried to call attention to this crucial matter in my Translator's Introduction to Vol. III of S.G. de Graaf's *Promise and Deliverance* (p. 12 footnote and pp. 15-17).

The incident recorded in Mark 2:1-12 is instructive here. The paralytic, lowered on a mat through an opening that had been made in the roof, came to lie directly in front of Jesus; his need was obvious to everyone crowded into that house, and it was clear what the man's friends expected of Jesus. Here, surely, was one of the world's "afflicted." But what was Jesus' response? He said, "Son, your sins are forgiven." And then, knowing in His spirit what the religious leaders were thinking, Jesus addressed them: "That you may know that the Son of Man has authority on earth to forgive sins," (turning to the paralytic) "I tell you, get up, take your mat and go home." In the currently recognized crises of our societies, this incident should teach us anew that the forgiveness of sins is not a matter for later consideration. In fact, according to the Word God Himself has given here, Jesus came to redeem us from the power of sin. We are being taught here the world's *real need.* Jesus underscores this point when He says what He does to the religious leaders who are criticizing Him. Forgiveness of sins – that is why He came into the world, this is what He had been commissioned and qualified to do, it was His vocation. For that He had come to suffer the wrath of God and to offer Himself voluntarily (John 10:17-18). The words to the paralytic to stand up, etc. are only the sign of the former, the lesser thing.

Back to the American continent. Another article in *Catholicism in Crisis,* entitled "Catholics and the Peace Movement," by James Finn, editor of *Freedom at Issue,* the bimonthly journal of Freedom House, shows how the Second Vatican Council (1962-65), the papal encyclical *Pacem in Terris* (*Peace on Earth*) and the increasingly unpopular and divisive Vietnam War enabled Catholic pacifists (*Pax Christi* is the American branch of the Catholic peace group) to seize the propaganda leadership from a troubled and uncertain episcopate. "A symbol of the changes that were taking place in how Catholics approach questions of war and peace," Finn tells us,

> is that during the Vietnam War the Catholic Association for International Peace – largely organized by thoughtful analysts of the just-war school – died a quiet and relatively un-mourned death, while lively

"Justice and Peace" offices began to spring up around the country. Far from rendering almost automatic support to U.S. policies, particularly concerning warfare, those attached to these offices tended to question and oppose. And frequently they viewed the world political scene through lenses that allowed them to describe the U.S. as a prime disturber rather than protector of peace in the world.

Novak too remarks that "the itch of the bishops to attack their own government is transparent... The hostility toward American government in the bishops' draft is muted but evident."

From an overall standpoint, considering both the two documents and the criticisms they have elicited in both countries, what a dividedness, and what confusion in this large segment of the Christian world! And, above all, what a threat to the future of the Christian religion on the North American continent!

In both Canadian and American continents, we have to do with a decided "shift to the left," as the phenomenon is commonly called, in the thinking of the Roman Catholic hierarchy. To help us Protestants, and any other readers of *Christian Renewal* not sufficiently acquainted with the relevant history, to understand the background of today's developments among Catholic clergy, I want especially to recommend a very recent book by Michael Novak, *The Spirit of Democratic Capitalism.*

In considering these developments in Catholic circles, we Protestants have no reason to mount our high horse. In fact, Gregory Baum, well-known professor of theology and sociology at the University of Toronto, writes:

What is remarkable and unique is that in Canada this shift of ecclesiastical teaching to the economic left has taken place on an ecumenical basis. The Christian churches in Canada have jointly sponsored inter-church committees to examine social issues from a Christian perspective.

What the perspective of the mainline Protestant denominations is, as it issues from their collective work in the World Council of

Churches (WCC) where we find words like "repugnant" being used to qualify the noun "capitalism" and encounter attitudes of outright hostility to the American government, we have all begun to realize in recent years, and could have vividly witnessed on national television when the program "60 Minutes," on January 23, 1983, aired a most informative segment "The Gospel According to Whom?" The viewer was there exposed to an interpretation of the Gospel which came down to something like this: church members, to live out their lives as Christians in the world, should be a part of any effort to benefit and improve the lot of the common man.

It is not only Catholicism that is in crisis. Christendom is. And it only confirms us who put out this magazine of the extremely urgent need for Christian renewal. Such renewal can only come when there is a return to biblical revelation in its fullness and completeness as the light by which we are to live our lives in this world. Human knowledge and practical wisdom always issue either from a heart darkened in unbelief, or one that has been enlightened by the renewing Power of the Word of God. That revelation, all of it, is God's Self-revelation, and it begins with God's gracious revealing to us of His act of creation. God is revealed as the Almighty Creator, the Lord of hosts, the sovereign Lord, *whose every word is the Law of His love for the created world of heaven and earth.* This sovereignty and holiness of Almighty God, and the fear of the Lord, that is, the ready acknowledgment of God's sovereign authority and His holiness and awful trust on the part of His creature man, are the foundation stories of the revelation by which all our life-acts are to be governed. It is a proper recognition of these foundations that is largely missing or only very vaguely sensed in the contemporary proclamation of the Gospel.

When this high and holy God created man, He entered into fellowship with him, establishing a relation of covenant which involved conditions. Obedience would bring divine blessing and life everlasting, disobedience, death and the wrath and judgment of Almighty God. This covenant relation, with its attendant blessing and judgment is the constant and abiding situation of all of us. Judgment in the creation is an expression of God's love, first for Himself as the

Holy One, then for His creation as bound to Him covenantally. In fact, biblical revelation in its integral wholeness, after the announcement of the creation and the establishment of covenantal fellowship, is the historically unfolding story of God's covenantal dealings with His creation, and specifically with His people. That is what the four volumes of *Promise and Deliverance* are all about. In this connection too I wish to direct the reader to the excellent and sorely needed article by John Bolt in the January 10, 1983 issue of this magazine, entitled "Is Yahweh a Man of War?" Let me simply add two New Testament passages: 1 Corinthians 3:16, 17, and 1 Thessalonians 4:1-8.

All this too is largely missing in the proclamation of the contemporary churches. That proclamation issues more from the thinking of the eighteenth-century Enlightenment, which, in assuming that the enlightenment of the mind comes from the mind itself and from the scientific method of studying the world of experience, was in principle the absolute rejection of God's Self-revelation and an expression of covenantal disobedience (autonomy) with the attendant curse of blindness and destruction. Today we hear from the World Council about sinful social "structures" which must be removed by social and political action. What seems to be forgotten here is that it was sinful men (covenantal beings!) who in the course of history gave those structures their structure. Once again, let me refer to my Translator's Introduction to Vol. III of *Promise and Deliverance*, pp. 15-17.

With that we must leave it for now. Let us all pray that God will give us patient endurance and faithfulness (Revelation 13:10b NIV). Let us be encouraged by the news in recent years of a reviving evangelical Christianity, and pray that these new Christians, also in China, Russia and the Eastern block, in Africa and Latin America, may be led to a greater measure of fidelity to the integral wholeness of God's Self-revelation. And let us pray for the Christendom that is in crisis.

The Spirit of Prophecy

Christian Renewal, May 23, 1983

THE MEANING OF ALL prophecy becomes clear in the coming in the flesh of the Son of God, the Messiah. The incarnation, the life and public ministry, the trial and death, the resurrection and ascension of Jesus Christ, is the culmination of prophecy because of the unique relation between Him and God. Matthew 11:27 reads: "All things have been committed to me by my Father. No one knows the Son except the Father, and no one knows the Father except the Son and those to whom the Son chooses to reveal Him." Geerhardus Vos, commenting on verses 25-27, says that this passage "expresses that God has devolved upon Jesus what is His own special prerogative: the task to reveal the whole truth in all its wide extent."

In Revelation 19:10b we read: "For the testimony of Jesus is the spirit of prophecy." Of it, Professor S. Greydanus has written: "For the testimony of Jesus, that is, what Christ the Lord says and witnesses about God, about Himself, about the Kingdom of heaven is the Spirit of prophecy, its intent, the working of the Holy Spirit, that Spirit Himself!" We might think in this connection of what the apostle John wrote in his gospel (15:26): "When the counselor comes, whom I will send to you from the Father, the Spirit of truth who goes out from the Father, He will testify about me." In his larger commentary on the Revelation passage Greydanus says this:

> These too are the angel's words by means of which he indicates the exalted station of them who have the testimony of the Lord Christ. In or with this testimony they have the spirit of prophecy. Thus they all are prophets and therefore are all equals with John and with the angel him-

self. Though there may be some difference of degree, there is no essential difference. The angel said that he is a fellow-servant with John and with his brethren who have the testimony of Jesus. To this he adds an illuminating remark to stress the exaltedness which is contained therein, namely, prophetic dignity and service, a worth equal to his own work. If the angel first came down, as it were, to all true believers by placing himself on one line with them, he now leads them up so to speak, to the height of his own service: they are what he is, just as he is what they are: each other's fellow-servants, all of them equally inspired and qualified by God for the same exalted service of being His prophets...

To possess in faith the testimony of Christ the Lord regarding Himself in such a way that it governs your inner being and very existence, all that you do and say, is to have the Spirit of prophecy. He of whom this can be said is a prophet. Since the Spirit of prophecy manifests itself in causing one to have and to speak about the Lord Jesus' testimony regarding Himself, all true prophets are witnesses of Jesus, and all who have the witness of Jesus in the highest sense are prophets.

All who have the Spirit will be witnesses of Jesus, and all who have the witness of Jesus are possessed by the Spirit of prophecy. Since Pentecost, the Spirit of God is poured out on all Christ's people, on each one of us, qualifying and enabling us to be prophets, to be witnesses of Jesus, that is, to have the witness respecting Jesus that Jesus had regarding Himself, a witness, as Greydanus remarked, about God, about Himself, about the Kingdom of heaven. On Pentecost, Peter, standing up and quoting the prophet Joel (2:28-32) said of the wondrous events of that day: "In the last days, God says, I will pour out my Spirit on all people. Your sons and daughters will prophesy, your young men will see visions, your old men will dream dreams. Even on my servants, both men and women, I will pour out my Spirit in those days, and they will prophesy" (Acts 2:17-18).

We who are Christ's men – we are called to be prophets, we are meant to be prophets, in our thinking, critiquing, writing, publishing, in our instruction of the new generation. That means that we are to be God-possessed, possessed by the Spirit of God, God-driven in our personal lives and work as members, and in our organized activities. Remember Professor Greydanus' words, "To possess in faith the testimony of Christ the Lord regarding Himself in such a way that it governs your inner being and very existence, all that you do and say, is to have the Spirit of prophecy. He of whom this can be said is a prophet."

Rediscovery of the Meaning of the Word of God

Christian Renewal 1984

WHAT IS THE Word of God? It may at first strike the reader as strange that this question has to be asked, particularly in our circles. Was the Protestant Reformation not first of all a rediscovery of the meaning of the Word of God? And are we not all agreed as to the meaning of that Word? I believe, however, that further reflection will convince all of us that we are here at the heart of our problem and of the cause of whatever devotedness there may be as to how we should go. Even we Christians of the Reformation very frequently have an inadequate understanding of the Word of God.

To be sure, we are familiar with this *book*, the Bible or the Holy Scriptures, a collation of sixty-six books written by many authors to whom the Word of the Lord came in diverse ways. But to know about this *diversity of fact* is not in itself to know the Word of God. Among my old "fundamentalist" friends there were those who could tell you at the drop of a hat how many chapters, even verses yes, even words there are in this collection of sixty-six books (at least in the King James Version).

Yet that is not in itself a knowledge of the Word of God. I know many persons who can tell me in the space of a lightning flash where a certain expression is to be found, chapter and verse. Now we certainly need also in this way to be thoroughly acquainted with the Bible, but even such knowledge is not yet the required knowledge of the Word of God. I have known people, converted in evangelistic meetings, who are at once instructed in so-called methods of personal evangelism, i.e. in ways of handling particular Bible verses to meet various types of objection to the call for a complete "surrender" to Christ.

Now I would not for a moment want to disparage the learning of specific Bible verses and their use in soul-winning. In our present discussion, I only mean to say that such acquaintance with diverse parts and moments of the Scriptures is not *by itself* the knowledge of the Word of God that we must have. It has been pointed out that it was of the experts in the Jewish law, the "*nomikoi*," that Jesus said (Luke 11:52): "You have taken away the key to knowledge." It is thus possible to be very much at home in the details of the Scriptures and yet not know the Word of God.

For the Word of God is *one*. Underlying all the diversity of the Scriptures, as we have them in this temporal life, is the unity of the Word of God. It is, after all, the WORD. How else could this big collection of sixty-six books be properly spoken of as the Word? And whence the "system" of systematic or dogmatic theology? It is not the mind of the theologian, going to work on the many texts of Scripture, that constructs for the first time out of many passages, a unity of meaning. This unity the theologian does not *make*; he *finds* it. The Divine Word *is* one, and *as such* is the POWER, living and active, that pierces to the heart and converts the soul (Rom. 1:16; Heb. 4:12; Ps. 19:7; James 1:18; cf. I Cor. 1:18, 24).

In the very first place it is not we who come with our understanding to the Word of God, but it is the WORD, which is the POWER of God, that comes to our hearts and opens our eyes so that we may understand the singleness of meaning of all the many Scriptures. In our exegesis or effort at getting at the meaning of this or that passage of the Bible *the Word is or is not already at work*. God is first with our souls, also here, and there is no sure ground for our lives in our methods. The Word of God is the only firm foundation of our life. A *proper* understanding of the Scriptures is only possible when we are *already* in the grip of the Word, the active, renewing Word of God.

Let us suppose that Christ Himself should suddenly appear visibly in His glory right here in our room. You know what would happen. Each one of us would be down on our knees. We would be vividly aware of three things: (1) that this Person is the Sovereign Lord; (2) that we are nothing in ourselves over against Him, but solely and wholly His servants; (3) that His Word is our Law. In effect we would be saying, "Speak, Lord; for your servant hears."

The Word of God is the POWER by which God opens our hearts to see our human situation in the framework of the whole of reality. This is to know the Truth. And to know the Truth is wisdom; for the fear of Yahweh, you will remember, is the starting-point of wisdom. Possessed of wisdom, we know how to live out our lives. We have the *regula* or principle by which to direct our goings.

But the Word of God does more. We are not only made aware of our place in the creation, but we are also convicted of our sin. In the presence of Christ we know not merely that we are nothing but servants; we know also that we are *unworthy* servants, not in part, but wholly. And, further, we know the total redemption of Christ. In a flash we know our place, that we have (in the first Adam) fallen from our place, and that in the second Adam we are restored to our place (though only in Him). It is not true that only part of us is fallen (e.g. the bodily passions), because there are no "parts." The *integrality* (wholeness) of the creation (particularly in the heart of man) brings with it the *radical* character of the Fall. In the Fall of man all created reality was directed away from the service of God. But it is also true that in the saving work of Christ in the heart of man all the creation is re-directed to the service and glorification of God.

The Reformation of the sixteenth century contributed much to help Christians regain this insight into the Word of God. For this we are deeply grateful to those who came before us. *Soli Deo Gloria.*

Introduction to McKendree Langley's "The Practice of Political Spirituality: Episodes from the Public Career of Abraham Kuyper, 1879-1918"

1984

In *The Practice of Political Spirituality* (Paideia Press, 1984) McKendree Langley has provided us with a significant little volume, simply written and very readable, about a subject which ought certainly to be at the heart of every Christian's interest today. Battles which go much deeper than the legal ones are being waged these days with regard to the separation of Church and State. As institutions, these may well be separate; statecraft (political activity) and spirituality (this in its biblical sense) *can*-not be. But today there is also the opposite threat of a Christianity that has become so politicized that the dynamic Good News of God, i.e., our liberation from the power, guilt and penalty of sin and restoration to a life of fellowship with God and our neighbour, becomes obscured. Is there a third route possible, between the Scylla of other-worldliness, and the Charybdis of a politicized Christianity? There is, as Professor Langley's book clearly shows – the way of political spirituality.

For this reason, Langley's book is extremely timely, providing a perspective that is badly needed but often missing from current American discussions. In it the author, of a Presbyterian and Anglo-Saxon background, reflects on what he felicitously calls the political spirituality of Abraham Kuyper. Kuyper was a prominent representative of the movement for the biblical renewal of life in the Netherlands in the last decades of the previous century, and indeed right up to the end of the First World War. While he is still too little known in American evangelical circles, he was without any doubt, one of the most important Christian thinkers and leaders of the modern period. He lived through times which, as to fundamental religious directions, were very much like our own, times of increasingly revolutionary rejection of the sovereign God and His revealed will, on the one hand, and, on the other, of a notable evangelical re-awakening and an increasing awareness, on the part of evangelical Christians, of their collective vocation to engage more actively (with spiritual weapons, of course) in the great Battle of spirits which has always, even when not sufficiently recognized, been the root driving force of human history.

That Battle, in Kuyper's day as now, involved in the first instance, the struggle of Christian parents to reclaim from the so-called religiously neutral and all-too-sovereign State their own God-given authority (thus, their right) to educate their children in all subjects and at all levels of instruction in accordance with the revealed will of God, and thus simultaneously to challenge the State's authority to determine the meaning or direction of life. Classical liberalism (from which our American conservatives and liberals both derive) did not, in this respect, differ from present-day totalitarian states.

In our own day, therefore, Langley's book should prove eminently useful to all Christians who confess, on the basis of the Scriptures of the Old and New Testaments, received as the authoritative Word of the living God, that the risen and ascended Christ is Lord, that He sits at the Father's right hand, possessing and exercising all authority both in heaven and on earth (Matthew 28:18; 1 Peter 3:22). Professor Langley expresses the hope

> that as believers in various countries and situations consider their own
> attitudes toward society, they will examine the legacy of political spir-
> ituality left by Abraham Kuyper, a legacy which provides not the final
> word on Christian political action, but a basis for reflection and discus-

sion (p. 160).

"Political spirituality" – there is a notion evangelical Christians are going increasingly to have to ponder in a more serious and sustained manner in the coming days, and Langley's book is an excellent place to start. He describes it as "an integrated Christian attitude" that provides "the ability to discern the directions sin and grace take in public affairs,"[1] and distinguishes it from political tactics. "Tactics change as times and situations differ, 'political spirituality' remains part of a Christian's obligation to do all things to the glory of God" (p. 3). Langley, who is an historian, not a philosopher or systematic theologian, does not attempt to analyze in any systematic way the meaning-content of the concept. What he offers us instead is an examination of the remarkable political career of Abraham Kuyper as an illustration of the practice of political spirituality. The book is not a biography of Kuyper either;[2] rather, it describes important episodes in his life which serve to demonstrate concretely Kuyper's political spirituality.

In America, Kuyper, where, if he is known at all, has been known almost exclusively as a theologian and devotionalist.[3] In itself that

1.   At a number of places throughout his book, Professor Langley makes the important point that the directions sin and grace take can only be detected against the backdrop of a revealed creation order (which includes creation norms). It is a point made frequently by Kuyper.

2.   Fortunately, we have in English a good popular biography of Kuyper: Frank VandenBerg, *Abraham Kuyper*, Eerdmans, 1960, now available in paperback from Paideia Press. Most recent is Dr. L. Praamsma's, *Let Christ Be King: Reflections on the Life and Times of Abraham Kuyper*, Paideia, 1985.

3.   This, in spite of the fact that the *Stone Lectures* Kuyper gave in the United States (at Princeton Theological Seminary in New Jersey in 1898) had as their main emphasis that Calvinism was a distinct and comprehensive outlook on man and the world, a worldview, one of the chapters being devoted to "Calvinism and Politics." A chief cause of the difficulty, without a doubt, has been the retreat of the body of believers in the course of the modern centuries so that the Christian community became restricted largely to ecclesiastical assemblies and theological institutions. In other words, the people of the

reputation is, of course, well deserved; what it fails to do is focus our attention on what was preeminently great and of unusual historical significance in Kuyper, on that which makes him an outstandingly important figure for Christians of our generation and of others yet to come, in all parts of the world. That was, without doubt, his richly informed perception that the secular humanism which, after the French and subsequent revolutions, was breaking out everywhere and assuming a position of dominance in government and cultural circles was an integral and comprehensive view of man and the world totally opposed in its direction to the Christian one, and that the ensuing situation in western societies required a new, more active, and more organized Christian stance in return.

But it was also the huge successes he reaped in this venture. God had placed just this man on the scene at just the right moment, and through his extensive journalistic and educational enterprises, and particularly his strenuous political activities (where he finally succeeded in breaking the stranglehold of Liberalism's long-held hegemony in his nation's political life – not, by the way, in the interest of conservatism – and rose to become Prime Minister), he aroused a large body of Christians to engage in the Struggle, beginning, as we said earlier, with their assuming their rightful *parental* responsibility for the religious direction of their children's education and, at the same time, with their entering the Contest, as a body of Christians organized on an accepted political program of principles, for the political direction of the life of the State.

The Battle *had* to assume this political aspect, because the rise of the modern socialist/communist movement had lifted up the idol of the Socialist Redeemer State, a totalitarian State which forcibly (by law or by arms or both) controls all of society and thus must eliminate the various social spheres which properly are free of state control. This is what the current struggle in Poland is all about, but, closer to home, the same battle is waged by law and in the courts. If

living God had become a kind of ghetto sub-culture in a largely rationalistic or naturalistic society. In such a situation Kuyper's message could scarcely be properly absorbed, far less acted upon.

in Poland it is the question of the right to exist of a labour union like *Solidarity*, free of State-domination, closer to home it is the question of the rights of parents in the institution of the family and of other non-public associations and institutions, of all those other spheres which do not owe their existence to the State and so must be allowed to fulfill their calling in the creation.

Kuyper was simply building, as Professor Langley points out,

> on the perspective inherited from Calvin's sixteenth-century *Institutes of the Christian Religion* and even from Augustine's fifth-century *City of God*. Augustine and Calvin made important statements about the comprehensive character of the kingdom of God and the task of believers in hostile pagan and apostate environments. Kuyper provided an updated version of this comprehensive Christian vision in our modern age of indifferent secularism[4] (pp. 163-164).

That is the importance of Kuyper for us today. The episodes Langley describes out of his long career of distinguished service to Christ the King were great and exciting moments in the history of Christ's people on earth, and we American Christians should know a good deal more about them than we do now. There is much for us to learn, and more to think about, in all those years of experience of our fellow-Christians who already more than a century ago were becoming aware of the new situation in the world which continuing critical events throughout the world are now forcing upon our attention.

Moreover, we American Christians, like Americans generally, have been inclined to view our struggle as engaging one particular issue at a time, and we are only now just beginning to be aware, as

---

4.   I am not exactly sure what Professor Langley means by the term "indifferent secularism." I suppose he is referring to the broad masses, whether a part of the believing community or not, which appear so lethargic, even supine, which, under the prevailing this-worldly, hedonistic worldview of Unbelief, seem so often to be without purpose or direction in their lives. On the other hand, since the Enlightenment of the eighteenth century and the French Revolution, there has been an increasing aggressiveness in a rapidly growing group of intellectuals committed to the Unbelief of the Left.

Kuyper was in his time, of the systematic denial, in our society, our schools and universities, *of the living God who has revealed Himself in Jesus Christ*. Consequently, we are only at the starting-point of considering how responsibly and effectively to bring a *corporate* and *integrated* Christian witness to bear on that situation. Professor Langley's book should be of help to us here by showing us that a piecemeal, one-issue-at-a-time approach is not so much a valuable national characteristic as it is a lack of sensitive, biblically inspired vision as to our Christian political-and cultural-calling in today's world.

Of course, there may be evangelical Christians in the United States – and elsewhere – who are still uncertain about, or even ignorant of, the comprehensiveness of the Struggle that is going on between what Augustine called the City of God and the city of this world. If there are such, they might well turn to the magazine *The Humanist* in its January/February issue of 1983 (Vol. 43, No. 1) and read the article by John Dunphy, "A Religion for a New Age" on pp. 23-26, the conclusion of which I quote here. "I am convinced," Dunphy writes,

> that the battle for humankind's future must be waged and won in the public school classroom by teachers who correctly perceive their role as the proselytizers of a new faith: a religion of humanity that recognizes and respects the spark of what theologians call divinity in every human being. These teachers... will be ministers of another sort, utilizing a classroom instead of a pulpit *to convey humanist values in whatever subject they teach, regardless of the educational level – preschool day care or large state university.* The classroom must and will become an arena of conflict between the old and the new – the rotting corpse of Christianity, together with all its adjacent evils and misery, and the new faith of humanism, resplendent in its promise of a world in which the never-realized Christian ideal of 'love thy neighbor' will finally be achieved" [emphasis mine, H.E.R.].

What, may I ask, is the difference between that and the religious mind-set of the communist rulers of the Soviet Union and the subjugated eastern European bloc of nations? Nor should we think that

Mr. Dunphy is an isolated case. On the contrary, he is representative of a broad movement, become increasingly militant, a movement of the human spirit (in rebellion against the living God and the authority of His ordinances) that has long been at work in our most prestigious prep schools and universities.[5]

No, the Struggle which Kuyper and the Christians of his day perceived to be present in society is a present reality for us also in our society. The important point is that it is a comprehensive, integral Struggle, proceeding from two opposing views on the world, man, the origin, and nature of authority. It is a Battle for which we Christians in America have yet to discover a suitable and effective strategy. About this Battle and the Christian strategy that Kuyper developed in order to cope effectively with it, Langley's book offers us, in chapter after chapter, much rich material for our thoughtful consideration, and our future study and discussion.

About the individualistic approach we have generally followed in America, Kuyper, who did have more than a little experience in political life, wrote:

> The influence which emanates from all these [modern secular] organizations is thus without exception destructive for our Christian confession. One reasons and acts out of principles which are absolutely opposed to ours. If now one allows oneself to enter into such organizations and if one mingles in such organizations with those who are of a wholly other mind, then what they think or judge becomes the starting-point of the decisions that are to be taken, and one supports by one's membership what one, in conformity with one's Christian confession, may not support but must combat. In such anarchistic, socialistic [or liberalistic so-called neutral] associations, a spirit is operative which never can or may be ours. The leadership in such organizations falls never to us, but always and inflexibly to our opponents. They carry out their intention,

---

5. It is illuminating, for example, to read Michael Straight's recently published book *After Long Silence* (N.Y.: W. W. Norton, 1983), which contains many revelations about the brilliant Communist circles of Cambridge University in the 1930s.

and whoever of us embarks with them ends up where *they* want to land but where we should never land. Thus *our* principle settles down at the point of non-activity, loses its position of influence and is pressed into the corner... mingling with these leaders of another spirit in the organization itself, leads always to a bitterly sad fiasco of the Christian principle and prepares the way for *their* victory and for *our* overthrow..."[6]

It would appear, judging from the record to date, that Kuyper wrote those words with a keen understanding and a broad, biblically grounded cultural sensitivity. The political spirituality Professor Langley is addressing in his book is one way in which this sensitivity finds expression. It is well to remember, in reading Kuyper's words, that by "Christian principle" Kuyper is referring to what has been revealed to us in the Bible about God the Creator, the Source of all authority in the creation, the divine ordinances for the creation, the religious nature of man and his covenant relation to God, and suchlike. Over against the latter he sees, as common to all the modern movements (though to differing degrees of consistency), the source of all authority and law in man himself, who is autonomous, (i.e., not responsible to Anyone beyond himself or the world of which he is a part). In other words, in present-day language, Kuyper is referring to the constant Struggle that goes on for control of God's creation between the people of God (who may do wrong) and the forces of secular humanism in its various forms (which are influenced in mysterious ways to do good by God's creation revelation and His restraining grace).

Those who fear that theocratic repression must be the result of any Christian group's obtaining governmental power – and that *is* a widespread fear (in large part due to the medieval legacy) – will most certainly want to familiarize themselves with Kuyper's views, and with what he persistently strove for and actually accomplished. Once again, he appears as a monumental figure in the history of the Christian movement. For Kuyper fought to achieve tolerance and an acceptance of public pluralism in modern society. On this most critical point too, Langley's book is instructive. Kuyper, he shows, was

---

6.   *Pro Rege*, 3 vols. (Kampen: Kok, 1911-12), III, 190.

not interested in excluding liberals or socialists from the government, to the extent that they really represented a segment of the Dutch electorate (the principle of proportional representation, as opposed to the American practice of winner-take-all).[7] As a matter of fact, Kuyper wished to secure and protect their legitimate rights, as opposed to the illegitimate monolithic hegemony the Liberals had long been enjoying. What he sought was equal acceptance for those citizens who wished to participate in government on the basis of their Christian convictions, something the Liberals' inflexible intolerance had worked to prevent.[8]

Professor Langley's brief summaries or comments at the close of each chapter are always helpful, and on the point we have just been discussing he gives us a most important consideration to reflect upon when he writes:

---

7. The idea of proportional representation, which had been supported by Kuyper's party for decades before it was instituted, "was accepted finally by all parties as a matter of simple justice. 'It was thought that Parliament should present a perfect mirror of the different groups that composed the nation.'" (Skillen and Carlson-Thies: see (a) in following footnote. The last sentence is quoted by them from an article by Hans Daalder, "The Netherlands: Opposition in a Segmented Society," in *Political Oppositions in Western Democracies.* ed. Robert A. Dahl (New Haven: Yale University Press. 1966), p. 207.

8. Some recent very informative literature on matters raised in the last paragraph:

    a. James W. Skillen and Stanley W. Carlson-Thies, "Religion and Political Development in Nineteenth-Century Holland," in *Publius: the Journal of Federalism*, Vol . 12, No. 3 (Summer, 1982), pp. 43-64;

    b. James W. Skillen, "From Covenant of Grace to Tolerant Public Pluralism: The Dutch Calvinist Contribution." Paper presented at the Workshop on Covenant and Politics of the Center for Study of Federalism, at Temple University, Philadelphia, 1980; James W. Skillen, "Societal Pluralism: Blessing or Curse for the Public Good," pp. 166-171 in *The Ethical Dimension of Political Life: Essays in Honor of John H. Hallowell,* ed. Francis Canavan, Durham, N.C.: Duke University Press, 1983.

Kuyper's assumption of power was an example of the paradox of partisanship. Assuming a partisan position and accepting the partisanships of others can open the way for public impartiality. Mutual respect for differences in a pluralism framework can make realities of governmental cooperation, mutual respect and the creation of a climate of trust and political stability (p. 78).

In the past when a book appeared having to do with Abraham Kuyper, it was quite generally assumed, I think, that the book was for a very restricted circle of readers – either Reformed theologians and pastors, particularly those of a Dutch stripe, or persons interested in Dutch ecclesiastical or national history. In these introductory remarks I have tried to place Kuyper where he belongs, at the very center of the history of Christ's people in our modern society where the Struggle constantly becomes more comprehensive and more integral. I have tried to show that a familiarity with the life and work of Kuyper at this time is vital to our clarifying to ourselves what our task is in America as evangelical Christians.

There is another reason why all evangelical Christians in America should embrace Kuyper's political spirituality, the theme of Langley's book, as an important chapter in their own history. Most of Kuyper's vision (though he worked it out farther and discovered many ways to apply it) he received from his noble predecessor in the faith, Guillaume (= Willem) Groen van Prinsterer (1801-1876). Groen, educated at the University of Leiden in law and the classics, was converted to evangelical Christianity in early manhood as a result of the Evangelical Awakening (the *Réveil*), which had its beginnings when the Scott, Robert Haldane (1764-1842), gave Bible studies in the book of Romans and conducted prayer meetings to stimulate a much needed spiritual revival among the theological students at the University of Geneva (Calvin's old Academy) in Switzerland. One of those students, Merle d'Aubigné, had been instrumental in the conversion of Groen.[9] The *Réveil* swept up the Rhine valley into the Lowlands and

9.   Because very little is known in America about this great Christian leader and
      his landmark labours in reviving the body of believers and their influence in
      the national life of the Netherlands, I should like to call attention to an ex-

Germany, affecting, among others, a number of men in positions of influence in several European countries.

It was Groen, for instance, who in his *Unbelief and Revolution* (1847), an historic book in the history of Christian thought, demonstrated that the deepest cause of the French Revolution, and of the revolutionary spirit abroad in Europe at the time, was the secular humanism of the eighteenth-century Enlightenment. It was he who then summoned his fellow-believers to the task of reforming political life on the basis of Christian principles in place of the revolutionary (i.e., unbelieving) principles of the Enlightenment. This aristocrat of the old stamp, now since his conversion a fellow-believer first of all, predicting the drift of Western politics to the left, was the first to call for the formation of a mass (Christian) political party in the Netherlands. He laid the foundations of Holland's oldest formal political party. It was his work and insight that Kuyper developed.

The work of Groen and Kuyper thus developed out of the Evangelical Awakening; in their work we see the awakening of the body of Christians, after centuries of accommodation to the emerging scientistic worldview, to the real threat of secular humanism as a comprehensive, an integrated attack on the Christian faith and the Christian way of life. Their work thus springs from reviving evangelical life. Both Groen and Kuyper wanted to be remembered simply as "*Evangelie-belijders*" (Gospel Confessors). For this reason, Professor Langley's little book ought to be read by every thoughtful evangelical Christian in North America. The book should serve as a bridge-builder between those who call themselves Evangelicals/Fundamentalists, and more specifically Reformed Christians. Against the secular humanist threat in our society and in God's world, we have a task that can only be accomplished if we find ways in our society of working closely together as servants of a common Lord.

There is one thing in Langley's discussion of Kuyper that leaves

---

cellent article about him in English in the Fall, 1982 issue of *The Westminster Theological Journal* (Vol. XLIV, No. 2), pp. 205–249. The article. "Guillaume Groen van Prinsterer and His Conception of History," was written by a Groen expert, J.L. van Essen, and translated by Herbert Donald Morton.

me somewhat dissatisfied. That is his discussion of grace, common and special, particularly in Chapters 14 and 16 (pp. 142-144, 165), where he speaks of "the realm (domain) of common grace" and "the realm (domain) of special grace." Kuyper's view on this subject has frequently been discussed in this way, and there has been much discussion of what precisely he meant. Men like Van Ruler, Schilder and S.G. de Graaf (author of the four-volume *Promise and Deliverance*, published in an English translation by Paideia Press) have offered criticisms. This is not the place to enter in any detail into the importance of these discussions for Professor Langley's theme. Nevertheless, this does constitute a matter of supreme importance. I shall make just two brief comments.

First, in perhaps the most important single article on this question – and how fortunate we are to have it in English – the late Professor S. U. Zuidema wrote:

> In summary I conclude that Kuyper gave Van Ruler [one of the critics] cause for writing what he did. But no less do I conclude that Kuyper more than once should have given Van Ruler pause in writing what he did (p. 100).[10]

He is referring to a statement he made previously: "...Van Ruler has not sufficiently, or rather not at all, taken into account the Kuyper who in principle overcomes and removes the polar tension between particular grace and common grace – precisely in his doctrine of particular grace. I am referring to the Kuyper who teaches – as he does in *De Gemeene Gratie* (Common Grace) II, 298 – that particular grace... in regeneration... works a deeply religious reversal of the 'innermost pivot' of our being... [and] next asks how this reversal of the 'invisibly small yet all-controlling central point' in man can possibly become effective on the *periphery*, that is to say, how a truly Christian life can

---

10. The article, "Common Grace and Christian Action in Abraham Kuyper" appears in a volume of essays by S. U. Zuidema on modern society and contemporary thought entitled *Communication and Confrontation* (Toronto: Wedge Publishing Foundation, 1972), pp. 52-101, but for the present point see particularly pp. 94-101.

blossom forth from such a regeneration..." "Here," Zuidema adds, "precisely in his doctrine of regeneration and particular grace, Kuyper radically rises above that haunting dilemma brought on by the polarly dialectical relation which he usually construed between re-creation [i.e., spiritual life in Christ or religion – H.E.R.] and creation" [i.e., activities in this world, or culture – H.E.R.]. In another place (p. 95) Zuidema makes the matter even clearer:

> ...Kuyper himself had already made this correction; that in fact the happy hour arrived that he set forth that Christ as the Mediator of Redemption not only may lay claim to the central, spiritual core of man, but also is in principle the new Root of all created reality and the Head, the new Head, of the 'human race.' With that, Kuyper had broken with his own polarly dualistic contrast between particular grace and common grace. That is why he could state more forcefully in his writings on *Pro Rege* than in those on *De Gemeene Gratie* that we are in the service of Christ throughout the entire domain of common grace" (*Pro Rege* II, 527).

My second comment is that, without ignoring the important writings of Klaas Schilder and others on the subject, I wish just now to call attention particularly to the work of S.G. de Graaf, especially (for those who can read Dutch) his important article "Genade en Natuur" (Grace and Nature), in the volume *Christus en de wereld* (Christ and the World) [Kampen: Kok, 1939, pp. 72–113] which deals in a brilliantly stimulating way with the subject of common grace.[11]

Happily, just at those points where Kuyper's scientific theological formulations were sometimes a bit less than satisfactory, it was his practical intuitive insights, nourished on the Scriptures, that direct-

---

11. In June, 1982 a theological master's thesis was submitted at the Free University of Amsterdam in the Netherlands on "Geschiedenis als Verbondsgeschiedenis: een onderzoek naar de visie van Simon Gerrit de Graaf (1889-1955) op de zin der geschiedenis" (*History as History of the Covenant: An Investigation into S. G. de Graaf's View of the Meaning of History*). It includes a discussion of de Graaf's view of common grace.

ed him to his political – and more broadly cultural – action. They even, as we have just seen, enabled him in time to correct some of his inadequate formulations. And I am glad that my friend, McKendree Langley, has brought *this* Kuyper to our attention.

When Professor Langley asked me to write an Introduction for his book, I joyfully responded; for it was when as a young man I, like him, a Presbyterian and partly Scotch-Irish, first went to Holland to study theology (a long time ago, in the Fall of 1939, arriving, in fact, on September 1, the day, early in the morning, that the Second World War broke out with Hitler's Stuka bomber attack on Poland) that I discovered, *in the patterns of everyday life there*, the colossal achievement that, in reliance upon God Almighty, had been realized by Groen and Kuyper and the hosts of faithful confessors of the Name who had entrusted themselves to their leadership.

A Review of *Kingdoms in Conflict* by Chuck Colson

Published in Christian Renewal, February 29, 1988

CHUCK COLSON'S latest and most ambitious book[1] holds the reader spellbound from beginning to end. From the fictional Prologue to the Epilogue at the end, Colson proclaims in the midst of worldwide darkness, of tumult and deep-seated fear, a message of hope in a manner fitting the glory of the Christmas festival, so recently celebrated and the looking ahead that traditionally accompanies the New Year (though on the part of many there may be a lesser degree of expectancy for 1988).

> Where then is hope? It is in fact that the Kingdom of God has come to earth – the Kingdom announced by Jesus Christ in that obscure Nazareth synagogue two thousand years ago. It is a Kingdom that comes not in a temporary takeover of political structures, but in the lasting takeover of the human heart by the rule of a holy God.

> Certainly,... the fact that God reigns can be manifest through political means, whenever the citizens of the Kingdom of God bring His light to bear on the institutions of the kingdoms of man. But His rule is even more powerfully evident in ordinary, individual lives, in the breaking of violence and evil, in the paradoxical power of forgiveness, in the actions of those little platoons who live by the transcendent values of the Kingdom of God in the midst of the kingdoms of this world, loving

---

1. Charles C. Colson, *Kingdoms in Conflict* (William Morrow and Company and Zondervan Publishing House, 1987).

their God and loving their neighbor.

Thus in the midst of the dark and habitual chaos of earth, a light penetrates the darkness. It cannot be extinguished; it is the light of the Kingdom of God. His Kingdom has come, in His people today, and it is yet to come as well, in the great consummation of human history. While the battle rages on planet earth, we can take heart – not in the fleeting fortunes of men or nations, but rather in the promise so beautifully captured in Handel's Messiah.

Stop. Listen. Over the din of the conflict, if you listen carefully, you will hear the Chorus echoing in the distance: "The Kingdom of this world has become the Kingdom of our Lord and of His Christ." Listen. For in that glorious refrain is man's one hope.

There, in summary, is the central message of Colson's new book. And there, in Colson's own words, is the Gospel, the momentous significance of God's becoming incarnate, that is, one with us in our earthly bodily existence, in Jesus. The effect of that is, as Colson says, and as his humility in ministry (servanthood) through Prison Fellowship, now a worldwide organization, unambiguously declares, that, as a result of a God-wrought change of heart, we can *take heart* – "*moed gegrepen*" is the way my beloved Dutch professor used to say it – and can *act*, act out of a love born of obedience to God's command to love Him with our whole being and our neighbor as ourself. Thus God's Kingdom is here among us now, developing and extending itself in the acts we undertake in Christ's name. All this is, of course, nothing new to those who have read earlier Colson books, particularly *Loving God*. Indeed, it is nothing new to whoever has understood the gospel as Jesus Christ, quoting the ancient prophet Isaiah, Himself first declared in that little Nazareth synagogue. But it is basic. And how many who call themselves Christians have understood it? Have you? Have I?

Laying the Groundwork

In the totally engaging way that is most familiar to readers of Colson's previous books, *Kingdoms in Conflict* interweaves with the book's developing message striking biographical sketches, incidents of daily life, and events of historical importance. In this respect this latest book is certainly the finest and most impressive. The story of Ernest Hemingway, the account of the rise of the Nazi movement (in short snapshot segments), of "the Troubles" of Northern Ireland, of "lesser cultural revolution" in the U.S.A. which has rendered God irrelevant, of Benigno and Cory Aquino and the non-violent overturn of the Marcos regime in the Philippines, of the influence of Nietzsche's more radical, activist, militant atheism on political life, and of Freud and Darwin upon our relativistic culture and the nihilistic conclusions drawn therefrom by more nearly contemporary writers like Jean Paul Sartre and Albert Camus – all this, worked into the development of the book's central theme, renders it a fine first introduction to a general education in a Christian spirit for any who may desire one in this way, and makes it a must reading for younger Christians trying to understand and place themselves in the world in which they are coming to responsible maturity, and for older Christians, seeking to get a hold on the sense of a world rapidly changing.

Human Action in the World

But now let us take a closer look at Colson's new book and at the concerns which compelled him to write it. For *Kingdoms in Conflict* is different from all the earlier books in that it focuses on a very specific theme of our culture, that of human action. That theme is the question of politics, of the Christian and political action, of the relation of church and state, of political life and the Kingdom of God. At this point in time that is a theme of pressing practical importance, for all Christian believers in the first place, and for all our citizens as well. It is a timely book Colson has given us. These questions are clearly a deep concern to any who understand the present world situation.

Unfortunately, Christians are, themselves, badly divided on these matters and "tensions run deep," Colson writes. "On one side are those who believe that religion provides the details for political agenda. On the other are those who see any religious involvement in the public arena as dangerous" (p. 43). In an article he wrote which was recently published in the volume *Piety and Politics*, Colson speaks pointedly about these divisions among Christians on the subject of politics: "...biblical Christianity declares that civil religion is idolatry and privatized faith is no faith at all. Both of these false options deny the truth of the Christian gospel – its unique character and its demand for the unrivaled lordship of Jesus Christ." Colson might well have in mind here the American Christian scene, where, besides the more radical Christian Reconstructionists, we find what he himself calls "the God-and-country, wrap-the-flag-around-the-cross mentality" and "the simply-passing-through mindset." He describes these on p. 246 of his book.

Timely the book indeed is, and not just for the United States. In Canada, the appearance on the scene of the Christian Heritage Party has placed a decision-demanding discussion of the question of the Christian's political responsibility squarely before the citizenry. All over Hispanic America, and elsewhere in the Third World, as well as here at home, we encounter liberation (or political) theologies. And in the Middle East we watch the spread of Muslim "fundamentalism" and its agents, sometimes called terrorists in the West. Referring to this larger world, Colson declares,

> Not since the Crusades have religious passions and prejudices posed such a worldwide threat – if not through a religious zealot or confused idealist whose finger is on the nuclear trigger, then certainly by destroying the tolerance and trust essential for maintaining peace and concord among peoples... I have brooded over this dilemma [he means, as is clear from the immediately preceding, how to balance the tension between the political and spiritual H.E.R.] since the mid-seventies...

So Colson tells us (p. 48):

> My concerns deepened each year as the conflict intensified between the body politic and the body spiritual. A variety of questions plagued me: To what extent can Christians affect public policy? Is there a responsible Christian political role? In a pluralistic society, is it right to seek to influence or impose Christian values? How are the rights of the nonreligious protected? Are there mutual interests for both the religious and the secular? Is it possible to find common ground? Friends urged me to

write on the subject since I've been on both sides – first, as a non-Christian White House official, and now as a concerned Christian citizen… But the task always appeared too daunting. I couldn't sort out all the questions raised in the blistering American debate. Both sides seemed hopelessly intractable.

Colson then goes on to tell how "it was on a visit to India in the fall of 1985 that I came to the unmistakable conviction that I must write this book."

The book is not only delightful reading; it is simply, crammed with valuable insights and wise suggestions that need to be heeded, and it is sincerely to be hoped that a large cross section of the Christian public will take it to hand.

Troublesome Ambiguity

At the same time there remains, in the opinion of this reviewer, a troublesome ambiguity in the book which if it is to be resolved, will require further attention. This is a matter of some consequence since it lies at the heart of the book's argument. Thus it appears in the very first chapter (after the Prologue) and then throughout the book. It affects how we are to understand even the book's title: *Kingdoms in Conflict*. For the question immediately arises, *What* kingdoms are in conflict? And is there merely a *tension* between those kingdoms that needs to be properly balanced (p. 48)?

The idea behind Colson's book is evidently derived from the great work of the North African church father, Augustine (AD 354-430), the *City of God*. There Augustine discusses the conflict (not tension) between the City of God and the city of man. Augustine's two cities are not to be identified with the Christian church (an institution) and the secular state, that is, with the spiritual and the political in the sense of two strictly delimited spheres of human functioning. Rather, they represent the conflict between the Kingdom of God and the kingdom of antichrist, that is, *between two religious directions in life that are all encompassing*. In his *City of God* Augustine expresses it this way:

two societies have issued from two kinds of love. Worldly society (i.e., the earthly city) has flowered from a selfish love which dared to despise even God, whereas the communion of the saints (i.e., the heavenly city) is rooted in a love of God and contempt of self.

The important thing is not to identify these two cities with distinct or separate spheres of human action. Each "city" manifests itself in the *entire range of human action*, because the love from which it grows is a love of the heart, that is, of man in his undivided, pre-functional root unity. It is clear that the question of religion and politics, of church and state, of politics and the Kingdom of God cannot be satisfactorily resolved apart from a consideration of the anthropological question, the question about the nature and composition of man. Augustine himself, although it is often overlooked, did begin to see the momentous significance of the biblical revelation concerning the "heart" of man (Hebrew, *lebh*; Greek, *kardia*) as the divinely inspired description of man's central religious selfhood in its undivided root-unity. He then employed the Latin word *cor* (heart) for this inner man.

The Heart of the Matter

It is important to be aware of this revelation in order to understand what the new birth, what getting a new heart, means. And the heart is the seat of religion. So the very meaning of the word "religion" is also involved here.

Faith, or belief, is not just worship and cultic acts generally; it is the new directedness of the heart in loving obedience to God in *all* things, *including* politics. Unbelief, far from being just a *lack* of faith, is faith directed to something other than God, an idol, *mis*directed faith, the heart's turning away from God in rebellious disobedience to worship self, *in politics as well as in public worship*. These two possible directions of the heart are what is meant by "religion" (although our use of the same word to indicate the world's religions reveals the confusion that is abroad on the subject), and these two ultimate relations to God are antithetically related to each other. Here there can be only conflict, the "enmity" of Genesis 3:15, but not tension. Religion, i.e., our spirituality, in the comprehensive sense of the word, does not and cannot stand over against politics as one sphere of our life over against another, but worship (the cult) does. Men's political activities too, just as in their worship, give expression to the religious orientation of their hearts. The two possible directions of the heart are the source of the two kingdoms of which Augustine speaks. There is a political sphere expression possible of the City of God as well as the city of man. So I find that what Colson writes at the top of page 48 is not in line with his use of Augustine's terms. He says there,

> Both the City of God and the city of man are vital to society – and they must remain in delicate balance. "All human history and culture," one historian observed, "may be viewed as the interplay of the competing values of these... two cities," and wherever they are out of balance, the public good suffers... This is why today's conflict is so dangerous. It would be a Pyrrhic victory indeed should either side win unconditionally. Victory for either would mean defeat for both.

Augustine's Confusion

Notwithstanding all we have said about his *City of God*, Augustine was never able to overcome entirely his early commitment to a form of Platonism, which divided man into a "higher" rationalism and a lower material body and which of course knew nothing of the biblical revelation of a religious heart, deeper than these and constituting man a unity. Likewise with respect to his two cities it is not at all surprising that, in an empire which had assumed absolute authority over all spheres of life and with the paganism of its ruling class largely prevailing, Augustine came to connect the "city of man" – though we saw that it really referred to all the ways in which man's *mis*directed faith-life can be expressed – with the Roman *political* authority, the government, while the isolated situation of believers in that empire brought them to depend increasingly on the church as an established institution with its bishops and synods and led to a confusion of the struggle between this *ecclesiastical* organization and the Roman *government* with the conflict between the kingdom of darkness and the Church Militant or kingdom of light. The Kingdom of God and the church organized for *worship* have here conceptually been gathered into one. So now we have a spiritual realm and a (secular!) political realm. The later medieval development, as we all know, brought the great struggle for power between the popes on the one hand and the secular power, on the other.

My point is that Augustine's great biblical theme of the two cities sometimes became submerged in the confusion of his times, and in the medieval contest between pope and emperor, got lost altogether. We have all been deeply affected by that development, and so has Colson. Many Roman Catholic writers of outstanding intellectual ability, a number of whom Colson cites, naturally belong to this tradition. However, there is also much in Colson's book that would appear to overcome the tradition, as when he writes (p. 83): "...that it is a rule not a realm makes it no less an actual kingdom, nor its laws less binding than those of nations and states." He states (p. 87): "The Kingdom of God embraces every aspect of life..." and refers in a footnote to a remark of R. C. Sproul that

> Americans, steeped in the tradition of democracy, find a monarchy, even with Christ on the throne, an alien concept. We think in terms of human rulers whose limitless lust for power is a constant peril to mankind. But God is not a mirror reaction of human rulers. He is God — and as such, is entitled to rule over all things. His character, as revealed in the Bible and in the person of Christ, reveals absolute justice, mercy, and love.

He declares (p. 91) that the "state was instituted by God to restrain sin and promote a just social order. One of the most common misconceptions in Western political thought is that the role of government is determined solely by the will of the people."

The Problem of Power

There is much more I should like to discuss. But we must begin to call a halt. Though Colson presents compelling reasons why Christians must be involved in politics and government (ch. 20), he yet speaks in this connection largely in terms of individuals, and (perhaps it is his close-up experience of government during the Nixon administration) appears to have a certain fear of power even while recognizing that it is abuse of power rather than power itself which is evil (p. 271). But if by power is meant simply the power of cultural formation which God has bestowed on His creature, man, in order for him to carry out the cultural commission (mandate) by giving form to material ready at hand in the creation to achieve a certain end, then we will have to recognize "power" as an integral aspect of creational life and acknowledge that the problem lies in whether or not power is used in accordance with the law-will of the Creator. Then we need not seek refuge in a distinguishing of "power" and "authority" (p. 275). Authority always involves power. Zechariah 4:6 is often quoted wrongly as opposing power; rather, it was God's assurance to Zerubbabel that they need not fear earthly powers; for a power that originates from the Spirit of God was with them in rebuilding the Temple. Again, we have to do with two powers, two Kingdoms in conflict with each other. With this Colson appears to be in agreement (p. 274).

The Little Platoons

And then there is that apparent restriction to the work of individuals. In the passage quoted at the beginning of this article, Colson speaks of a Kingdom "that comes not in a temporary takeover of political structures, but in the lasting takeover of the human heart by the rule of a holy God." Good enough. But then, after assuring us that God's reign "can be manifest through political means," he asserts that this rule "is even more powerfully evident in ordinary, individual lives... in the actions of those little platoons who live by the transcendent values of the Kingdom of God in the midst of the kingdoms of this world." However, the Kingdom of God is not a mere collection of individuals; it is a Body, a communion of faith. I presume that communion is what comes to light in those "little platoons." Why then no suggestion of a Christian political party as one such little platoon? Why is God's rule "even more powerfully evident in ordinary, individual lives... who live by the transcendent values of the Kingdom of God"?

In the volume *Piety and Politics* already mentioned, James Skillen of the Association for Public Justice, writes (p. 168):

> Christian politics will mature in America when Christians recover the biblical vision of the communal responsibility they have for others. When we begin to see that the body of Christ is not a 'part-time' or 'private' organism unrelated to political realities, we will be able to break away from the individualistic conception of political responsibility which presently dominates our democratic political system. We will no longer be willing to have the major political parties practice all of our politics for us on their terms – terms which presuppose the individualistic character of political responsibility, the rule of the majority for determining what justice is all about, and the neutral secularity of the political dimension of life. Instead, we will be driven by the Spirit of Christ to begin working together as a political community and not just as an ecclesiastical community or as an educational community. We will see that politics is our business as a community with a distinct view of life unlike the views of other communities. We will begin to practice politics as unto the Lord.

In Colson's article in the same volume (p. 184-185), he seems to be very close to saying the same thing. Let me, in closing, quote some of his sentences. "Secular politics simply cannot compete with the body of Christ when it is empowered by the Holy Spirit in His service." (Of course, I am not taking "secular politics" to mean politics directed by unbelief, and the opposition of these two to mean not two merely distinguishable dimensions or spheres of life to be kept in balance, but two heart-directions of human life in its entirety that are in antithetical conflict.)

From the same article, as a conclusion to this review:

> In ancient Rome... religion was considered an acceptable and important aspect of culture. Therefore, as long as Christians fit the mold and allowed themselves to be defined by the society, they were accepted. It was when the church began to express its unique calling, refused to be defined by popular images, and proclaimed in word and deed that Christ is Lord, that it came into open conflict with the world...

Yet the early Christians had one great advantage over us: then it was clear that the surrounding culture was groping in the darkness of paganism, and that the culture should have no hand in defining the role of God's people in the world. But today, we have grown accustomed to thinking of ourselves as part of the 'Christian West' and as a 'Christian nation.' That habit is hard to kick, because it has the narcotic effect of easing the painful reality of the stark contrast between twentieth-century American culture and the calling of Christ to his church. Yet we must kick that habit, if by serving heaven we are to be any earthly good. Our challenge is clear: we must reject the illusions, seductions, and false alternatives of the current political scene and reassert the ageless truth that Christ is Lord of lords and King of kings. With Athanasius, the great fourth-century champion of the faith, we must stand for Christ *contra mundum*—against the world. In the very moment of our clearest opposition to the world, we will find that, as witnesses to the Truth and Life, we will have the inestimable privilege of helping to make Christ's invisible Kingdom, visible in the world.

Here we have Colson returned to Augustine's biblical best. A good ending for this review.

Glenn Andreas

January 29, 1917 – November 5, 1993

EARLY ON November 5, 1993, my very good friend of almost 60 years, Glenn Allen Andreas, of Pella, Iowa, passed away quietly in his sleep. His death was totally unexpected, and while a great gain for him, it is a loss that will surely be felt by the Reformed/Reformational movement not only in Canada and the United States, but throughout the world. I would like the readers of "Christian Renewal" to know something more about this stalwart but modest Christian warrior, and because Glenn's life and mine have for so long been so intimately intertwined, I shall also have to talk – if you will forgive me – about myself.

Glenn and I had met in a most unusual way. It was February, 1934, and the place was Wheaton College, a Christian College just west of Chicago, Illinois. I was a second semester sophomore, living in the spatially somewhat limited men's dorm on the fourth floor of the administration building. Inside stairs led down to the lower levels of laboratories, classrooms, and offices, but we very often used the fire escape at the far end of the other hall to get down to the ground quickly.

A dorm gathering the evening before Glenn came had informed us he would be arriving the next afternoon and that we should be expecting him. And it just so happened – is that a proper word for God's providential leading? – that once the next afternoon when I looked out my door, a noise at the fire escape entrance got my attention and I saw a rather short figure of a fellow with a pile of books on his one arm and a radio sitting on top trying to open the door to get into our hall. That had to be the new student, I thought. I ran down the hall to his aid, relieved him of the radio and walked this total stranger down to his room, which was close to mine but on the other side of the hall. Then I left; we had scarcely spoken to each other.

Towards evening I again looked out my door and I saw that the new student's door was wide open. I walked over, looked around to see how he was getting his room in order, and finally asked him if he would like to go with me over to the girls' dorm, where we had our meals. He agreed, and when later we had returned to our rooms I asked him to go with me to the Tuesday evening student prayer service over in the new chapel. A bit to my surprise he again agreed, but when halfway down the fire escape he turned to me and said he would rather go to a restaurant downtown and talk. I hesitated, but decided it might be best to take the time to get a bit acquainted.

Over milkshakes Glenn told me something of his life on an Iowa farm, and I told him something about my growing up in Philadelphia, PA. And that was the beginning – although neither of us knew it then – of our 60-year long friendship. In the next couple of weeks I learned, for one thing, that Glenn had been raised a Mennonite. And I remember telling him about a book I had been given by an unusual lady in our Presbyterian church when I left home to go to Wheaton, and which in the year just past had greatly influenced my thinking. I asked him if he would like to look at it. Again, to my surprise, he agreed to read it – I believe now that God had prepared us for each other – and he did just that. The book was Loraine Boettner's *The Reformed Doctrine of Predestination*. For weeks that book was the center of our discussions, and our common interest in those discussions – although I was scarcely aware of it at the time – was drawing us closer together. From the beginning, though we had quite different backgrounds, we had very similar reactions and leanings. Now Glenn is gone, but I marvel still at the way the Lord brought us together so quickly.

Just before the spring vacation, Glenn asked me if I would go with him to his home in Lisbon, Iowa. I was delighted. I had never been that far west and was eager to see the Mississippi River, but I especially wanted to continue our talks and to meet Glenn's mother. With her I had long conversations and found her to be a wonderful Christian lady. Unfortunately, she died not too long after my visit, but her Christian character undoubtedly had had a great influence on her son.

At the end of that sophomore year I decided, for a couple of reasons, to go home to Philadelphia and attend the University of Pennsylvania. For one thing, the Depression had struck us, and it was much cheaper to stay at home. The other reason was that, unlike most American high school graduates of the time, I had enjoyed three years of ancient Greek in addition to the usual four years of Latin, and had therefore had to take junior and senior Greek at Wheaton. I felt that I needed more Greek. When I told Glenn of my decision, he decided that then he would also go home to work with his father and brothers in their fast-growing grain business. And that is what took place. But we did correspond with each other throughout the year.

What happened next strikes me now as an unusual working of God's providence. I heard that Wheaton was acquiring a new professor in the classical language department, a young lady who had just obtained her Ph.D. degree under the most distinguished classics scholar of the University of Illinois. I therefore decided to go back to Wheaton; after all, I wanted a *Christian* education. When I told Glenn that I was planning to return to Wheaton for my senior year, he decided that in that case he would go back too. So we had another short time together. I even persuaded him to take the beginning course in Greek. We spent a lot of our free time together that last year. I remember telling Glenn of my plan to attend Westminster Theological Seminary in my hometown of Philadelphia. I was enthusiastic about that, and I wanted my friend to understand how I felt.

My attachment to Westminster was a matter of long standing. Let me take the time to say just a word about that; for the school was to have a great influence also on Glenn's life. Westminster Seminary was founded in 1929 when several professors at Princeton Theological Seminary in New Jersey left because of the reorganization of that seminary to allow room for more liberal theological instruction. The new seminary, which was to continue the orthodox Reformed theological position of historic Princeton, was to be situated in Philadelphia. My parents, who had been following developments in the General Assembly of the northern Presbyterian Church with some dismay, took me with them to the very first opening exercises held in the Witherspoon Building in downtown Philadelphia on September 25; I was thirteen years old and in the 10th grade. I still have a vivid memory of that evening; of seeing march across the platform in full academic regalia: Dr. J. Gresham Machen, who had played and was still to play a leading role in the battle against theological liberalism in the northern (U.S.A.) Presbyterian Church, and the previous summer had led the break with Princeton[1]; Robert Dick Wilson, the internationally well-known Semitic scholar (Hebrew, Arabic and related languages) and great defender of the faith, who would live only one more year; Dr. Oswald T. Allis, who as Old Testament scholar and editor of the scholarly Princeton Theological Review had gained an international reputation for his exact and thorough grasp of orthodox Christianity; the young Ned B. Stonehouse, who had just returned from obtaining his doctorate in theology at the Vrije (Free) University of Amsterdam, and who was to assist Machen in New Testament studies; and Dr. Cornelius Van Til, who had just completed his first year of teaching at Princeton in the department of Apologetics (philosophical defense of the Christian faith).

In the next couple of years, while still in high school, I had also heard Drs. Wilson and Machen preach in my home church in Philadelphia. And then in my sophomore year at Wheaton, in the course I was taking on medieval philosophy, the professor had suggested that Plato's philosophical views provided a natural basis for Christian theology. At the time I knew little of the long history of Christian theologians' dependence on Plato or Aristotle or even the Stoics, but the very idea that the philosophical position of any Greek philosopher could serve as a foundation for the construction of a Christian theological system was utterly repugnant to me. I believe that the many

---

1.   See his important little book *Christianity and Liberalism*; and Edwin H. Rian, *The Presbyterian Conflict* (Eerdmans, 1940).

years of instruction in the Summer Bible School of my home church during the four weeks of July and the great quantities of Scripture passages we had had to memorize, along with the Westminster Shorter Catechism, played a significant role in establishing my conviction on the subject.

In any case, I chose to write my required term paper on the relation of theology to philosophy. So when I went home for spring vacation I got up the nerve to go downtown to Westminster Seminary to ask to speak with Dr. Van Til. The syllabus material he lent me only corroborated and strengthened my feeling on the subject at issue. My professor was unhappy with the resulting term papers and indicated that by the grade he gave me. But this experience I had had with Westminster Seminary only strengthened my determination to study there.

All of this was the subject of our conversations while Glenn and I were still together in my senior year at Wheaton. It may appear that I have been talking too much about myself just now, but, believe me, the experiences I had had played a big role in those discussions we were having, and they undoubtedly had much to do with Glenn's later becoming such a vigorous supporter of a worldview and of a philosophy that are *thoroughly grounded biblically.*

In the summer of 1936, and under Machen's leadership, the Presbyterian Church of America (later called the Orthodox Presbyterian Church) was organized, and I with my parents became charter members of one O.P.C. congregation. And then in the fall I entered Westminster Seminary. It was not long before Glenn came on a visit to see everything for himself. When he was ready to return home, he had purchased a good number of books on the subject of Reformed theology and Reformed Christian living; among them I remember, was the 10-volume collection of B.B. Warfield's works.

From then on, largely at home, Glenn grew rapidly in his knowledge of the Reformed faith and in his desire to promote it. At the same time, he was working with his father and brothers in their rapidly expanding grain business. Later visits to the seminary were bringing him to the attention of a number of the professors, including especially Van Til, John Murray (systematic theology) and Stonehouse. I remember that a number of luncheons and dinners were arranged in order for Glenn to talk with faculty and board members and for them all to become better acquainted with one another.

In the second semester of my senior year at Westminster the faculty invited Professor Klaas Schilder of the Kampen Theological School of the Netherlands, who was coming on a visit to the United States, to give a week-long series of lectures on the early history of Reformed theology. His lectures were most inspiring, and Dr. Van Til, knowing that I was wanting to go to Germany for further study (my mother was partly Pennsylvania Dutch, and even in high school I had several times gone downtown to the central library to read books about the various German universities), suggested that because Nazi Germany was rapidly approaching a situation that would likely bring war to the West I should give consideration to studying in the Netherlands, at least at first. He thought I should talk with Professor Schilder about it, which I did. And when at my graduation I was offered a year's fellowship for further study in Europe, I chose to study with Schilder (dogmatic theology) and Prof. Greijdanus (New Testament) in Kampen.

War did indeed break out in Poland on the day our ship arrived in Rotterdam (on Friday, Sept. 1, 1939), and two days later (on Sunday) England and France declared war. But I was young (23), and, since I wanted to become acquainted with Europe, I decided to stay on in the Netherlands. I spent four and a half months of study at Kampen, and I learned very much from both Schilder and Greijdanus.

Particularly Schilder's lectures on the doctrine of God showed me how much ancient and medieval theologians had based their views on the theologies of Platonist, Meso-platonists, and Neo-platonists, until Thomas Aquinas also introduced into Christian theology the thinking of Aristotle on the subject. Through Schilder's lectures I also became a bit more familiar with, and interested in, the extensive work of Profs. Vollenhoven and Dooyeweerd of the Free Reformed University of Amsterdam, who, following the lead of Abraham Kuyper, were developing a *Christian* philosophy, one based not on Plato or Aristotle or the Stoics but solely on the Scriptures and the creation-order therein revealed. At last I was finding what I had been searching for at Wheaton, i.e., a biblical foundation for the entire philosophical enterprise. By November, however, and particularly in January, 1940, increasing Nazi violation of the Dutch-German border convinced me that Germany would very soon attack the Netherlands. With great regret I made the decision to return home, and left at the end of February.

Scarcely had I got home when Glenn sent me tickets to visit him in Iowa. This was typical of him. He wanted to know all about my experiences in Europe; he wanted especially to hear what new things I had learned from *Greijdanus* and particularly from Schilder's lectures on dogmatic (systematic) theology. It revealed Glenn's growing passion to understand and to live the Reformed faith.

In the meantime, Glenn, who for years had been a member of a local Presbyterian (U.S.A.) church, because of the continuing situation in that denomination, had withdrawn and become a member of the Orthodox Presbyterian Church. But since there was no O.P.C. congregation in Cedar Rapids where he now lived, he became a member of one in Waterloo, Iowa, some 70 miles away, and attended it faithfully. The month that I now spent with him I rode along, and while driving had extensive time to talk with him about my experiences in Europe, about the church situation in the U.S.A. and what we were going to do further with our lives. Glenn was now making a very good living, but his first concern was with the spiritual life and how he could best serve Christ's kingdom. When I returned home to Philadelphia I found that I had been offered a year's scholarship to study at the Harvard Divinity School in Cambridge, Massachusetts.

(Meanwhile, the war had extended itself to the West.) At the end of that year, on the recommendation of two of my professors (neither of them orthodox Christians) I was interviewed by professors in the university graduate school for a place as a Junior Fellow in the Society of Fellows of Harvard University. I was elected to membership, and for two years had the great honour of working closely with Professor Werner Jaeger (formerly of Berlin University, perhaps the greatest

Greek scholar of the western world – he had escaped Germany with his Jewish wife) on a critical edition of the preserved writings of Gregory of Nyssa (a Cappadocian church father, c. 330-c. 395). Glenn came to visit me in Cambridge, and again I informed him of the significance of the work I was doing. He always seemed to sense the importance of whatever work I was doing, and showed a real personal interest. (If anyone might wonder at this, let me say that when I was teaching a Greek class in Wheaton's summer school I looked up his I.Q. and found it recorded as 168, which is genius.)

Because of the wartime need of a Latin teacher in the Christian High School of Paterson, N.J., I taught Latin (and Greek on the side) for two of the war years, but got home to Philadelphia most weekends. It was at this time that I became candidate for the Th.M. degree at Westminster, specializing now in church history. Professor Schilder's lectures on dogmatics had shown me the great need for a better knowledge of the history of the church and particularly of the history of dogmatics and its philosophical orientation. Professor Woolley was very supportive of my plan and allowed me a good bit of freedom in my research, which concentrated on two areas of the church's history: (1) the first four – i.e., 2nd through 5th-centuries, and (2) the history of Reformed dogmatics in the 16th and 17th centuries.

It was about this same time that among some men in both the O.P.C. and the C.R.C. a concern was growing as to how to provide for our American youth a genuinely Christian higher education. A committee was formed to investigate the possibility of erecting a Reformed Christian university in the United States. Dr. Ned B. Stonehouse, whose origins had been in the Christian Reformed Church and who therefore knew leading men in both church communities, was a key initiator of the idea. By this time Glenn and he had become very good friends, and Glenn was immediately invited to join the committee. Very soon he became its secretary-treasurer, I suppose because of his increasing financial experience in the prospering grain business of his brothers.

I received my Th.M. degree in the spring of 1946, but in the meantime I too had become a member of the committee for a Christian University. There was such enthusiasm and determination in the committee that even the luxurious Widener estate in Philadelphia, which we discovered had to be sold, was reasonably purchased by the committee.

Unfortunately, or so it seemed, the Christian Reformed members of the committee, soon feeling extreme synodical pressures, resigned from the committee. The result was the immediate selling of the property, and finally the end of the committee's life. But Glenn had played a very important role in the life of that committee, and the experience had only convinced him of the great need for taking further measures in the future to advance *scripturally grounded higher education.*

It was some time after I received the Th.M degree, in the early summer of 1946, that Glenn and I attended a concert by the Philadelphia Symphony Orchestra and afterward went to a nearby Horn and Hardart's restaurant next to City Hall for some refreshment. I remember talking to him about my growing conviction that something really radical had to be done to rid the theological world of its unhealthy, even deadly, dependence on one or another of the unbelieving Greek philosophers, and to face up to the more fundamental structural question of whether there really is an independent Reason/reason or whether our reason*ing*, like all the rest of our bodily activity is ultimately an expression of our inner-most being, what the Scripture designates as the "heart" (Hebrew "*lebh;*" Greek "*kardia*"). I told him something of what I had learned in the Netherlands of the reformation of philosophy that was being undertaken, especially by Professor Vollenhoven and his brother-in-law Professor Dooyeweerd, at the Free Reformed University of Amsterdam (a development that seemed to come as an answer to prayer once offered in a public gathering by the then old Abraham Kuyper, who had been instrumental in the founding of that university in 1880).

Imagine my surprise when Glenn suddenly reared back in his chair, looked me straight in the eye and said, "Evan, if you think that some study at the Free University will help you in your further reflection on this subject, I'll pay your passage over. But then after that you will have to take care of yourself." I could not believe what I was hearing, but immediately I promised him that I would look into the matter.

Dr. Van Til, who knew both Dutch professors well, arranged for me to speak by phone with Professor Vollenhoven – it was a stirring experience – and many details were worked out, including the assurance that if I came, I could count on some financial aid. That did it.

But when I went to an office of the Holland-America Line, I discovered to my consternation that all state-rooms were reserved for many months ahead. Both men in government and businessmen were making up for five years of war and broken contact with Europe. Yet here again I was amazed at how the Lord was working things out for me. For just a few days after that I happened to mention my predicament to Professor R.B. Kuiper (who had been my professor of practical theology at Westminster Seminary) and he said he might be able to help. And only a few days later he phoned to tell me that he had contacted Michigan's Senator Vandenberg, and that an August passage would be available for me. Again, I could scarcely believe my ears, but I thanked the Lord, told Glenn and made plans.

There followed a good year and a half of study with Vollenhoven and of occasional visits with Professor Dooyeweerd (Professor in the law faculty) and other leading figures of the movement for a consistently biblically grounded philosophical position. I was ecstatic; I had found what for years I had been searching for,[1] and I passed my doctoral exams in November, 1947. I also found the girl who was to become my wife, and Glenn came over to stand with me at our wedding in December. Very important for him was that he quite independently spent time in discussions with both Vollenhoven and Dooyeweerd. Those discussions completely convinced him of the need to develop a specifically scripturally grounded philosophical position which would also serve as the philosophical component involved in every one of

---

1.   The interested reader can follow the development of this position in the magazine *Philosophia Reformata* (1936 to the present). The general reader can consult Dooyeweerd's *In the Twilight of Western Thought* (1960), and his *Roots of Western Culture* (Wedge, 1979).

the special sciences, from the mathematical ones up to the ethical and including theology. From both professors I learned how delighted they both had been to make his acquaintance and how pleased they were with his support of the Free University.

Early in the new year (1948) wide-spread concern about a possible Soviet invasion of Western Europe drove me, who now had a Dutch wife, to obtain a visa for her and to find a passage back to the United States. I had passed my doctoral exams and was free to work on my dissertation.

After a year with my parents in Philadelphia, Glenn invited us, in the early summer of 1949, to find a little house in Pella, Iowa, to which he had moved his family so his children might have Christian schooling. We lived there for slightly less than a year, enjoying almost daily contact with Glenn and his family and becoming acquainted with the Christian Reformed Church, with which Glenn and his family had become associated. Several times I was invited to speak to the men's societies of the several Christian Reformed churches in the area, and that is how my name came to be mentioned as a possible professor for Calvin College. In fact, a recommendation to that effect was sent to Calvin's board of trustees, and, since I was little known in these circles, Glenn sent my wife and me his plane and pilot that we might spend some time in Grand Rapids, Michigan in order to talk with some professors there. I also met with some members of Calvin's board of trustees, who showed some interest but told me that they would like to talk to me after I had obtained my doctor's degree.

In the spring of 1950 we returned to the Netherlands and my weekly contacts with Professor Vollenhoven. Our first child was born in May, and I struggled to finish writing my dissertation. With the doctor's degree granted in April, 1951, we returned to America and I went to Grand Rapids to meet Calvin's board. To my amazement and great joy I was appointed an assistant professor of philosophy to begin in September, the first non-Dutchman, I discovered, to a full-time faculty position at Calvin. Glenn was very pleased with my appointment, and when we had moved came to visit us.

Several years now passed without our seeing each other; we were both very busy with our work. Glenn had bought a bank in Pella, worked with his brothers (now ADM, Archer Daniels Midland), and did much to help the local Christian schools. In the beginning of my second year at Calvin there was a new development: the first three of the children of post-war Dutch immigrants to Canada came to study at Calvin and at the request of their pastors looked me up. Many a Sunday evening they spent at our home; I remember the many conversations we had about the different social conditions they had experienced among Christians back in the Netherlands and now in Canada and the U.S.A. Especially the lack of a Christian political movement here struck them as strange. My own studies of American political life had persuaded me of the dire need of a Christian political witness in the U.S.A. As a result of our conversations together I decided to organize a student club to study these issues, and in September, 1953 such a club was begun.

From the beginning we met strong resistance from American students, but after a couple of years we had solid support from an increasing number of Canadian students, who began to see the connection between the question of a scriptural approach to philosophy and the question of political organization on a scriptural basis. I persuaded the club members to study the thought of a most important 19th-century Dutch Christian leader, Guillaume Groen van Prinsterer, as laid down in his fundamental work *Ongeloof en Revolutie* (Unbelief and Revolution) published in 1847,[2] just one year before the much smaller but also much more influential *Communist Manifesto* of Karl Marx and Friedrich Engels. We translated the book as we went along. As a result of their study the students decided to name their club the Groen van Prinsterer Society, and it became known popularly as the Groen Club. After Glenn had visited the club a number of times he too became strongly supportive of the idea of Christian political organization for North America, as well as of the ever increasing need

---

2.   A later member of the Groen Club, Harry Van Dyke, now a professor at Redeemer College, translated and commented on the book. His doctoral dissertation, *Groen Van Prinsterer's Lectures on Unbelief and Revolution* (Wedge, 1989) is must reading for anyone interested in these matters.

for Christian higher education.

During the 50's I became acquainted with some of the leaders of the reformational[3] movement in Canada and Glenn and I always talked over these developments whenever we were together. By the end of the 50's there was evidence of livening spiritual life in Canada, at least in Dutch immigrant circles. The first Unionville (Ontario) conference for college students was held in 1959,[4] and about that time Bernie Zylstra, a former president of my Groen Club, finished his law studies at the University of Michigan (originally he had intended to study for the ministry but our studies in the Groen Club had convinced him of the great need for Reformed Christian leadership in the world of law and politics) and had a strong desire for further study of law in a Christian philosophical setting with Professor Dooyeweerd in Amsterdam. I mentioned it to Glenn, and he immediately offered financial help to Bernie whenever he would need it. That was increasingly characteristic of Glenn; the money he had belonged to the Lord, and would be freely given to promote the Lord's cause wherever he saw a need.

Glenn had not been present at that first Unionville Conference, but while on a visit to our home in December, 1959 he read the manuscript of my lectures and was so taken by them that he asked if he might take them home and get them printed. (I am sure it had not occurred to any of us how valuable that might be for our future organizational development.) The resulting volume[5] made available all the lectures given at that first conference. In a Preface to the volume the Rev. François F. Guillaume wrote, "I wish to extend my feelings of deep appreciation to Mr. Glenn Andreas of Pella, Iowa, one of our

---

3. The word "Reformational" I use to refer to the movement to have the biblically Reformed view of life extend in fact to all of our life, in particular to our scholarly and political life, and the life of the labour union.

4. See H. Evan Runner, *The Relation of the Bible to Learning*, 5th rev. ed., 1982 (Paideia Press), especially the Preface by Bernard Zylstra.

5. *Christian Perspectives*, 1960, Pella Publishing, Inc., Pella, Iowa (February 1960), with a preface by the Rev. François Guillaume and an introduction by the Rev. P. Y. De Jong.

board members, for the excellent work that he has done in helping to get this book printed and published."

Yes, Glenn's settled conviction of the need for Reformational action had brought him into the board of the Association for Reformed Scientific Studies (later called the Association for the Advancement of Christian Scholarship) headquartered in Toronto, and his generosity in getting this volume published promptly had much to do with the future advance of the movement towards a university of Reformational persuasion in Canada. For shortly after that first Unionville Conference students who had been deeply moved by what they had heard there began to organize themselves into clubs, at first at a couple of universities in Ontario. Also, the publication and study of the lectures heightened the sense of need and led to the determination to hold Unionville Conferences annually at least for the present.

In 1960 Glenn himself attended the second conference, and then also the third, to which Professor Vollenhoven had been invited. At these conferences Glenn would invite the lecturers, Association board members and other leaders to a dinner at a Toronto hotel, and the entire evening would be spent discussing how best to meet the growing need for Christian university education in North America. Meanwhile, similar conferences were organized in Alberta and British Columbia, to which some of the Unionville lectures were sent, and representatives from Western Canada came into the Association for the Advancement of Christian Scholarship. After the first year the conference lectures were published in Canada itself.

The Association board had begun to work on a plan to open an Institute for Christian Studies in Toronto as a beginning. I was asked to formulate an educational creed for the Institute; then Glenn took the paragraphs I had written and worked them into the creed's present form, except for a couple of very minor changes made by a board committee. Glenn and I asked Professor Vollenhoven to write a preamble for it, which he did in his room some time during the sessions of the third Unionville conference. The resulting document the board adapted with thankful enthusiasm.

I must bring this article to a close, but first I must mention one more thing. I began the article by saying that Glenn's life and mine have for so long been so intimately intertwined. In 1980, the year before I would be officially retired, Glenn and I both attended the celebration in Amsterdam of the 100th anniversary (October 20) of the founding of the Free University. On October 17, I was invited by Glenn to a dinner party at the Amsterdam Hilton Hotel, where Glenn was staying. I got there at the appointed time, and immediately I noticed that there was quite a gathering of people I had known over the years. And then when I had found my place at one of the tables I heard to my amazement that Glenn had made plans for a "Groen Club"-like gathering of about 40 people, either from the original Calvin College Groen Club or from a similar club my former students had organized at the Free University and which included some Dutch and South African students.

Of course, everyone present knew that Glenn and I had long been personal friends, but that is not why we were all gathered there. Glenn gave the dinner, it was clear, to honour the work I had done with those students over the years. The same was true of the financial and other assistance he gave for the publication of the two Festschrifts, *Hearing and Doing* (Wedge, 1979) and *Life Is Religion* (Paideia, 1981). This, I must say, was typical of Glenn his lifelong; his mind (heart) was always thinking of ways to strengthen and extend Reformational thinking and living in the world.

So much more could be written, but this is enough to show the great and important influence Glenn Andreas has had in very significant developments in our Reformed life for more than half a century. Besides all he did in and for the A.A.C.S. and its book publishing program, there were his years of service to Westminster Theological Seminary, to Calvin College and Seminary, to the Christian Schools of Pella, Iowa, to Dordt College, to Redeemer College and its recent plan to erect a Dooyeweerd Centre on its campus. As I think back over my 60 years of close friendship with Glenn, I can only thank the Lord Jesus Christ for the wonderful privilege He extended to me of learning to know this man and of being associated with him for so many years in the Lord's work. And now he is with the Saviour.

But he left behind him a host of good works and the most precious memories. To God be the glory!

The World-Historical Importance of Dooyeweerd's Christian Philosophy

Address at Redeemer College on the occasion of the official opening and dedication of the Dooyeweerd Centre for Christian Philosophy on Saturday evening, November 5, 1994

PRESIDENT COOPER, permit me first of all to offer you my congratulations on your becoming the new president of this increasingly important university college on our North American continent. I, and all of us here tonight, pray God's richest blessings down on you in the important work you have to do here. May He keep you faithful in searching out the fullness of His revelation in Christ Jesus, and in finding ways of applying the same in this new office in which your fellow believers have placed you. I am sure you understand that by "*office*" I mean not the room in which you work, but the office, that is, the *ambt*, to use a Dutch word, in which God has placed you and with which your fellows have honoured you.

President Emeritus De Bolster,
Members of the Board of Governors and of the Academic Council, and of the Advisory Council of the Dooyeweerd Centre,
Members of the faculty,
Mr. Herman Dooyeweerd, Jr.,
Dr. Daniel Strauss,
Students of Redeemer,

Friends and supporting community,

Ladies and gentlemen,

How thankful I am, dear friends, first of all to our sovereign Lord through Jesus Christ our Saviour, that I am privileged to be here at Redeemer College this evening to witness this wonderful occasion of the official opening and dedication of the Dooyeweerd Centre for Christian Philosophy. What a joy it is to me to be able to have a part in this momentous event. And may I take just a moment to recall that a most enthusiastic supporter of the action to establish this Centre here went to his heavenly home just one year ago today. I speak of my very good friend of 60 years, Mr. Glenn A. Andreas, of Pella, Iowa, whose grandson, Jonathan Andreas, is with us here tonight.

And now I want, first, to express my deep appreciation to the members of the Board of Governors of Redeemer College and to the members of the Academic Council for the support they have given to the action that has led to the event we are celebrating here this evening, an action that makes Redeemer College the first in the North American world to assume such a vital work.

I also have the great pleasure of congratulating you, Mr. Herman Dooyeweerd, Jr., on the opening of this Centre, named in honour of your illustrious father, who, along with his distinguished brother-in-law, Professor Dirk H. Th. Vollenhoven, for *the first time in history* developed a way of systematic philosophical thinking and gained a much better insight into the history of philosophical thinking now more thoroughly grounded in divine revelation as given to us in Holy Scripture. Herman, when I speak of your "illustrious" father, you know that I mean, in the first place, to thank the Lord for the tremendously important gifts He gave your father and the terribly significant work He permitted him to do, for His own glory, first, and for the enrichment of His people on earth. All that goes too for Professor Vollenhoven, your uncle. This is what causes these men to stand out and shine in human history. I see that Professor Dooyeweerd's oldest daughter, Maria, is also present here this evening with her husband, Magnus Verbrugge, strong supporters of this work. To them too my hearty congratulations.

Finally, I want to welcome to our North American shores and to Redeemer College my old friend from South Africa, Dr. Daniel Strauss, or Danie Strauss, as we all for so long have known him, to congratulate him on this joyous occasion, and to thank him from the heart for his willingness to leave his beloved fatherland and the scene of his outstanding philosophical accomplishments in order to take up the direction of the work here in this first Dooyeweerd Centre for Christian Philosophy, a work very much more important than most people realize for the advancement of God's kingdom.

So now, ladies and gentlemen, I want to take the rest of the time I have to demonstrate the *world-historical importance* – no, friends, I am not exaggerating – the world-historical importance of what we are doing here this evening in dedicating this Dooyeweerd Centre for Christian Philosophy.

I realize that to some here tonight this may indeed sound right now like a little bit of an exaggeration, perhaps even more than a little bit. Why does it make sense to open a Dooyeweerd Centre here, and now? Weren't both Dooyeweerd and Vollenhoven Dutchmen? And didn't both these men begin to publish their work about the same time they both became professors in the Free Reformed University of Amsterdam in 1926? And Professor Dooyeweerd's life ended on February 12, 1977 – almost 18 years ago – and Vollenhoven's on June 6 of the following year. Haven't there been significant developments in the field of philosophy since then? Why *now* a Dooyeweerd Centre? And how could this be a matter of *world-historical importance?* But it is true, and if you will permit me, I shall attempt to explain. Let me first, however, read to you two tributes to Dooyeweerd and his work by two outstanding Dutch humanists.

On the occasion of Dooyeweerd's 70th birthday, Prof. G.E. Langemeijer, a man, please note, of *socialist* persuasion, for many years professor of legal philosophy at the University of Leiden, prosecutor general of the Supreme Court of the Netherlands, and for several years president of the Royal Academy of Science and Letters, had this to say:

It may seem strange that on the 70th birthday of a philosopher of such pronounced religious and political persuasion as Dooyeweerd... tribute is paid by a jurist with an entirely different worldview and political persuasion... However... there is every reason to put the question what the significance of this philosopher is for Dutch philosophy of whatever persuasion, or even for philosophy in general without any restriction of nationality. For without any exaggeration Dooyeweerd can be called the most original philosopher Holland has ever produced, Spinoza himself not excepted.

Another writer linked Dooyeweerd with Johan Huizinga, author of *Erasmus* and the very well-known *The Waning of the Middle Ages,* and with Gerardus van der Leeuw, author of *Religion in Essence and Manifestation,* as one of the four most encyclopedically learned men in the Netherlands in the 20th century.

The plain implication of Langemeijer's assessment is that in Dooyeweerd the Church of Jesus Christ possesses a man of the quality of mind that appears but rarely in the space of several hundred years.

And now, in the very recent issue of *Trouw* of Saturday, October 8, 1994, Professor Mr. Dr. P.B. Cliteur, a humanist, president of the *Humanist Society (het Humanistisch Verbond)* writes,

> Herman Dooyeweerd without doubt is the greatest Dutch philosopher of the 20th century. As a humanist, I have always looked for such persons in my own tradition. They are not to be found... In the case of Herman Dooyeweerd we may speak of a philosopher of international importance, too great for the Dutch way of doing philosophy... Dooyeweerd is a philosopher, [he writes,] who wishes to do justice to the variety in reality.

From my article in the Christian Reformed *Banner* of April 22, 1977, "Dooyeweerd's Passing: An Appreciation": "What ultimately attracted so many of us students to him" – I'm speaking of myself – "was his Christian faith, at once simple and profound, and particularly the bold consistency with which, using all his many talents, he set it forth and worked it out in his philosophical writings..." Mainly,

Dooyeweerd was a witness as almost no other man in modern times, to the power of the Word of God to liberate (from non-Christian traditions), to redeem our intellectual work, to reclaim that part of a lost creation and through men to actualize creational potentials.

Becoming biblically based in our philosophical work is one important witness to the world. Philosophy is important: working everywhere in the scientific world by the light of the Scripture; living always and everywhere by the Word of God. The fact is that the gradual development of philosophy in the great universities of the modern world has played a huge role in the developing collapse of our society. I know, from my years at the University of Pennsylvania and at Harvard University. There must come a Christian antidote: Christians who believe God's Word, even if they differ on some things, must find a way by Scripture to combat the gradual historical development of our time – the secret Oxford University society of British and American scholars to get concentrated control of our national societies in order to force anti-Christian ideas and ways of living on us all! Let us pray that the Dooyeweerd Centre will be an important early and beginning moment of that struggle!

But haven't many scientists, you may yet ask, been coming to the conclusion that no philosophical explanation of our world of experience is possible – all the philosophies have failed – and that therefore we shall have to be satisfied with whatever the several special sciences like physics, chemistry, the biological sciences, economics, the law sciences, can give us? Of course this is something that will have to be dealt with in the Dooyeweerd Centre itself, but let me say now just this, that *none* of the results of any of the special sciences are ever the same as the world of *concrete* or *actual* things that you and I experience every day, the world of institutions, of marriages, of families, of stores and banks and churches, the world of people and plants and animals. Science always involves abstraction; so there has to be something there first, from which we abstract. And it is the concrete world, the real world we all, including the scientists, live in that has to be accounted for.

But we'll leave all that to the people who will be working here.

So now, ladies and gentlemen, let me get on with my task tonight of demonstrating to you the world-historical importance of the work of Professors Dooyeweerd and Vollenhoven, and of the work lying before the Dooyeweerd Centre for Christian Philosophy now, here at Redeemer.

Their work, and yours here, is of world-historical importance simply because it has to do with our life-purpose of living by the light of God's revelation as given in His Word. In that connection I want to speak to you for just a moment about Groen van Prinsterer, who died in 1876. Some of the younger people here tonight may be inclined to think of that as a long time ago, and may wonder what he might have to do with us here now. The answer is: just about everything. And it's not just people of a Dutch background who have to know about Groen. I who am speaking to you am not Dutch, I'm Scotch-Irish, Welsh, English, and German – a good American "mix" – but I became acquainted with Groen when I was studying in the Netherlands, and it is I who am saying that all of us have got to know more about Groen van Prinsterer. We Christians have got to wake up, and read, and fight. A major battle is on.

For those of you who may not be very much acquainted with the man, all those words – Groen van Prinsterer – are only the family name. His first name was Willem – our William – although his baptized name was Guillaume, the double 'l' sounding like a Y. But of course, I'm forgetting that I am here in Canada, where you all know (some) French. And of course the older ones here tonight will remember the Rev. François Guillaume, whose last name is the same as Groen van Prinsterer's first. And some of you, I'm sure, will remember that I had a Groen van Prinsterer study club at Calvin College, where for years we studied that extremely important book of Groen's, *Ongeloof en Revolutie* (Unbelief and Revolution), which at that time had not received an English translation. Incidentally, we do have one now, an excellent one together with most helpful historical discussions, done by a man well-known here at Redeemer, namely Professor Harry Van Dyke, who is here tonight with his wife, Nienke. It is important that everyone involved with the work of the Dooyeweerd Centre — and, for that matter, everyone here tonight, whether from Canada or the U.S.A. or elsewhere — become familiar with this book and this man. For though he lived in 19th-century Holland, his writings are essential for the lives of Christian persons and others today in all parts of the world, in Asia and Africa, in Australia and New Zealand, in Central and South America, and in Europe.

The Groen I wish to say something about right now is not, however, the Groen who wrote that book. I have in mind the *young* Groen, born in the year 1801, in the time of Napoleon, just twelve years after the outbreak of the French Revolution. Voltaire (1694-1778), Rousseau (1712-1778), great scientific advances and revolution all characterized the years just preceding his birth. In the Netherlands too it was a terribly unsettled time of political conflict. Then in 1801, the year of Groen's birth, Napoleon signed a *Concordat* with the pope, recognizing, undoubtedly for political reasons, the Catholic Church, and at his order a somewhat more conservative government was set up in France.

In June of 1806 – Groen was five years old – the Kingdom of Holland came into being when Napoleon proclaimed his brother, Louis, king of Holland. But difficulties quickly developed between Napoleon and his brother, and in 1810 Napoleon sent French troops against the Dutch capital. On July 1, 1810 Louis abdicated and fled. Napoleon annexed Holland to France. Just three years later, however, in 1813 Napoleon himself was defeated at the battle of Leipzig, and in Holland a national revolt broke out. The result: the Prince of Orange was recalled from exile and William VI, who was to become William I, was inaugurated (without a coronation!) in Amsterdam on March 30, 1814. In July (1814) he undertook the provisional government of the southern Belgic provinces of the Netherlands. On March 16, 1815 (and from 1815-1830) William proclaimed himself king of the United Netherlands with its now increased territory. It was a firm monarchy, the states-general (parliament) now consisting of two chambers, and the seat of government was to alternate yearly between The Hague and Brussels.

All this was happening during the years that Groen was growing up. But quickly opposition grew up between the largely traditionally Calvinistic northern and the Catholic southern parts of the country, and finally, as we all know, in 1830 the Belgian Revolution broke out, (the second rupture in the "Great Netherlands," after the split between the north and the south in the 16th century). All these momentous events were a matter of deep concern to Groen, now in his late twenties and closely connected with the Court.

Groen's mother came from a wealthy Rotterdam banking family and his father was now court physician at the court of William I. He was a member of the Reformed Church, but as was very common among the upper classes in those days, he was a man of what were then called "progressive" views, holding a moderately rationalist approach to religion. He did see to it that Groen was given catechetical instruction by the court preacher, and Groen himself did make public profession of his faith at the age of 17. But, as he himself testified many years later, his profession was sincere but *conventional,* which at that time meant that it was shallowly optimistic and moralistic.

That is what many Reformed churches, and what theological instruction in the (Dutch) universities, had come to. Many of you will remember that Abraham Kuyper's theological education at the University of Leiden was also like that.

So I want to speak to you briefly about what had happened in earlier Reformation circles that will serve to explain this widespread moderately rationalist approach to religion in the time of Groen's youth. And – important for this evening – what had happened had to do *very directly with philosophy.*

We've just celebrated another Reformation Day. I love the Reformers – and their return to the Scriptures was also a matter of world-historical importance – but there is a very important aspect of the Reformation that is too often overlooked, but which we must know, and reflect upon more. For the Reformation, that we associate with the names of Luther and Calvin, had been preceded by a number of developments in Italy which we speak of as the Italian Renaissance, the revival of the classical languages and learning of antiquity, and especially of the texts of ancient philosophy. Just before the

Reformation movement began, this revival had begun to spread out to the various European lands, and especially to Switzerland and Germany. John Calvin speaks frequently of "the philosophers," meaning the Greek and Roman philosophers being revived in his time in Renaissance Italy.

Let me just quote a few sentences from Calvin's *Institutes*, where he himself at first is quoting the Roman philosopher, Cicero.

> This is the sum of the opinion of all philosophers: reason which abides in human understanding is a sufficient guide for right conduct; the will, being subject to it, is indeed incited by the senses to evil things, but since the will has free choice, it cannot be hindered from following reason as its leader in all things (*Institutes*, bk. 2.2, 2-9 and also bk. 3.19).

Then Calvin himself continues:

> All the ecclesiastical writers have recognized both that the soundness of reason in man is gravely wounded through sin, and that the will has been very much enslaved by human desires. Despite this many of them have come far too close to the philosophers

– there's that term that Calvin uses so frequently. "Of these," he goes on, speaking of the ecclesiastical writers, "the early ones" – he means those we call the Church Fathers of the early Christian centuries –

> seem to me to have, with a two-fold intent, elevated human powers for the following reasons. First, a frank confession of man's powerlessness would have brought upon them the jeers of the philosophers with whom they were in conflict...

That, friends, is still the case with so many Christians. "Therefore, that they might teach nothing absurd to the common judgment of men, they strove to harmonize the doctrine of Scripture halfway with the beliefs of the philosophers."

Just a half page later Calvin writes, "A little later it will be quite evident that these opinions to which we have referred are utterly false." In *Inst.* 2. 2. 6 Calvin declares, "...how far I disagree with the sounder Schoolmen" (the medieval theologians, like Thomas Aquinas) and then adds, "I differ with the more recent Sophists to an even greater extent," which expression apparently refers to William of Ockham, the great English Franciscan of the 14th century, and his later interpreters, such as Gabriel Biel – two philosophers who had greatly influenced Luther – and the Sorbonne theologians of Calvin's own university years. In *Inst.* 2. 2. 22 Calvin says, "Plato seems to have been compelled to consider (in *Protagoras* 357) that we sin only out of ignorance. But Augustine" – he considers Augustine on this point an exception to all those early Church Fathers –

> so recognizes this inability of the reason to understand the things of God that he deems the grace of illumination no less necessary for our minds than the light of the sun for our eyes. Not content with this, he adds the correction that we ourselves open our eyes to behold the light, but the eyes of the mind, unless the Lord opens them, remain closed.

Notice the use of the word "mind"; we'll have something to say about that shortly.

Calvin, however, was a wonderful exception among the Reformers. I cannot take the time to discuss Luther any more than I already have. But I must say something about the Frenchman who succeeded Calvin in Geneva and who in 1559 became the first rector of the newly organized Geneva Academy. Five years after the Academy was opened Calvin died; and this Frenchman, Theodore Beza, would become one of the leading educators, theologians, and statesmen of the Reformation movement, effective especially in French-speaking Switzerland – Beza had early on taught Greek in Lausanne – and in France, the land of his birth and where, as a 12-year-old, he had studied Greek with Melchior Wolmar, living, it seems, along with Calvin, in Wolmar's house. It took a firm faith and plenty of guts in those days to espouse the Reformation, and I do not wish at all to minimize the importance in so many respects of the work of Beza for the Reformed Churches. Philosophically, however – and that is our special interest this evening – Beza was an Aristotelian in his theological method, and he contributed in a very important way to the development of Aristotelian philosophical structures in the scholastic Reformed theology of the 17th century.

Again and again, as the authority of Calvinian theology was dissolving, scientists appeared on the scene with a sense of the sheer order of natural events, the inscrutable will of nature whose decrees were to be discovered and accepted as facts. And, it was no accident that the chief seat of this development was at the University of Leiden in Calvinistic Holland. The law of God, in perfect conformity to which man finds his salvation and his chief end, turned out to be the law of nature.

Like Beza in the Calvinistic world, in the widespread Lutheran areas Philipp Melanchthon (1497–1560) was important in matters philosophical. His actual family name was Schwarzerd ("black earth"), but his great-uncle, Johann Reuchlin, a famed student of the classics and an early European Hebrew scholar, following a contemporary custom among the more highly educated of the time, in recognition of his great nephew's achievements in the Greek classics, named him Melanchthon, which in Greek means the same thing as Schwarzerd ("melan" being Greek for "black" or "Schwarz," and "chthon" a Greek word for "earth" or "erd").

In 1518 the Elector of Saxony asked Melanchthon to teach Greek at Wittenberg. There Melanchthon immediately set the stage for a new educational program. He proposed to rejuvenate society and regenerate instruction by dropping traditional methods and returning to original sources.

Luther was greatly impressed with him, and soon the force of Luther's personality swept Melanchthon into the evangelical movement, and in 1519 he openly broke with Reuchlin, his great-uncle, who had contributed so much to his education. But he could not long forget his scholarly and intellectual interests in the Greek philosophers and his plan to publish Aristotle, and since he had never had Luther's intense experience, he gradually brought back into the body of Lutheran teaching, which he proceeded to formulate, much of the intellectual system of the Schoolmen and much of the ethical spirit of the Humanists. He became known as *praeceptor Germaniae*, the one who organized Protestant education in the German-speaking countries. But his program was along humanistic lines. He reinstated the idea of natural law, which Luther had opposed to the Gospel, set natural theology once more beside revealed theology, and crowned the educational ladder with a systematic philosophy. It was not, however, the Platonism of so much of the Renaissance; it was Aristotle as those Humanists understood him, with a strong Stoic and Ciceronian admixture in ethics. He published a long series of textbooks in which he arranged this Aristotelian system with neatness and precision. "There is need of philosophy not only for method," he writes, "but the theologian must take many things from physics," and in physics he followed Aristotle closely, with strong emphasis on a natural theology of final causes. As a Humanist, he now finds the will free, and in Ethics the natural law of the Stoics coincides with the Gospel teachings.

Melanchthon's influence was very extensive, and the many schoolmasters who built on him in the 16th and 17th centuries added a metaphysics, to make a well-rounded theological Aristotelianism with few traces of originality or philosophic interest. Even in controversy with the Reformed theologians, they borrowed from the Jesuit Thomists and from Zabarella and the Padua Aristotelians.

For a century and a half the Protestant universities in the Germanies were given over to a sterile Aristotelian scholasticism that shut them off from all contact with the currents of modern philosophy or the beginnings of natural science.

This Protestant Scholasticism combined with the economic destruction of the religious wars, was to delay for two centuries any independent development of German thought. In the second half of the 17th century, interest in theological argument began to decline, and at the same time the primacy in matters intellectual passed to lay scientists and philosophers. Clergy, not only in Protestant lands but also for the first time now in Catholic countries, were slowly crowded into the background. Inevitably, an anti-Christian, a so-called non-religious type of thinking gained an increasing body of adherents as soon as the barrenness of theological discussion was contrasted with the positive results obtained by the natural scientists.

Such was the authority of theology, however, that the whole succession of scientists from Copernicus to Newton paid homage to it, sincerely in some cases, perfunctorily in others, with a view to buying immunity from a power which still ruled the universities and looked upon itself as the crown and glory of the edifice of learning.

Only very gradually did men become more courageous. At first an occasional rare scholar paraded a certain indifference to theology, to be followed gradually by others who directed a moderate criticism against the various theological systems, whether Catholic or Protestant; finally, still bolder spirits advanced to the position that every closed intellectual system was hopelessly incompatible with the perpetual search of science for new truth. What greatly sustained these pioneers in the battle for intellectual freedom (as they called it) was the strong revulsion against dogmatic rigor that followed in the wake of the ruinous religious wars, together with the rise of a body of tolerant men interested in mediating between the rival faiths. Deism grew.

There had to come a reaction. Spener (the founder of what became known as the pietist movement), stressed the Christian priesthood of all believers, and taught that the laity (as non-clergy were called and often still are) should share in the spiritual government of the church, which was not the case in the Lutheran churches. He sought a reorganization of the theological training of the universities, giving more prominence to the devotional life and urging a different style of preaching, namely, in the place of pleasing rhetoric, the implanting of Christianity in the inner man, the soul of which is faith, and its effects the fruits of life. Large numbers of so-called orthodox theologians and pastors were deeply offended by Spener's teaching. But an increasing number of the common people were influenced.

We're back now to Groen van Prinsterer, who at the end of the 1820s was working at the Court and had easy access to the King. On November 1, 1827, just a half-year before his marriage to a well-educated and very pious young lady, Groen was appointed reporting clerk to the royal cabinet; in the spring of 1828 he became its director. The Belgian situation moved him, who had made profession of faith, deeply, concerned him intensely, and drove him to deep reflection. In fact, the Belgian Revolution constituted a turning point in his thinking, Indeed, it was a crucial event in his formative years; it drew the scales from his eyes and set his feet on a path that he would travel the rest of his days.

In that same year (1828) – how the sovereign Lord was arranging all this! – there was a new chaplain at the court. (You know him from his work *The History of the Reformation*.) His name was Merle d'Aubigné. Merle had gone to Geneva to study, and it was the time that the Haldane brothers had come from Scotland to Geneva, and had discovered the extent to which modern anti-Christian thought had penetrated the university, begun, you will remember, by Calvin and Beza. Especially Robert Haldane got a number of students together to study Paul's Epistle to the Romans. Merle d'Aubigné was in that group, and those discussions changed him. Back at the Dutch court Groen and his new wife were strongly attracted to Merle's preaching, and a closer contact came about between the two couples, which developed into a life-long friendship.

Living in the midst of the political conflicts of the revolutionary (Napoleonic) period, Groen felt the need for firm guidance, both for mind and heart. World events shook up his worldview. Coming out of an atmosphere of much lukewarm Christianity, he sensed that he did not have what his wife and friends had: a personal relationship with Christ. And so, he could not measure up to what seemed to be the criteria of a true Christian, as defined by the revivalists: total commitment, inner joy and peace, a readiness at all times to testify of the hope within one and to renounce the world of refined culture and pleasure.

The Belgian revolt constituted a turning point in his thinking. He began to change in his inner man. He read Edmund Burke and French Catholic opponents of contemporary unbelief. More and more he found himself disagreeing with the government's vacillations, and he communicated this to the King.

In the fall of 1829, back in The Hague, Groen felt driven to edit a new small journal of political comment, *Nederlandsche Gedachten* (*Dutch Reflections*). He urged the government to persevere in its language and educational policies repressive of its French and Catholic subjects in the south, and not to give in to the cry for parliamentary sovereignty, which was just another name for *popular* sovereignty. But at the same time, he criticized the government for not consulting parliament seriously and regularly, in fact for wielding an excessively centralized and autocratic regime.

Under mounting influence of the growing redirection in his personal outlook, Groen's journal grew more critical of the views common to both sides of the dispute. For he saw that King William's state centralism had liberal roots that had led to the French Revolution no less than did the views and program of the rebels in Brussels. The year 1830 was to him a point of no return. He recommended making a clean break, cut all ties with Belgium, and recognize its independence *before* the revolutionary ideas and struggle would spread northward.

It's a measure of Groen's greatness, and the index of his historical significance, that while his whole milieu was pulling him in the direction of a *conservative* reaction (most Christians in the U.S.A. and Canada?), he persisted in his ponderings until he had gained a firm hold of the key insight that would unlock the secret of his revolutionary times. This insight once gained, he never looked back.

This spiritual turnabout in his life was the result of two potent injections: a re-reading of modern history through the eyes of men who wrote against the French Revolution of 1789, and a new reading of the Scriptures under the fresh impression of weekly sermons by revival preachers like Merle d'Aubigné.

So, with growing conviction Groen came to see a link between the day-to-day occurrences and the underlying ideology of liberalism with its roots in the revolutionary philosophy of the Enlightenment, and to lay another crucial link between that revolution and unbelief. (See his book *Unbelief and Revolution,* noted above.) He came to see that the intellectual revolution of the 18th century was directly related to the decline of Christianity after its short-lived revival in the 16th century, that in fact it represented a wholesale substitute for Christianity, aiming at founding a new society, one without God. We're living, folks, very much in such a world, as is becoming increasingly clear.

For lack of time, let me jump now to Abraham Kuyper, and then we'll see the connection between Kuyper and Groen.

I haven't the time to speak of Kuyper's early half-liberal views which his university education had given him or of his final ultimate commitment to a thorough Calvinist Christianity. It is characteristic of a number of leading men of the middle 19th century.

Let me quote from the Preface I wrote to McKendree Langley's *The Practice of Political Spirituality* (Paideia 1994):

> In America, Kuyper, if he is known at all, has been known almost exclusively as a theologian and devotionalist. In itself, that reputation is, of course, well deserved, but that is not Kuyper. What that view fails to do is to focus our attention on what was preeminently great and of unusual historical significance in Kuyper, on what makes him an outstandingly important figure for Christians of our generation and of others yet to come, in all parts of the world. That was, without doubt, his richly informed perception that the secular humanism, which, after the French and subsequent revolutions (of 1830 and 1848), was breaking out everywhere and assuming a position of dominance in government and cultural circles, was an integral and comprehensive view of man and the world totally opposed in its direction to the Christian one, and that the ensuing situation in western societies [and that includes us, folks, in Canada, the U.S.A. and much more!] required a new, more active and more organized Christian stance in return. [Have we, folks, studied that history, learned that lesson, and acted accordingly in faithful obedience?]
>
> But it was also the huge successes he reaped in this venture [where Groen had little support all his life, though he was preparing hearts]. God had placed just this man [Kuyper] on the scene at just the right moment, and through his extensive journalistic and educational enterprises, and particularly his strenuous political activities... he aroused a large body of Christians to engage in the Struggle... as a body of Christians organized on an accepted political program of principles, for the political direction of the life of the State.

(Shall we get such Christian leaders, folks, in our countries and will the Christian people listen and work?)

Through the work especially of Groen van Prinsterer, the Reformed, Calvinistic Christian school movement had its nation-wide association, the Society for Christian National Education, founded on October 30, 1860, just 134 years ago. This society was to meet in national convention in Utrecht on May 19 and 20, 1869. Mr. Guillaume Groen van Prinsterer, the society's honourary chairman, traveled to Utrecht to attend the convention (now in his 68th year, his health failing, his followers not numerous, and the harvest of many years of devoted labour painfully meager). Dr. Abraham Kuyper, then only 31 years of age, delivered the pre-convention address. Groen was very deeply moved by it. Though the two men had previously corresponded, they had never met. Kuyper said later,

> When I met him afterwards in the consistory room, he took such a strong hold on me and so profoundly impressed me that from that hour I became his spiritual associate, no, more, his spiritual son.

A few months later, on September 1, 1869, Groen in a published article pointed to Dr. Kuyper as the future leader of the Anti-revolutionary political party. In those days, Kuyper wrote something we need badly to hear. "Politicophobia (fear of engaging in politics) is not Calvinistic, is not Christian, is not ethical." *Listen, folks!*

Well, we have a connection with Groen, but what is Kuyper's connection with Dooyeweerd? Dooyeweerd was born just 100 years ago, in 1894. In October of 1898 – just four years later – the 60-year-old Abraham Kuyper gave his six *Stone Lectures* at Princeton Theological Seminary in New Jersey. In the first of those lectures, entitled "Calvinism: a Life-System," Kuyper speaks of

> that point in our consciousness in which our life is still undivided and lies comprehended in its unity, not in the spreading vines, but in the root from which the vines spring. This point, of course, lies in the antithesis between all that is finite in our human life and the infinite that lies beyond it. Here alone we find the common source from which

the different streams of our human life spring and separate themselves. Personally, we experience repeatedly that in the depths of our hearts,

– "heart" not "body-mind" or "body soul-spirit" (dichotomy or trichotomy) –

at the point where we disclose ourselves to the Eternal One, all the rays of our life converge as in one focus, and there remain that harmony which we so often and so painfully lose in the stress of daily duty.

Dooyeweerd, in the Foreword to his main philosophical work, *A New Critique of Theoretical Thought* (page v), writes:

The great turning point in my thought was marked by the discovery of the religious root of thought itself [instead of "mind" or "reason"], whereby a new light was shed on the failure of all attempts, including my own, to bring about an inner synthesis between the Christian faith and a philosophy which is rooted in faith in the self-sufficiency of human reason. I came to understand the central significance of the "heart," repeatedly proclaimed by Holy Scripture to be the religious root of human existence. [Again, a break with both dichotomy and trichotomy.] On the basis of this central Christian point of view I saw the need of a revolution in philosophical thought [from the Aristotelianism or Platonism in Christian theology] of a very radical character. Confronted with the religious root of the creation, nothing less is in question than a relating of the whole temporal cosmos, in both its so-called "natural" and "spiritual" aspects [There's that dualism again, as opposed to the unity of man in the Scriptures], to this point of reference . . . . From a Christian point of view, the whole attitude of philosophical thought which proclaims [its own] self-sufficiency [i.e., what happened among the Reformers], turns out to be unacceptable, because it withdraws human thought from the divine revelation in Christ Jesus.

Of his brother-in-law Dooyeweerd writes: "I am very thankful that from the outset I found at my side my colleague Dr. Vollenhoven, professor of philosophy at the Free University of Amsterdam, whose name has been inseparably joined to my own."

But many of the other professors at the Free University had been raised in and taught the traditional views that we have just discussed, and the coming of Dooyeweerd and Vollenhoven to the Free University in 1926 produced great conflicts among the professors and the students.

Dooyeweerd appeals in truly Christian humility to his critics, saying that "the question is not a matter of a 'system'" – he's not asking them to accept all the thoughts he has developed – [subject to all the faults and errors of human thought], "but rather it concerns the *foundation* and the root of scientific thought as such." He means not "the mind" or "the reason" of the philosophers, neither of which actually exists, but the rational expression of the human heart in its openness to the God Who speaks in His Word – the battle with the philosophical tradition from the Greeks on.

In the same Foreword (p. viii) to *A New Critique* he writes:

I am fully conscious that any method of criticism which tries to penetrate to the religious motives [i.e., what drives you; motivation] of a thinker is in danger of causing an emotional reaction and giving offence. In tracking down a philosophical train of thought to its deepest religious foundations I am in no way attacking my adversaries personally, nor am I exalting myself in an *ex cathedra* style. Such misunderstanding of my intention is very distressing to me... I have continually laid emphasis on the fact that the philosophy that I have developed, even in the sharp penetrating criticism that it exercises against non-Christian immanence-philosophy, constantly remains within the domain of *principles*. I wish to repudiate any self-satisfied scientific attitude in confronting immanence-philosophy. The detailed criticism of the Humanistic immanence-philosophy... must be understood as self-criticism, as a case which the Christian thinker pleads *with himself*. Unless this fact is understood, the intention of this philosophy has not been comprehended. I should not judge immanence-philosophy so sharply were it not that I myself have gone through it and have personally experienced its problems. I should not pass such a sharp judgment on the attempts at a synthesis of non-Christian philosophy and the Christian truths of faith, had I not lived through the inner tension between the two and personally wrestled through the attempts at synthesis.

These, my friends, are amazing words. I hope all of you too feel that. And especially pertinent to tonight's gathering are these words of Dooyeweerd:

> It is certainly obvious that those interested in the Christian foundation of theoretical thought should not be concerned with personal success, which is after all of no value. Rather they should be willing to carry on a long and difficult labor, firmly believing that something permanent can be achieved with respect to the actualization of the idea concerning an inner reformation of philosophy. For, as a matter of fact, the precarious and changing opinion of our fellow-men is not even comparable with the inner happiness and peace that accompanies scientific labor when it is based upon Christ, Who is the Way, the Truth and the Life! (*A New Critique*, I p. ix).

These words of Dooyeweerd are the words I want to leave with the Dooyeweerd Centre for Christian Philosophy. The establishing of this Centre is a most important stage in an utterly fundamental Struggle that has been going on since the Fall of man. May Almighty God bless this new undertaking, to His own glory and to the spiritual edification of men everywhere. Amen.

APPENDIX

Brief Chronology of the Life of Howard Evan Runner

Supplement to Christian Renewal, *March 10, 2003,
Brief Chronology of the Life of Howard Evan Runner, compiled by
Kerry John Hollingsworth*

1916   Born 28th January, the only child of Howard and Sarah Watterson-Runner in Oxford, Pennsylvania.

1932   Graduates with Honors from West Philadelphia High School. He writes a section of the Commencement program. Enrols at Wheaton College. Strikes up a lifetime friendship with Glenn Andreas.

1935   Studied Classical Greek and Philosophy for a year at the University of Pennsylvania. He took copious notes in Philosophy and began to dabble in Syriac.

1936   Graduates with Honors in Philosophy from Wheaton College. He earns an A for a paper on *Plato's Concept of Ideas.*

1936 – 1941 Attends Westminster Theological Seminary where he earns a Bachelor's degree in Theology. It is here that he sits under the teaching of Cornelius Van Til, Ned Stonehouse, and Edward Young. Van Til begins to direct Runner's interest in the influence of Greek thought on a number of the second- and third-century theological controversies.

1939   Runner travels to Kampen to study Theology for a year with Klaas Schilder. The outbreak of the War forces him to return after only six months.

1941 – 1943 On the 12th of March he receives an invitation to become a Junior Fellow of Harvard University, a very prestigious position. It is during this period that he becomes an assistant to Prof. Werner Jaeger, at the time, one of the world's leading Classical Scholars. He maintains a lively and cordial relation with Jaeger right up until his departure to the Netherlands in the Fall of 1946. It is under Jaeger's guidance that Runner's longtime interest in Greek thought is brought to focus on the influence of Classical Greek Philosophy on the writings of the Early Church Fathers.

1941 – 1949 Publishes seven review articles including books by Dooyeweerd, Etienne Gilson, and Mels Ferré. The latter review precipitates a meeting and a number of cordial letters from Ferré.

1946   Runner is awarded a Masters degree in Theology from Westminster Theological Seminary.

1946   In the Fall Runner leaves for the Free University of Amsterdam to work in the Philosophy Department as a candidate for the Ph.D. degree. His intention is, "to make the history of Greek and Roman philosophy my primary subject." He subsequently goes on to write a dissertation on Aristotle.

1947   In early February Runner meets Elisabeth Wichers and they are married later in December.

1948   Runner is invited to become a board member of the Christian University Association of America.

1950   The Runners' first child Evan Jr. is born on May 17.

1951   Defends his Ph.D. thesis on the topic, *The Develop-*

ment of Aristotle Illustrated from the Earliest Books of the Physics.

1951 Begins in the Fall semester teaching Philosophy at Calvin College.

1953 With the public address, *Rudder Hard Over*, on the 3rd of February there were inaugurated a number of very significant beginnings; first, the Calvinistic Culture Association, second, a firestorm of controversy over his remarks, and, later in the Fall, the Groen Van Prinsterer Society.

1953 Delivers the controversial paper, *The Christian and the World: An Historical Introduction to a Christian Theory of Culture*, to the Faculty Board Conference of Calvin College at the beginning of the Fall semester.

1953 Also in the beginning of the Fall semester he delivers another public lecture entitled, *Cui Bono, To What End Men's Societies?*

1954 The Runners' first daughter Cathy is born on October 3.

1954 Writes a substantial polemical article in *Torch and Trumpet* entitled, *Christian Witness Requires Christian Organization.*

1956 The Runners' second daughter Joselyn is born September 6.

1956 As the Centennial celebration of the Christian Reformed Church approaches, Runner delivers a public address entitled, *Year of Decision: One Faith or Two?*

1957 Delivers a major essay entitled, *The Development of Calvinism in North America on the Background of Its Development in Europe*, to the Calvinistic Action Association in Calgary, Alberta, Canada.

1958　　　Writes a review of Dooyeweerd's, *A New Critique of Theoretical Thought*, for the *Westminster Theological Journal*.

1959 – 1960　Delivers the Unionville Lectures, *The Relation of the Bible to Learning*, which are subsequently published through the financial help of his close Wheaton College friend Glenn Andreas.

1961　　　Delivers the Unionville lectures, *Scriptural Religion and Political Task*, which are also published through the assistance of Glenn Andreas.

1962　　　Writes the article, *The ARSS and its Reorganization*, for the weekly *Calvinist Contact* Magazine.

1965　　　Writes the consequential essay, *Place and Task of an Institute of Reformed Scientific Studies*.

1967　　　Writes and delivers the stirring address, *Can Canada Tolerate the CLAC?*, April 29, on the occasion of the Fifteenth Anniversary Convention of the Christian Labor Association of Canada.

1967　　　October 7. Delivers the keynote address, *Point Counter Point*, on the occasion of the opening of the Institute for Christian Studies.

1968　　　Writes and delivers, *Christianity and Humanism*, for the annual meeting of the Christian Freedom Foundation.

1969　　　Writes a never to be completed manuscript for the Trinity Invitational Meetings, *Introduction to the Encyclopedia of the Sciences*.

1972　　　Delivers the lecture, *The Radical Christian Facing Today's Political Malaise*, for the student group at Calvin College, Students for Political Education through Christian Thought and Renewing Action, on Oct.

26.

1973	Sensing the less than whole-hearted support from some faculty members at the Institute for Christian Studies, Runner declines an appointment and remains at Calvin College until his retirement. However, for some years he does travel to Toronto to teach Introduction to Philosophy on a bi-weekly basis during the academic year.
1976	Writes the invited article for Calvin College's *Prism* Magazine, *Some Observations on the Condition of Calvin College at the Celebration of its Centennial.*
1977-1996	Runner became a very proud and devoted grandfather, beginning with his oldest daughter Cathy who produced two grandchildren, then Joselyn with five, and Evan Jr. with twins.
1977	Runner, along with his wife Ellen, embarks upon a major translation project, the 4-volume work of S. G. de Graaf, *Promise and Deliverance*, in an attempt to provide the sort of material that can radically change the religious heart direction of the body of Christ and hence truly ground the development of a fundamental Christian philosophical insight into the order of Creation.
1977	Writes an article for *The Banner*, April 22, entitled, *Dooyeweerd's Passing: An Appreciation. Christianity Today* declined to publish the article intimating that it was of little interest to its readers.
1979	On the occasion of his 60th birthday Runner is presented with a (belated) collection of essays entitled, *Hearing and Doing*, in which he contributes an in-depth interview on his own development.

1979   Delivers a major speech in Amsterdam, the Netherlands, entitled, *On Being Anti-revolutionary and Christian-historical at the Cutting Edge of History*, on the occasion of the 100th anniversary of the founding of the Anti-Revolutionary Party, April 3.

1981   In May, Runner officially retires from Calvin College as Professor of Philosophy. He is presented with a book of essays from former students entitled, *Life Is Religion*.

1982   Delivers a major speech for the Second International Symposium sponsored by the Association for Calvinistic Philosophy in the Netherlands on August 23 entitled, *The Christian Philosophical Enterprise in the Light of Biblical Prophecy.*

1983   Writes *Christendom in Crisis*, for *Christian Renewal.*

1984   Writes three articles for *Christian Renewal* on contemporary Church Life.

1984   Writes an introduction to McKendree Langley's book, *The Practice of Political Spirituality.*

1993   Writes a substantial essay for *Christian Renewal* commemorating the sixty-year friendship and support of Glenn Andreas on the occasion of his passing

1994   Writes and delivers *The World-Historical Importance of the Christian Philosophy of Herman Dooyeweerd* on the occasion of the opening of the Dooyeweerd Centre at Redeemer Christian College, November 5.

2000   Ellen, Runner's wife of 52 years, dies on October 13.

2002   After a two-year bout with cancer Howard Evan Runner goes to be with his Lord on March 14.

About the Author

HOWARD EVAN RUNNER (1916-2002) graduated with honours from Wheaton College. He earned a Bachelor's degree in theology from Westminster Theological Seminary. He subsequently received an appointment as a junior fellow at Harvard University. After earning a Master's degree in theology at Westminster he travelled to the Free University of Amsterdam where he earned the Ph.D. degree. Runner taught Philosophy at Calvin College from 1951 until his retirement in 1981.